Ultimate Festival & Travel Guide Milan & Lombardy

Unforgettable Experiences, Unmissable Events, Unique Destinations, Inspiring Tours, Best Times to Travel, The Italian Lakes, 2026 - 2027 Edition

Katerina Ferrara

IMMERSION TRAVEL PUBLISHING

ISBN (Paperback): 978-1-966874-11-9

ISBN (Hard Cover): 978-1-966874-12-6

ISBN (eBook): 978-1-966874-10-2

Audible (AudioBoook)

Library of Congress Control Number: Pending

DISCLAIMER

The author is not a travel agent. All opinions, experiences, and views expressed in this book are based on personal travel experiences.

Festival and event dates are set by local comuni and may change with little or no notice due to weather, logistics, or local decisions. Some festivals follow variable calendars tied to religious feasts or seasonal events. For this reason, it is strongly advised to confirm dates directly with official sources before booking travel.

Businesses and websites recommended in this book may also change, change ownership, rebrand, or close. The author has received no compensation or sponsorship for any recommended businesses.

Contents

Explore More and Stay Connected

Let's keep exploring together

Welcome to the real Italy! This guide is designed to unlock unforgettable experiences, from Milan's grand Duomo to Lake Garda's festivals and Lombardy's hidden villages. Wherever you turn these pages, may they inspire you to travel deeper and savor the magic of Italy.

Unlock the Secrets of Italy with Insider Expertise!

Sign up for my **free monthly newsletter** at www.KaterinaFerrara.com and unlock a world of exclusive travel guides, inspiring itinerary ideas, and expertly curated monthly updates filled with insider tips, festival highlights, and immersive experiences designed to make every journey truly unforgettable.

KaterinaFerrrar
a.com

First, A Few Words About the Author

In the late morning of August 18, 1982. I was minding my own business at the kitchen table of my parents' home, where I was residing temporarily, when four policemen entered the house, and without any explanation. dragged me out to their cruiser and rushed me to the psych ward of a local hospital.

That was the day my life took a sharp left turn from which it has never fully righted itself. My mother's psychiatrist, who had seen me only once following my return from the Middle East with a mysterious illness, had hastily diagnosed me with bipolar disorder (manic depressive illness), without performing a medical exam or listening carefully to my story. and now he was hospitalizing me against my will so he could forcefully treat me with the anti-psychotic medication he wrongly claimed I needed.

Years later, I uncovered the actual cause of the symptoms I brought home from the Persian Gulf, but it was too late to change the course of events. I had already been incorrectly diagnosed as mentally ill, and that diagnosis, by then, and the falsehood-ridden records that went along with it would dog me for the next four decades, negatively changing the entire trajectory of my life.

Before the nightmare began, I was a regular, hardworking guy, a young man with goals and dreams and better than average prospects. I had a loving family, and I lived in a close-knit community. I worked my way through a private high school as a busboy at Bishop's, a popular Lebanese American restaurant in Lawrence. Massachusetts, and then hustled tips as a waiter there on weekends as I earned my accounting degree from Merrimack College in 1977 and later my MBA with distinction from the Business School at Suffolk University in

Lt. Prosecutor Daniel Kaffee (Tom Cruise): - "Colonel, I only want TRUTH from you!"

Col. Nathan R. Jessep (Jack Nicholson): "Prosecutor, you can't *HANDLE* the *TRUTH!*"

From the movie: "A FEW GOOD MEN"

With your complimentary newsletter subscription, you'll enjoy:

- Monthly updates with insider secrets, seasonal highlights, and hidden gems

- Practical travel tips and Vatican/Italy news you can use

- Early access to new book launches and bonus content not found anywhere else

Don't miss out on the chance to travel smarter and deeper.

Join today at www.KaterinaFerrara.com

Travel Italy Book Series

Available now:
Book 1: *Ultimate Festival and Travel Guide Sicily (Available in English, Italian, & Dual-Language)*
Book 2: *Rome 2025 Jubilee Year Travel Guide*
Book 3: *Ultimate Festival and Travel Guide Rome and Beyond*
Book 4: *Ultimate Festival and Travel Guide Puglia*
Book 5: *Ultimate Festival and Travel Guide Venice and the Veneto*
Book 6: *Ultimate Festival and Travel Guide Milan and Lombardy*

Arriving in 2026:
Book 7: *Ultimate Festival and Travel Guide The Italian Lakes*

Arriving in 2027:
Book 8: *Ultimate Festival and Travel Guide Florence and Tuscany*
Book 9: *Ultimate Festival and Travel Guide Naples, Amalfi and Beyond*

CHAPTER ONE

The Joy of Festival Travel

Experience Italy in Celebration

Picture yourself sipping an espresso under the soaring glass roof of the Galleria Vittorio Emanuele II, when the quiet hum of the city is replaced by a marching band and a swirl of color. Flags wave, music rises, and you are swept into a celebration that transforms Milan from modern metropolis to living tradition. A few days later, you find yourself on the shores of Lake Como, watching fireworks explode over the water as bells ring out from hillside chapels. This is festival travel. It is not just about visiting. It is about experiencing.

Welcome to a side of Milan and its region, Lombardy, that most travelers never see. This is a world of centuries-old traditions, village fairs, lakeside processions, and city-wide celebrations that reveal the soul of northern Italy. Over the last twenty-five years of traveling through Italy, I have found that the region comes alive in unexpected ways during festivals. From the fashion capital's patron saint celebration to food sagre in alpine towns, each event offers the chance to witness and take part in something deeply rooted and joyfully shared.

Festival travel lets you become part of a story still being written. In Italy, these stories stretch back to Roman times, carry through the Middle Ages, and echo in today's celebrations. In a single summer, you might take part in an illuminated boat procession on Lake Iseo, a Renaissance pageant in Vigevano, and a cheese festival in the alpine village of Preghera, where artisans gather to share mountain flavors passed down for generations. These are not reenactments for tourists. They are vibrant moments of community and celebration, where travelers are welcomed as guests, not observers.

Your Key to Milan and Lombardy

This guide goes beyond a standard travel guide. It is your invitation to immerse yourself in the rhythm of Italian life. While it includes all the essentials like walking tours, city highlights, restaurant recommendations, maps, accommodations, it is shaped by the unforgettable festivals and sagre that transform Lombardy throughout the year.

You will discover the grandeur of Milan's Duomo and the artistic genius of Leonardo da Vinci, but also the intimacy of a small-town festival or the thrill of a medieval joust in a fortified town. The region is rich in history, from Roman ruins and Romanesque churches to Renaissance villas and contemporary design districts. Yet it is in the festivals that you will feel the pulse of this land. These celebrations are when the cobbled streets echo with music, the piazzas fill with laughter, and the kitchens turn out once-a-year delicacies you will never forget.

What This Guide Offers:

- **City Highlights:** Explore Milan, Bergamo, Brescia, Como, Pavia, and more through the lens of their most vibrant traditions.

- **Historical Insights:** Understand how the Roman, medieval, and Renaissance eras continue to shape daily life in Lombardy.

- **Natural Beauty:** Discover the spa towns with their thermal waters, the Alpine peaks above Lecco, and the serene beauty of Lake Maggiore.

- **Local Experiences**: Uncover authentic experiences, from mountain cycle paths to bustling markets to quiet, off-the-beaten-path locations.

- **Transportation and Accommodation Information:** For each town and each event there are suggested accommodations and also transportation information.

- **Local Restaurant Recommendations**: Through our travels and our friends in Italy, we have curated restaurants that specialize in local specialities and offer the best value.

- **Festival Focus:** Each chapter is centered on specific events that bring these places to life. Plan your trip around the festivals or find one that fits your travel style.

Finding Festival Culture

Because of my love for Italy and our goal to move there one day, I started studying Italian in 2020 when our son Augustus left for university. I don't do anything halfway, so when I decided to learn Italian, I really committed myself to it and became fluent quickly (somewhat thanks to lockdowns). What began as a personal challenge soon opened up a whole extra dimension of Italian culture to me.

Every morning, I tune into Di Buon Mattino on TV2000. What started as a simple language immersion exercise blossomed into a genuine passion. The show broadcasting from Rome goes beyond typical news coverage; it journeys across Italy, discovering festivals, traditions, and local specialties. Between watching Italian TV series, chatting with Italian friends, reading Italian newspapers, and my daily dose of Di Buon Mattino, I kept discovering one fascinating festival after another. Even now, each day the show transports me to a new celebration somewhere in Italy, revealing another region's unique culture. It's a daily way to learn about new cities, regions, saints, or celebrated foods.

As I explored deeper, I realized these festivals truly embody Italian culture; they're living celebrations of community, history, folklore, and tradition. This sparked an idea: why not experience these festivals firsthand? When I began planning our travels around them several years ago, I was thrilled that my husband, son, cousins, and friends were just as excited to join the adventure.

While there are cultural festivals in the U.S., they're different. Festivals in Italy are lifelong commitments, drawing people back year after year, even from far away. These aren't just celebrations; they are cherished reunions with family and friends.

A huge part of what makes these festivals special is the food, dishes and desserts you can only find during these celebrations, flavors that stay hidden from restaurant menus the rest of the year. As I researched these festivals for our trips, the cuisine emerged as a crucial part of the story, deeply woven into local traditions and memorable experiences.

I'll never forget hunting down the Testa del Turco at the Festa della Madonna delle Milizie in Scicli. Following the enticing aromas through the centro storico, my anticipation grew with each step. That first bite, the delicate, crisp pastry with its rich, creamy filling, was unlike anything I had tasted before. It was not just delicious; it was a gateway into the festival's spirit, a flavor that captured the essence of celebration and tradition. Don't worry, I have included all these special festival foods in the chapters.

Surrounded by the festival's sights, sounds, and smells in the town square, I felt a change, something delightful. The locals welcomed me with such warmth and pride in their traditions that I couldn't help but be drawn in. That moment sparked my love for Festival Travel: a way of engaging with Italy that goes beyond sightseeing to truly becoming part of its living traditions.

Each festival since has only deepened this connection. There's nothing like the scent of roasting chestnuts leading you to a tiny village square on a crisp fall day, or the sight of a solemn religious procession casting flickering light down a medieval street. Rather than simple memories, these experiences provide intimate glimpses into the heart and soul of Italy, uncovering the genuine spirit of its people. They've inspired me to create the **Travel Italy Book Series**, which will eventually grow to include 22 Festival and Travel Guides covering all of Italy's diverse regions.

My friend Annalisa's story perfectly captures the festival spirit. Like many Italians, she moved to Rome for work but returns to her hometown every year for her patron saint's festival. When I asked to join her one year, she laughed and said, "Katerina, you wouldn't be able to keep up! I run all over town just to see the procession of Sant'Ambogio at every important viewpoint!" Her enthusiasm showed me how deeply these festivals are woven into Italian life.

Understanding Feste and Sagre

What Sets a Festa Apart from a Sagra?

As you explore this guide, you will naturally pick up some Italian along the way, starting with two essential terms: "festa" and "sagra."

A **festa** (plural: feste) often grows from Roman Catholic traditions, such as Milan's Festa di Sant'Ambrogio or Como's Festa di San Giovanni. Yet not all feste are religious. They include major cultural events such as Milan Film Festival, the Bergamo Donizetti Opera Festival, and the Monza Grand Prix celebrations. Among the most vibrant are the Palio di Legnano, a medieval reenactment complete with jousting and pageantry, and Vigevano's Renaissance fair that transforms the town into a sixteenth-century spectacle.

While Catholic traditions shape many Italian festivals, these celebrations welcome everyone, regardless of faith. They are joyful expressions of history, tradition, folklore, and community spirit where all can create lasting memories.

A **sagra** (plural: sagre), by contrast, springs from ancient harvest celebrations. The word itself derives from "sacro," meaning "sacred" in Latin. Originally held in temple yards to thank the Roman gods for bountiful harvests, these festivals live on in small towns and villages across Lombardy as community fundraisers for schools and local projects, powered entirely by volunteers.

While feste celebrate various aspects of culture, sagre focus specifically on local cuisine. From the sweet torrone in Cremona, the risotto celebration in the Valtellina region or the Polpenazze del Garda's Wine Festival, these events spotlight regional specialties. Other sagre honor bresaola, pizzoccheri, cheeses, porcini mushrooms, and local wines.

Here is my essential sagra tip: arrive hungry. Purchase your meal ticket at the event booth. For twelve to fifteen euros, you will enjoy an exceptional zero kilometro meal with local wine. "Zero kilometro" refers to food produced within roughly 150 kilometers, ensuring peak freshness and supporting local farmers.

For feste, I recommend staying two to three nights minimum, as celebrations often continue into the late evening. Sagre, however, work perfectly as day trips, since they often occur in small villages that may not even have hotels. Many visitors base themselves in nearby towns and venture out to experience these local food festivals.

Whether you are traveling solo, with family, or planning a multi-generational trip, these festivals offer rich experiences for everyone. Photographers, influencers, and creatives discover endless possibilities, from vibrant processions to intimate cultural moments. Music festivals showcase Italy's performing arts, while markets built around the festivals highlight local artisans creating unique treasures. Many festivals offer hands-on experiences with traditional crafts or cooking techniques.

Families particularly appreciate the child-friendly atmosphere, complete with puppet shows, parades, special treats, and kids running free in the piazza. Just as importantly, these events support sustainable tourism and directly benefit local communities, helping to preserve cherished traditions for future generations. Think of this guide not only as a travel companion but also as your personal planner for creating authentic journeys beyond the typical tourist path.

Why Festival Travel?

- Experience cities at their most alive and authentic.

- Join in centuries-old traditions and celebrations.

- Taste once-a-year dishes tied to seasons and saints.

- Connect with communities that welcome you into their traditions.

- See places transformed by music, costumes, food, and light.

- Support local artisans, performers, and small towns.

What to Expect in This Book

Now that you understand the magic and significance of festival travel, let me show you how this guide will help you experience it firsthand. In the chapters that follow, we will explore Milan and Lombardy's most captivating festivals, diving into their origins, meaning, and the best ways to join in.

Whether you are timing your visit to coincide with centuries-old traditions or crafting your own adventure through this diverse and enchanting region, the insights you find here will help you make every moment count. Festival travel transforms ordinary tourism into an extraordinary experience. Instead of seeing Italy through the eyes of a typical tourist, you will experience it through celebration, through local connection, and through traditions that continue to thrive. Let this guide lead you to unforgettable experiences rooted in place, history, and community.

The Magic of Milan and Lombardy's Festivals

Picture yourself walking beneath the towering spires of the Duomo as a saint's feast day unfolds in candlelight, swaying to music in a lakeside town as fireworks reflect over the waters of Lago Maggiore, or tasting freshly stirred risotto at a harvest sagra in the hills above Bergamo. These are the moments most travelers miss. The true rhythm of Italian life rises to its peak in celebration.

This guide opens doors most visitors never even notice. Beyond simply telling you when and where festivals occur, I will share the small secrets that help you move from observer to participant. You will find the quiet courtyards where Milanese families gather for processions, the cafés that serve once-a-year sweets only during festival days, and the local volunteers who keep ancient customs alive.

Let me invite you to look beyond museum tickets and shopping boulevards, and into a world of living tradition. Let's begin this journey together, where every bell tower holds a story, every local recipe reflects a season, and every celebration invites you into the center of Europe's living heritage. Join me in discovering the real Italy: one festival at a time.

Welcome to Festival Travel.

Your most extraordinary adventure is about to begin.

CHAPTER TWO

How to Use This Unique Travel Guide

Plan, Explore, Enjoy

While festivals make this guide unique, its purpose goes far beyond event calendars. This book is designed to help you explore Milan and Lombardy with depth, curiosity, and ease. Whether you're planning your first visit or returning for a deeper connection, this guide serves as your trusted travel companion, offering insights into the region's history, architecture, culinary heritage, and cultural spirit. Festivals might set the rhythm, but the spirit of this book lies in its immersive experiences, insider tips, and thoughtfully curated adventures that elevate any journey.

Each chapter offers a complete guide to a specific town, with historical background, must-see sites, walking tours, restaurant recommendations, travel logistics, and authentic suggestions. Even if your trip doesn't center on a festival, you'll discover hidden gems, local flavors, and off-the-path treasures that help you experience the region like a knowledgeable traveler, not just a tourist.

If you're interested in festivals, you'll find a curated calendar by month and location to help align your trip with local celebrations. Festival chapters include detailed descriptions of what to expect, from historic processions and sacred rituals to jazz concerts, food markets, and centuries-old traditions. Even if you don't attend a festival, the city chapters offer cultural richness, suggested day trips, and personal travel insights to help you make the most of your time.

Use this book in whatever way best suits your travel style. You may design a full itinerary, plan one unforgettable day, or flip through pages while enjoying a cappuccino in a Milanese café.

Quick Start Guide

Want to include a festival? Follow these steps:

1. Check the Festival Calendar (Chapter 51) to see what's happening during your visit.

2. Read Chapter 1 to understand the joy of festival travel and the difference between religious festas and food-based sagras.

3. Use the maps to visualize festival locations and plan your route.

4. Pick one or two festivals to start with, don't try to fit in too many on your first trip.

5. Book accommodations early for popular events like Milan's Feast of Sant'Ambrogio or the Festa del Torrone in Cremona.

6. Arrive the night before a festival for the best experience.

Already chosen your cities? Use the alphabetical index of towns to find festivals happening in places you're already visiting.

Planning a festival-focused trip? Start with the Calendar of Events and build your itinerary around multiple celebrations using **FestaFusion** techniques.

Chapter Organization

Each chapter is designed to give you everything you need for a complete experience.

1. Town Overview

2. Festival Overview and Event Guide

3. Must-See Sights in Walking Tour Order

4. Logistics, including how to arrive and get around

5. Restaurant Recommendations

6. Day Trips or nearby sights

7. Year-round events and cultural highlights

Accommodation information can be found in the Stay in Style: Accommodation Recommendations, Chapter 46.

Maximize Your Festival Experience with #FestaFusion

Why see just one festival when you can time your trip to catch several? FestaFusion is your guide to discovering the magic of multiple celebrations in one journey. Thanks to its great train lines, Lombardy is the perfect place to experience:

- FestaFusion Milan during Sant'Ambrogio and the Oh Bej! Oh Bej! Christmas market

- FestaFusion Bergamo, combining Fiera di Sant'Abbondio with the Palio del Barello

- A summer of lakeside fireworks and jazz festivals around Lake Como and Lake Iseo

Every celebration reveals new layers of Italy's diverse traditions, food, and customs.

Immersion Experiences: Beyond the Festivals

Italy's beauty doesn't stop when the music fades or the candles are blown out. That's why you'll find Immersion Experience chapters throughout the book, designed to guide you toward meaningful cultural experiences outside festival dates.

These year-round activities invite you to:

- Make risotto or polenta with local chefs in Bergamo or Pavia

- Take a break in the thermal waters near the Alps

- Cycle through the vineyards of Franciacorta or along Lake Garda's shoreline

- Explore Roman ruins in Brescia or ancient monasteries in the Valtellina

- Walk the Pilgrimage to Pavia or hike the sacred Sacri Monti

Each Immersion chapter includes:

The Full Story: What makes the experience special and what to expect

How to Make it Happen: Booking tips, websites, perfect timing, and travel details

Insider Secrets: Little-known tips to elevate your experience

Planning Your Festival Travel

Want to make the most of your trip? Arrive the evening before the festival begins. This gives you time to settle in, walk the streets, enjoy an aperitivo, and find the main piazza and church, almost always the heart of the celebration.

How Long to Stay:
For major festivals, plan three or four nights. Outside Milan, hotels in Lombardy are often very affordable. Longer stays mean you can enjoy evening events and won't feel rushed.

For smaller food festivals (sagre), a day trip might be enough; many happen in villages that don't have extensive lodging options.

Early Bird Tips:

- Follow the suggested walking tour to uncover local history

- Sample regional dishes like risotto alla Milanese or tortelli di zucca

- Visit a café and chat with locals, they often offer insights not found in any guidebook

- Track down the event flyer which is most likely near the door of the main church in town

Consider Booking a Local Guide
In cities like Cremona, Bergamo, and Varese, local guides can enhance your experience with stories, personal knowledge, and historical context. I recommend platforms like Tours by Locals or With Locals.

Feel the Rhythm of the Festival

Once the celebration begins, put away the camera and jump into the experience. Eat the festival treats, join the processions, and connect with the community. These are the moments you'll remember most.

Timing of Festivals

Festivals in Lombardy, as elsewhere in Italy, fall into two categories:

Fixed-date events like Sant'Ambrogio (Dec 7) or The Epiphany (January 6)

Movable feasts tied to harvests, seasons, or the liturgical calendar, such as wine sagre or Easter processions

Each listing includes expected dates, and my website, katerinaferrara.com offers sample itineraries and updates to help you plan effectively.

Final Note

While the focus is on festivals, this guide is also your essential companion for exploring Milan and Lombardy. From Renaissance palaces to alpine vineyards, Michelin-starred meals to village trattorie, you'll find what you need to make your trip meaningful.

With this book in hand, you're ready to go beyond the surface and embrace Italy's rich cultural heritage. Let the stories unfold, one piazza and one celebration at a time.

CHAPTER THREE

Discover the Lakes, Milan, and Lombardy

Innovation & Eternal Elegance

M ilan: Gateway to Modern Italy

There is nowhere in the world quite like Milan. Rising from the fertile plains of Lombardy with Gothic spires piercing the sky and sleek glass towers reflecting centuries of ambition, this pulsating metropolis seduces visitors with its intoxicating blend of ancient grandeur and cutting-edge innovation. Life here unfolds not in hushed reverence but in the purposeful stride of impeccably dressed executives crossing cobblestones, where the aroma of fresh espresso mingles with the scent of fine leather and every corner hums with possibility. It is a city where fashion, finance, and faith converge, a testament to human ingenuity that has reinvented itself countless times while never losing its soul.

For over two millennia, Milan has stood at the crossroads of Europe, a strategic position that has made it wealthy, embattled, and eternally dynamic. From Roman Mediolanum to the powerhouse of the Visconti and Sforza dynasties, from the industrial revolution to today's global fashion capital, Milan has always been a city that looks forward while honoring its past.

Each of Milan's neighborhoods tells its own compelling story. In the historic Brera district, art galleries nestle beside aperitivo bars where creatives gather to debate and dream. The Quadrilatero della Moda pulses with the energy of international fashion week, while the Navigli canals echo with laughter from canal-side trattorias and buzzing nightlife. Porta Nuova stretches skyward with sustainable architecture that rivals any global city, and the Isola district vibrates with young energy and innovative cuisine.

The Six Zones of Milan

Centro Storico revolves around the magnificent Duomo, where Gothic pinnacles reach toward heaven and La Scala's curtains rise on world-class performances. Here, history lives in every marble facade, and modern luxury finds its most elegant expression.

Duomo di Milano

Brera and Garibaldi balance bohemian charm with cosmopolitan sophistication, home to the Pinacoteca di Brera and tree-lined streets where artists, students, and fashion insiders create Milan's intellectual heartbeat.

Porta Venezia and Porta Garibaldi showcase the city's evolution, where Art Nouveau mansions stand beside contemporary towers, and diverse communities bring global flavors to traditional Milanese tables.

Navigli flows with the energy of Milan's historic canals, designed in part by Leonardo da Vinci, where aperitivo culture thrives and young Milanese gather along waterways that once carried marble for the Duomo.

Porta Nuova and Isola represent Milan's future. A vertical city of sustainable skyscrapers, innovative restaurants, and cutting-edge design that proves Milan's commitment to reinvention.

Porta Romana and Ticinese blend student energy with historic charm, where universities meet medieval churches and the aperitivo hour extends well into the night along ancient Roman roads.

But Milan is more than its famous sights. It's the thrill of discovering a hidden courtyard where fashion shoots unfold against Renaissance frescoes. It's the satisfaction of a perfect cappuccino at 11:00 a.m. in a bar where regulars have gathered for decades. And it's the spectacle of festivals that celebrate everything from design innovation to ancient traditions.

Yet, to truly appreciate Milan, one must understand that its story extends far beyond the city limits. It's merely the gleaming center of a region that has shaped European civilization for centuries.

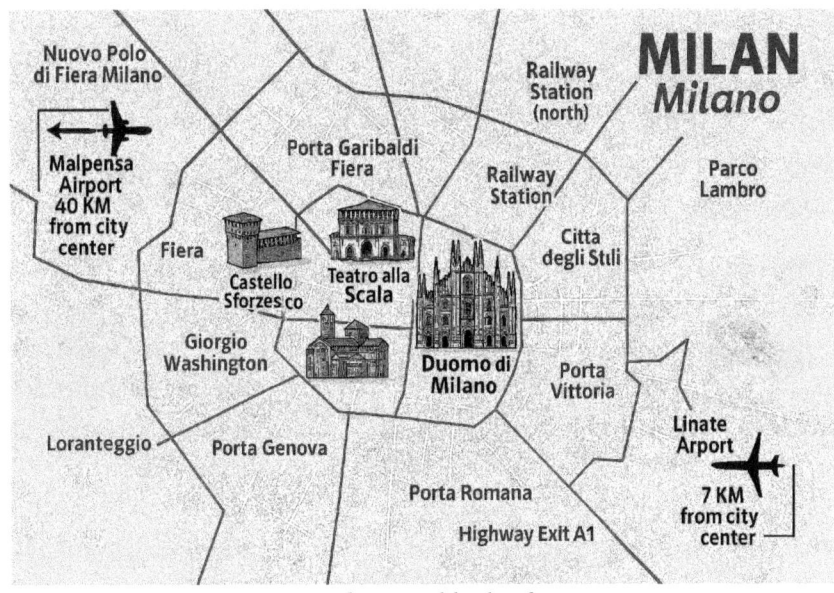

Milan Neighborhoods

Exploring Milan and Beyond: The Rich Tapestry of Lombardy

Milan may feel like a universe unto itself, pulsing with fashion weeks and financial markets, but one of the greatest discoveries of traveling through Lombardy is just how easily it reveals its other treasures.

I remember one warm September day when a friend and I came into Milano Centrale to connect to a train to Lago di Como, specifically the lakeside town of Varenna for the day. The weather was sunny and inviting, perfect for spur-of-the-moment adventures; in an hour, we arrived in a postcard village.

We wandered through Varenna's narrow medieval streets, where flowering bougainvillea spilled over stone balconies and the scent of lemon trees drifted from hidden gardens. The colors were intoxicating; the deep blue of the lake contrasted with pastel houses and the dramatic backdrop of mountains rising on all sides. We stopped at a waterfront café for fresh lake fish and risotto, watching elegant ferries glide between ancient villas while swallows dipped and soared above the water.

Later, we explored the romantic gardens of Villa Monastero, where exotic plants from around the world have found a home in this microclimate, and discovered that this unassuming lakeside village had been attracting artists, writers, and dreamers for centuries. We could understand why; there was something magical about the interplay of water, mountains, and Mediterranean vegetation that felt almost otherworldly.

There was an easiness to the day, a joy in discovering somewhere so close to Milan yet utterly transported from the urban energy. We spent the afternoon ferry-hopping between the lake's most enchanting towns. In Bellagio, we explored elegant villas and silk boutiques on the promontory where the lake's three arms meet. In Menaggio, we strolled along the palm-lined promenade overlooking the Alps. And in Tremezzina, we discovered the breathtaking Villa del Balbianello, its gardens tumbling down to the water. Each ferry ride offered new perspectives on the lake's dramatic beauty, and later we shared an aperitivo as the setting sun painted the water gold and the church bells of ancient villages echoed across the lake.

Why Venture Beyond Milan?

Milan may be the gleaming star of Lombardy, but it is far from the complete story. Just beyond the metropolitan bustle lies a region of extraordinary diversity, from the Alpine grandeur of Valtellina to the gentle hills of Franciacorta, from the Roman splendor of Brescia to the lake-kissed romance of Como and Sirmione.

Venturing beyond Milan reveals layers of Italian culture that the cosmopolitan capital only hints at. Here, you can sip world-class wines in the shadow of snow-capped peaks, explore medieval fortress towns that seem untouched by time, or cruise pristine lakes where Roman emperors once built their villas. You'll encounter artisans preserving centuries-old crafts, festivals rooted in mountain traditions, and piazzas where locals still gather to share stories over aperitivo.

Whether you're drawn by art, cuisine, history, outdoor adventures like hiking and cycling, or simply nature itself, Lombardy offers something richer: a deeper connection to the forces that have shaped northern Italy's prosperity, creativity, and enduring appeal.

Concise History of Lombardy

To understand the festivals and traditions of Milan and greater Lombardy, one must first journey through their layered past, rich with imperial grandeur, medieval innovation, Renaissance brilliance, and industrial transformation.

Roman Foundations and Imperial Glory

The story of Lombardy begins with the Romans, who recognized the strategic importance of the fertile Po Valley. Around 222 BC, they established Mediolanum (modern Milan) as a key military and commercial hub. The city's name, meaning "in the middle of the plain," reflected its position at the crossroads of trade routes connecting Rome with the Alpine passes and northern Europe.

By the 3rd century AD, Mediolanum had become so important that Emperor Diocletian made it the capital of the Western Roman Empire. The city flourished under imperial patronage, acquiring magnificent buildings, extensive walls, and a hippodrome that could seat 35,000 spectators. It was here in 313 AD that

Emperor Constantine issued the Edict of Milan, granting religious tolerance throughout the empire and effectively legalizing Christianity.

The region's Roman legacy extended far beyond Milan. Cities like Brescia (Brixia), Bergamo (Bergomum), Como (Comum), and Pavia (Ticinum) thrived as Roman municipia, connected by a network of roads that facilitated trade and cultural exchange. Their legacy remains visible today in ancient amphitheaters, forums, and archaeological treasures that dot the Lombard landscape.

The Lombard Kingdom and Medieval Rise

Following the fall of the Western Roman Empire, Lombardy experienced waves of barbarian invasions before the Lombards (Longobards) established their kingdom in 568 AD. These Germanic peoples gave the region its modern name and established Pavia as their capital. The Lombards proved to be capable administrators, blending Germanic traditions with Roman legal and administrative systems.

The medieval period saw the rise of powerful city-states throughout Lombardy. Milan emerged as the leader of the Lombard League, a coalition of northern Italian cities that successfully resisted the attempts of Holy Roman Emperor Frederick Barbarossa to assert imperial control. The victory at the Battle of Legnano in 1176 marked a turning point in the struggle between imperial authority and municipal independence.

During this period, each major Lombard city developed its own character. Milan became a center of religious and political power, while Como specialized in silk production, Bergamo controlled mountain trade routes, and Brescia emerged as a center of metalworking and arms production.

Visconti and Sforza: The Age of Ducal Power

The late medieval and Renaissance periods brought the dominance of two great dynastic families: the Visconti and the Sforza. The Visconti family began their rise to power in Milan during the 13th century, gradually extending their control over much of Lombardy. Under rulers like Gian Galeazzo Visconti, the Duchy of Milan became one of the most powerful states in Italy.

The Visconti commissioned the construction of Milan's Gothic Duomo in 1386, a project that would span centuries and become the symbol of the city's ambition and faith. They also initiated the construction of the Navigli canal system, designed in part by Leonardo da Vinci, which connected Milan to major rivers and facilitated trade.

When the Visconti line ended in 1447, the Sforza family inherited control of Milan through marriage. Under Francesco Sforza and his successors, particularly Ludovico il Moro, Milan became a major center of Renaissance culture. The Sforza court attracted artists like Leonardo da Vinci and Bramante, who left masterpieces including The Last Supper and contributed to architectural marvels like Santa Maria delle Grazie.

Foreign Domination and Austrian Rule

The Italian Wars of the early 16th century brought foreign powers into Lombardy. The region passed between French and Spanish control before eventually falling under Austrian rule as part of the Duchy of Milan. Under Empress Maria Theresa and her son Joseph II, the Austrians implemented administrative reforms and fostered cultural development.

Austrian rule in Lombardy was relatively enlightened compared to other parts of the Italian peninsula. Investments were made in infrastructure, education, and the arts, with Maria Theresa notably expanding schooling to include girls. The La Scala opera house, inaugurated in 1778, became a symbol of Milan's cultural prestige during this period. The Austrian administration also promoted economic growth, laying the groundwork for Lombardy's later industrial success.

Risorgimento and Italian Unification

Lombardy played a crucial role in the Italian unification movement. The region's prosperity and strategic importance made it a key battleground between Austrian forces and Italian patriots. The revolts of 1848, particularly the "Five Days of Milan," demonstrated the strength of nationalist sentiment.

The decisive moment came in 1859 during the Second Italian War of Independence, when French and Piedmontese forces defeated the Austrians at the battles of Magenta and Solferino. The Kingdom of Piedmont-Sardinia annexed Lombardy, which became part of the unified Kingdom of Italy in 1861.

Cities throughout Lombardy contributed to the Risorgimento cause. Bergamo was known as the "City of the Thousand" for its contributions to Garibaldi's expedition, while Brescia earned the nickname "Leonessa d'Italia" (Lioness of Italy) for its fierce resistance to Austrian rule.

Industrial Revolution and Modern Transformation

The late 19th and early 20th centuries transformed Lombardy into Italy's industrial heartland. Milan became the center of Italy's textile industry, while cities like Brescia developed heavy industry and precision manufacturing. The region's network of waterways, improved transportation links, and skilled workforce attracted investment from across Europe.

During World War II, Lombardy was part of the Italian Social Republic and experienced intense fighting during the resistance movement. Milan became a center of partisan activity, and the region paid a heavy price for liberation.

The post-war economic miracle transformed Lombardy into one of Europe's wealthiest regions. Milan evolved into a global fashion and design capital, while maintaining its position as Italy's financial center. The region's cities specialized in different industries: Como in silk and luxury goods, Brescia in precision manufacturing, Bergamo in textiles and services.

Lombardy Today: Innovation and Tradition

Today, Lombardy generates nearly a quarter of Italy's GDP and remains one of Europe's most economically dynamic regions. Milan has successfully reinvented itself as a global city, hosting Expo 2015 and the 2026 Winter Olympics.

Key Subregions of Lombardy

Metropolitan Milan: The Engine of Innovation

This subregion encompasses the fashion capital itself with its Gothic cathedral and world-class museums, the industrial heritage of Sesto San Giovanni, and the expanding urban landscape that reaches toward the Alps. Once the seat of the Western Roman Empire, Milan has continuously reinvented itself as a center of commerce, culture, and creativity.

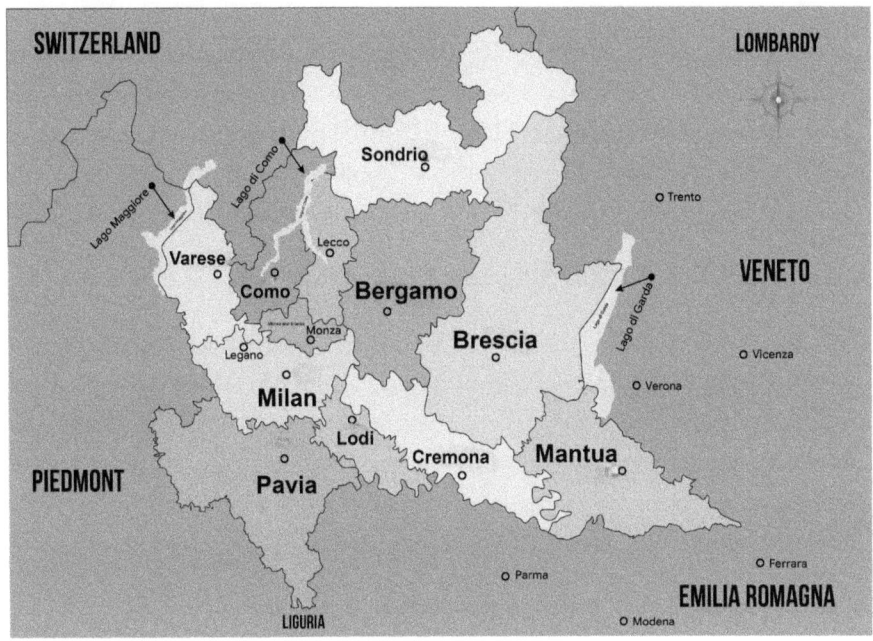

Map of Lombardy and its Provinces

Bergamo: Where Medieval Walls Embrace Modern Dreams

Two cities in one, Bergamo offers both the intimacy of a medieval hilltop town and the energy of a modern commercial center. The Città Alta, encircled by Venetian walls and accessible by funicular, preserves Renaissance palaces and ancient squares, while the Città Bassa pulses with contemporary business and cultural life. This province has given the world commedia dell'arte, the Donizetti opera tradition, and countless emigrants who carried Lombard traditions around the globe.

Brescia: The Lioness Where Roman Glory Meets Alpine Majesty

Romance, ruins, and industrial prowess define Brescia, a land where Roman theaters stand beside medieval castles and modern factories. Brescia, nicknamed the "Lioness of Italy" for its fierce independence, offers extraordinary Roman remains, including the UNESCO-protected monastery of San Salvatore. The province extends from the wine hills of Franciacorta to the pristine shores of Lake Garda and into the ski slopes of the Adamello mountains.

Como and the Lakes: Where Silk Roads Lead to Azure Waters

Elegant villas, pristine lakes, and centuries-old silk traditions define the Como region, a landscape of refined beauty and artisanal excellence. Lake Como, with its cypress-lined shores and palatial gardens, has attracted emperors, artists, and Hollywood stars for centuries. The nearby lakes of Lugano and smaller alpine waters create a paradise of reflection and renewal, while the city of Como maintains its global reputation for silk production and luxury craftsmanship.

Cremona: Where Violins Sing and Rivers Flow

The musical heart of Lombardy, Cremona resonates with the legacy of Antonio Stradivarius and the continuing tradition of violin-making that has made it a pilgrimage site for musicians worldwide. Set along the Po River, this province blends agricultural abundance with extraordinary artistic heritage, where master craftsmen still shape instruments using techniques perfected in the Renaissance.

Mantua: Renaissance Jewel in the River's Embrace

Surrounded by lakes formed by the Mincio River, Mantua stands as one of Italy's most perfectly preserved Renaissance cities. The Gonzaga family transformed this strategic location into a cultural powerhouse, commissioning masterpieces from Mantegna and Giulio Romano. Today, this UNESCO World Heritage site maintains its architectural harmony while celebrating traditions that span from courtly festivals to robust agricultural heritage.

Varese and the Pre-Alps: Where Sacred Mountains Meet Modern Innovation

Rolling hills, sacred mountains, and pristine lakes define the Varese region, where Alpine foothills create a landscape of spiritual and natural beauty. The Sacro Monte di Varese, with its baroque chapels climbing toward a sanctuary, represents centuries of pilgrimage tradition, while Lake Maggiore and Lake Varese offer tranquil waters and elegant nineteenth-century villas.

Sondrio and Valtellina: Alpine Heights and Ancient Flavors

A dramatic realm of peaks and terraced vineyards, Sondrio province rises into the heart of the Alps, where nature and tradition reign supreme. The Valtellina Valley, carved by the Adda River, leads to Switzerland through landscapes shaped by glaciers and cultivated by generations of mountain farmers. Here, ancient grapes create prestigious wines like Nebbiolo, while traditional dishes celebrate the marriage of Alpine and Mediterranean influences.

Pavia and the Southern Plains: Where Learning Flows Like Rivers

The scholarly spirit and agricultural abundance of Pavia province reflect its position along the Po and Ticino rivers, where medieval universities meet fertile farmlands. Pavia itself, once capital of the Lombard kingdom, maintains its prestigious university tradition, while nearby Certosa showcases Renaissance architectural perfection. This is Lombardy's rice heartland, where paddies flood each spring in a transformation that has defined the landscape for centuries.

Why Journey Beyond?

I found that in Italy, history isn't confined to museums; it flows through everyday life. Entering the walls of Bergamo Alta, I stepped into a world where medieval stones frame views across the Po Valley, where local restaurants serve casoncelli that taste of mountain traditions, and where the evening passeggiata follows routes walked by merchants and pilgrims for centuries.

Life moves to a different rhythm. Imagine yourself on a ferry over Lake Garda, with the morning mist lifting from villa gardens, or enjoying Franciacorta sparkling wine as harvest light filters through vineyard rows. Here, festivals aren't performances but living traditions, where you're welcomed not as a tourist but as a temporary neighbor sharing in celebrations passed down through generations.

This journey beyond the Duomo offers something precious: the chance to experience northern Italy not just as a destination, but as a living story you get to step into. Let this exploration be your guide as you uncover the hidden wonders of Milan and Lombardy. Adventure awaits, and it's just a train ride away.

Note on Ruling Families and Glossary

Because I want to keep the history sections concise and get you to the festivals and travel information as quickly as possible, I have included two chapters in the **Quick Reference Guide** section of this book. They are **Rulers and Dynasties of Lombardy** and **Glossary of Terms**. If you come across a ruling family, architectural style, Italian word you don't recognize or historical reference that is not fully covered in a chapter, check this section.

CHAPTER FOUR

Maps of Milan, Lombardy and the Lakes

Lakes, Mountains and Cities

Navigating Milan

Understanding Milan's layout is essential to making the most of your visit. This city map highlights the key districts and landmarks to help you get oriented quickly.

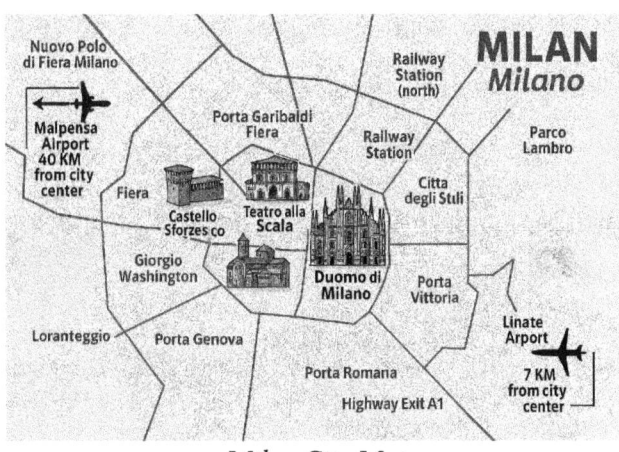

Milan City Map

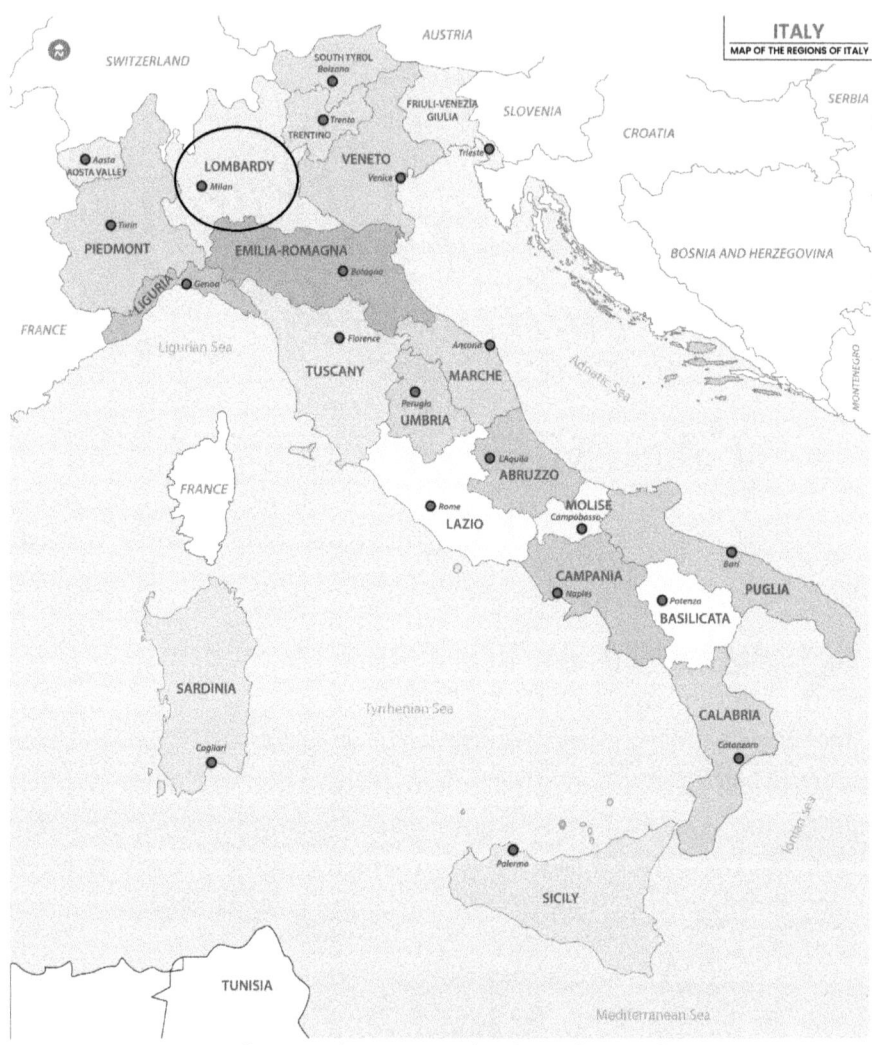

Italy Map showing Lombardy in the North

Lombardy, in northern Italy, borders Switzerland to the north and fans out across the Lombard plain, where snowcapped Alps give way to rolling hills, glittering lakes, and the cosmopolitan energy of Milan.

Map of the Provinces of Lombardy

To better understand the diversity of Lombardy, it helps to see the region laid out visually. The map highlights each of Lombardy's provinces, ranging from the alpine peaks of Sondrio to the fertile plains of Cremona and Mantua, showing their capitals and geographical position within northern Italy. Milan, at the heart of the region, anchors the network of historic towns, lakes, and cultural centers that surround it.

The map also places Lombardy in context with its neighbors Switzerland to the north, Piedmont to the west, Emilia-Romagna to the south, and Veneto to the east, illustrating how history, trade, and traditions have long flowed across these borders.

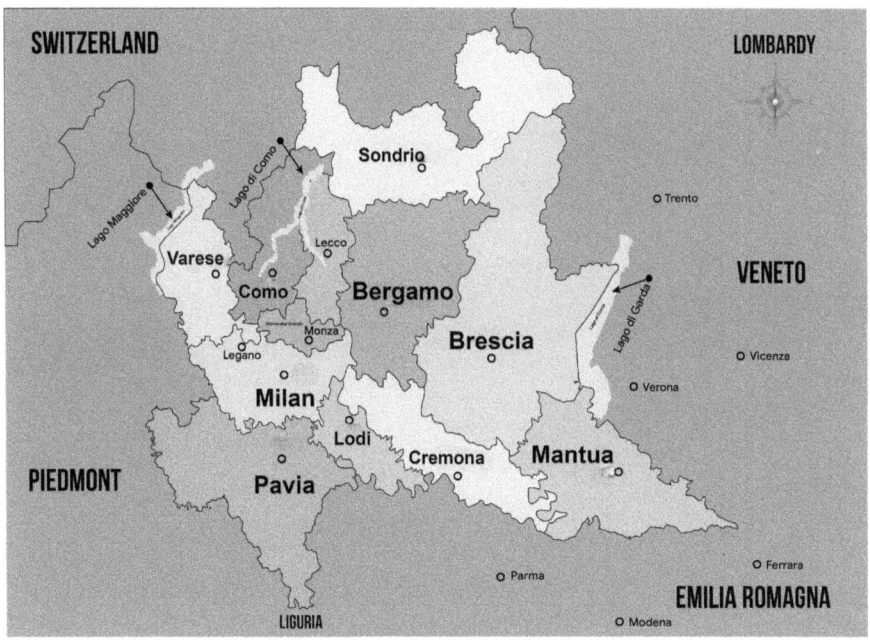

Lombardy, the Lakes, and Key Cities

Lombardy's Northern Lakes

This map highlights the northern Lombardy lakes, a region where Italy meets Switzerland and alpine beauty merges with cultural charm. Lago di Como, shaped like an inverted Y, is famed for its dramatic mountainsides, elegant villas, and towns such as Bellagio, Varenna, and Tremezzo that line its shores.

To the west lies Lago Maggiore, stretching into Switzerland with destinations like Stresa, Verbania, and the Borromean Islands, celebrated for their gardens and palaces. Between them, Lago di Lugano straddles the border, offering a blend of Swiss precision and Italian flair, while smaller lakes such as Lago d'Orta, with its romantic island of San Giulio, and Lago di Varese provide quieter escapes. Together, these lakes form one of Lombardy's most enchanting areas, inviting exploration by ferry, hiking trail, or lakeside promenade.

Lago d'Orta, Lago Maggiore, Lago di Varese, Lago di Lugano, Lago di Como

Lombardy's Eastern Lakes

This map highlights Lombardy's eastern lakes, which form some of the region's most scenic landscapes. At the heart lies Lago di Garda, Italy's largest lake, shared by Lombardy, Veneto, and Trentino-Alto Adige. Along its Lombard shores are celebrated towns such as Sirmione with its Roman ruins and Scaliger Castle, Desenzano del Garda with lively piazzas and a harbor, and Gardone Riviera known for the Vittoriale degli Italiani estate.

Smaller lakes nearby add to the region's charm: Lago d'Iseo, framed by mountains and the island of Monte Isola, hosts towns like Iseo, Sarnico, and Lovere; while Lago d'Idro and Lago di Ledro provide quieter retreats for hiking, cycling, and outdoor adventures. Together, these lakes showcase Lombardy's blend of culture, history, and natural beauty, offering visitors everything from medieval castles and historic villas to lakeside promenades and water sports.

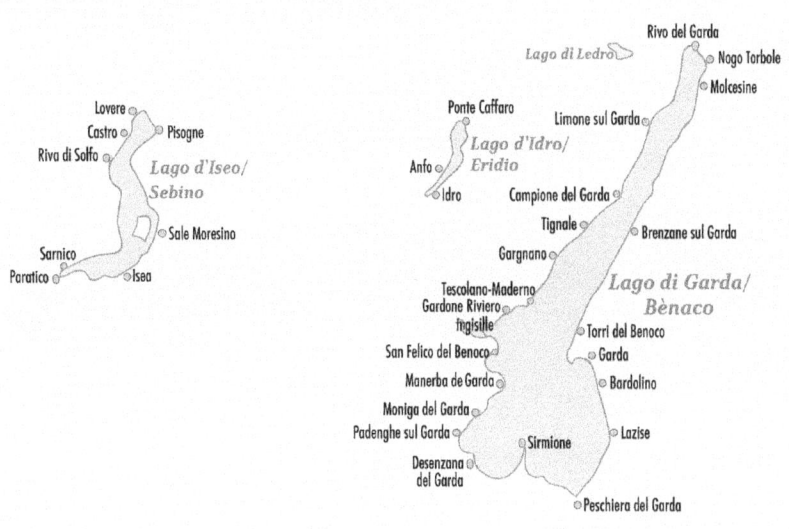

Lago d'Iseo, Lago d'Idro, Lago di Garda

CHAPTER FIVE

Map of Must See Celebrations

Interactive Maps for the Festivals

Festival & Sagra Map: Your Essential Guide

Immerse yourself in Italy's most cherished traditions. Our detailed festival map pinpoints vibrant celebrations across the region, from ancient religious processions to mouthwatering food sagre. Each marker reveals event dates and locations, making it easy to weave these authentic Italian experiences into your journey. Find the map here: https://katerinaferrara.com

Interactive Google Map: Plan Your Adventure

Take your exploration further with our comprehensive Google Map. This dynamic tool brings the festival cities to life, helping you visualize your route, estimate travel times, and preview each destination through local photos. From North to South, plan your journey here:
https://maps.app.goo.gl/Q3XcDdLDeqjuvQmC7

The Festival Map is also available in color on the book's page.

https://katerinaferrara.com/

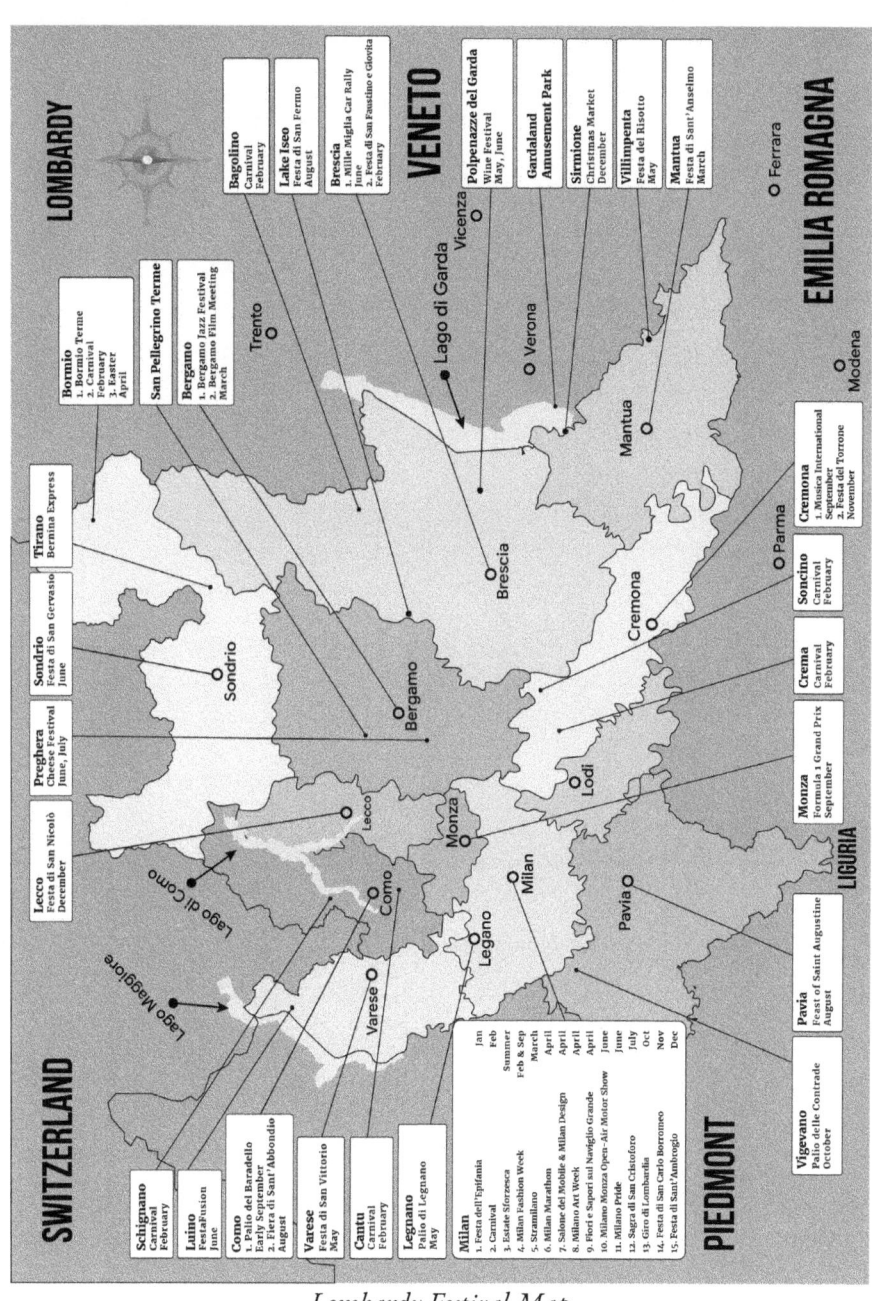

Lombardy Festival Map

Chapter Six

Arrival Made Easy: Airports, Bases, Beyond

Introducing Milan

Milan is Italy's dynamic capital of fashion, finance, and design. But it is also a deeply cultural city of ancient churches, sprawling piazzas, canals, and artistic treasures. Whether you are arriving from overseas or traveling by train from within Italy, this chapter offers a brief overview to help you settle in, get oriented, and prepare for unforgettable excursions.

Getting to Milan

Milan is served by three primary airports:

- **Malpensa (MXP)** for international and intercontinental flights

- **Linate (LIN)** for domestic and short European routes

- **Orio al Serio (BGY)** near Bergamo, ideal for low-cost carriers

From each airport, travelers can reach the city center by express trains, buses, taxis, or ride apps. Milan Central Station is the primary hub for train travel, with high-speed and regional trains connecting the city to the rest of Italy and Switzerland.

For complete transportation logistics, including how to navigate Milan's metro, tram, and train systems, see Transportation Detail, Chapter 47.

Choosing Your Base in Milan

Where you stay will shape your experience. Milan's neighborhoods are as varied as its architecture. The Duomo area puts you steps from major landmarks. Brera offers cobbled lanes, art galleries, and boutique shopping. Navigli charms with canals and nightlife. Isola is modern and creative. Porta Venezia is elegant and residential.

Each district offers a different mood. We've stayed near the Duomo for access to the cathedral and museums, and in Navigli for evening strolls and late-night cafés. On quieter visits, we have loved Brera's refined ambiance and slower pace in the early mornings.

For specific neighborhood recommendations and hotel suggestions, see Chapter 46: Stay in Style, Accommodation Recommendations.

Getting Around Milan

Once you are settled in, Milan is easy to explore. The city's **metro** is fast and well-connected. **Trams** offer scenic rides through elegant neighborhoods. Walking between historic sites is pleasant and efficient. Bike and scooter sharing options are also widely available.

To explore beyond Milan, regional trains connect quickly to cities such as Bergamo, Como, Pavia, Mantua, and Brescia. Day trips to Lake Como or the wine country are simple to arrange. For travelers with a rental car, Lombardy's roads are well maintained, but be mindful of limited traffic zones in historic centers.

Explore with Ease

Whether you are coming for Fashion Week, a quiet getaway, or an immersive cultural journey, Milan rewards those who explore beyond the postcard landmarks. Let the neighborhoods guide your mood. One day may begin with espresso under the arcades of Piazza del Duomo and end with a sunset aperitivo beside the canal.

For detailed information on Milan's train lines, public transit, airport connections, day trips, and accommodations across the city, refer to the back of this guide:

- **Chapter 46: Stay in Style: Accommodation Detail**

- **Chapter 47: Transportation Detail**

Traveler Tips
- **Download Before You Go**: ATM Milano (metro/tram/bus), Trenitalia and Italo for trains.

- **Airport Transfers**: The Malpensa Express train is the fastest way into Milan; Linate is closest to the center; Orio al Serio near Bergamo is ideal for budget flights.

- **Money Matters**: ATMs are plentiful; credit cards are widely accepted in Milan, but carry cash for small cafés or village stops.

- **Local Transit**: Validate tickets on metros, trams, and buses because fines are strictly enforced.

- **Language Note**: English is common in Milan hotels, restaurants, and airports; less so in small towns, knowing a few Italian phrases goes a long way.

Buon viaggio!

Summer Celebrations

May Through August

CHAPTER SEVEN

Varese: Victory and Veneration

Faith, Fireworks, & Festivities

Festa di San Vittore

Where: Varese

When: May 8

Average Festival Temperatures: High 22°C (72°F). Low 12°C (54°F).

Varese: A Garden City of Faith and Culture

Picture a city where Alpine peaks pierce the morning mist, where baroque spires rise from gardens thick with azaleas and rhododendrons, and where the shimmer of Lake Varese reflects centuries of noble villas and sacred pilgrim paths. This is Varese, la Città Giardino, the Garden City, nestled at the foot of Monte Campo dei Fiori just an hour from Milan's bustling streets.

Long before it earned its floral nickname, Varese's story began with pre-Roman settlements that archaeologists still uncover today. Roman roads once carried legions through these hills, leaving behind traces of villas and the earliest whispers of the Christian faith. Through the medieval centuries, the city flourished as a crossroads where merchants, pilgrims, and nobles converged under the watchful eye of the powerful Visconti and Borromeo families. At its heart stood the Basilica of San Vittore, a beacon for the faithful.

Walk through Varese's historic center and you'll find the same baroque facades and elegant piazzas that have welcomed visitors for generations. But climb higher, toward the Sacro Monte di Varese, and you'll discover why UNESCO declared this holy mountain a World Heritage Site, one of only nine Sacri Monti scattered across Piedmont and Lombardy.

Today, with nearly 80,000 residents calling it home, Varese strikes that rare balance between provincial energy and lakeside tranquility, serving as the perfect gateway to northern Italy's most breathtaking landscapes.

The Feast of Saint Victor

The celebration of San Vittore, Saint Victor, has been central to Varese's identity for centuries. Records show that devotion to the saint dates back to the early Middle Ages, when the basilica that bears his name became the base of the community. By the thirteenth century, May 8 was firmly established as the city's patronal feast day, and since then generations of Varesini have honored their protector with solemn processions, liturgies, and community gatherings.

Over time, the celebration expanded beyond the religious sphere, blending faith with civic pride. By the seventeenth and eighteenth centuries, fireworks, concerts, and public feasts had become part of the festivities. Today, the festival continues for an entire week, usually from May 4 to 11, filling the historic center with pageantry, music, and devotion. The focus of the feast remains the liturgical celebrations inside the Basilica of San Vittore and the solemn procession through the streets, but the week also includes concerts, folk performances, markets, and nightly fireworks that draw both locals and visitors from the region.

Who Was Saint Victor?

Saint Victor is venerated as one of the early Christian martyrs of northern Italy. Tradition holds that he was a soldier in the Roman army during the reign of

Emperor Maximian at the end of the third century. Refusing to renounce his Christian faith, he endured imprisonment, torture, and finally martyrdom in Milan around the year 303 AD.

His courage and steadfastness quickly inspired devotion among the Christian community of Lombardy. Milan became the principal center of his following, and the Basilica of San Vittore al Corpo was built in his honor. Varese soon adopted him as its patron and protector, placing his name upon the city's basilica and dedicating the annual feast to his memory.

Festival Traditions

Pilgrimage to the Basilica di San Vittore

Each day of the novena leading up to May 8 begins with prayers and pilgrimages to the Basilica di San Vittore. Parish groups, confraternities, and families gather to honor the city's patron, filling the nave with flowers and votive candles.

Basilica di San Vittorio

May 8: Saint Victor Feast Day Events

Morning

The morning opens with the Pontifical Mass, presided over by the Bishop of Varese. Clergy, civic leaders, and delegations from nearby towns join in attendance. The basilica resounds with sacred music as hymns in honor of San Vittore echo beneath the painted dome.

Late Morning Children's Procession

Schoolchildren dressed in white and carrying banners of their parishes parade through the main piazza, a tradition that emphasizes passing devotion to the next generation. The procession ends with a blessing on the steps of the basilica.

Evening

Solemn Procession of San Vittore

The most important event of the feast day takes place in the evening. The statue of San Vittore, adorned with flowers and candles, is carried from the basilica through the streets of the historic center. Clergy in ceremonial robes, confraternities in traditional attire, and civic representatives accompany the image. Incense drifts through the piazzas while choirs sing litanies in honor of the martyr.

Balconies and windows are decorated with banners and lanterns, and the faithful line the route with candles in hand.

Fireworks Display

As the statue returns to the basilica, the night sky over Varese erupts with fireworks. Reflected in the waters of nearby Lake Varese, the spectacle marks the joyful conclusion of the feast day. Families gather in the main piazza and along the lakeside promenades to watch the colors illuminate both the city and the surrounding mountains.

Walking Tour of Varese

#1. Basilica di San Vittore

The Basilica di San Vittore, dedicated to the city's patron, is a striking example of Lombard Baroque architecture. Its tall neoclassical bell tower, built in the eighteenth century, rises proudly above the rooftops and has become a symbol of Varese itself. Inside, the church glows with frescoes, gilded altars, and side chapels filled with works of devotional art.

The grand nave draws the eye upward to a richly painted ceiling, while the chapels hold centuries of local history in marble and canvas. During the feast, the statue of St. Victor is displayed here, surrounded by flowers and candles, before being carried through the city streets in solemn procession.

#2. Baptistery of San Giovanni Battista (St. John the Baptist)

Next to the basilica stands the octagonal Baptistery of San Giovanni, one of the oldest and most precious monuments in the city. Dating from the twelfth century, it preserves the simplicity and strength of Romanesque stonework. Step inside to find frescoes that tell the story of baptism and salvation, their faded yet vibrant colors linking modern pilgrims with medieval worshippers. The font itself, carved in stone, has welcomed countless generations into the faith.

#3. Piazza Monte Grappa

A short walk brings you to Varese's main square, a lively hub framed by arcades and civic buildings. It is the perfect place to pause for a coffee and watch the rhythm of city life, with the Alpine peaks visible in the distance.

#4. Corso Matteotti

Stroll along Corso Matteotti, the city's elegant shopping street lined with boutiques, cafés, and historic buildings.

#5. Palazzo Estense and Gardens

Continue toward the Palazzo Estense, an eighteenth-century residence built for Francesco III d'Este, Duke of Modena. Today it serves as the town hall, but its true gem lies behind: the formal Italian gardens, often compared to a smaller version of Versailles. Fountains, flowerbeds, and sweeping avenues make this a peaceful place to stroll after the bustle of the festival.

Logistics

Train: Varese is well connected to Milan by frequent regional and suburban trains. The journey from Milano Cadorna or Milano Porta Garibaldi takes about one hour, arriving at Varese's main station. From there, it is a 15-minute walk to the Basilica di San Vittore and the historic center.

Bus: Local buses run from the train station to the main squares and the basilica area. During the festival week, additional routes and extended evening hours often operate to accommodate visitors attending concerts and fireworks.

Car: From Milan, take the A8 Autostrada dei Laghi north toward Varese. Exit at Varese Centro and follow the signs into the historic center. The drive takes about one hour depending on traffic.

Parking: Much of central Varese is a restricted traffic zone (ZTL). Visitors should plan to park outside the ZTL and continue on foot. Paid parking is available at Piazza della Repubblica and at the multi-level garages near Piazza Monte Grappa, both within a short walk of the basilica and festival events.

Restaurant Recommendations

Ristorante Teatro. Via del Carlo Croce, 3

An elegant dining spot near the historic center, offering refined Lombard and Mediterranean cuisine. Known for creative risotto dishes, seasonal tasting menus, and an excellent wine list. Perfect for a celebratory dinner after the fireworks.

Osteria di Piazza Litta. Piazza Litta, 2

Historic osteria just steps from the basilica, popular with both locals and visitors. Homemade pasta, Lombard cured meats, and simple yet flavorful regional plates are served in a setting that recalls old-world Varese. Ideal for a relaxed lunch between festival events.

Day Trips from Varese

Lago di Varese. Just 5 kilometers (3 miles) south of the city center, Lake Varese is a beautiful escape surrounded by villages, wooded hills, and views of Monte Rosa. A cycling and walking path circles the lake for about 28 kilometers (17 miles), making it one of the most popular outdoor activities in the area. Visitors can also rent kayaks or small boats in summer, and birdwatchers flock to the Brabbia Marsh Nature Reserve, a protected wetland on the eastern shore.

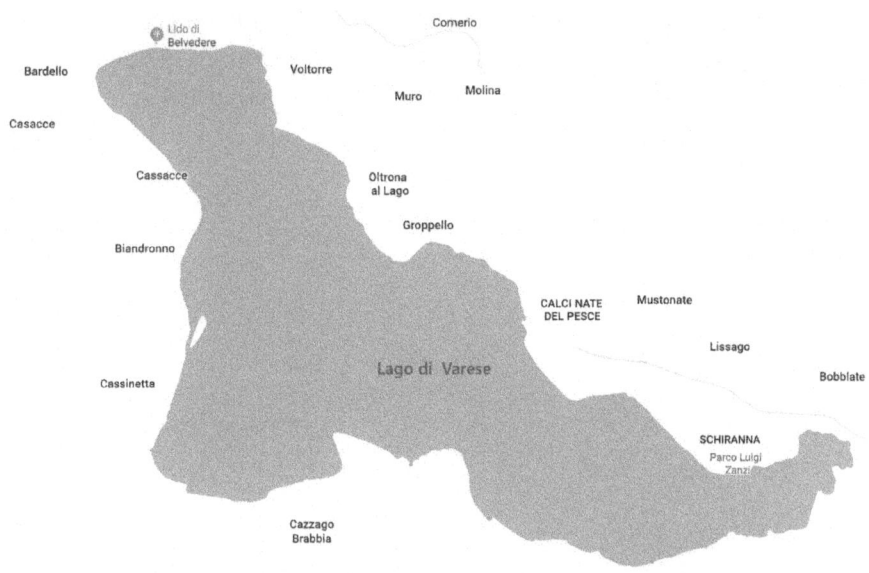

Lago di Varese

While Lago di Varese does not have large ferries like the major northern lakes, small excursion boats and rowing clubs animate the waters, especially in the warmer months. The lake is also famous for its rowing regattas and was a training site for Italy's Olympic team.

Laveno Mombello. About 30 kilometers (19 miles) northwest of Varese, Laveno sits on the eastern shore of Lake Maggiore. This charming lakeside town is known for its ceramics tradition, colorful harbor, and sweeping views across the water to Verbania and the Borromean Gulf. From Laveno, car ferries and passenger boats cross to Intra and Verbania, making it an excellent gateway for exploring Lake Maggiore.

A cable car climbs from the town to the summit of Sasso del Ferro, offering breathtaking panoramas of the lake and Alps. The harbor area is lively with cafés and gelaterie, perfect for relaxing before or after a ferry excursion.

Locarno, Switzerland. Located 70 kilometers (43 miles) northwest of Varese, across the Swiss border, Locarno is a historic lakeside city on the northern shore of Lake Maggiore. We enjoyed 10 days at Lago Maggiore, staying in Baveno, and Locarno was one of the most beautiful spots. We arrived by car and returned by boat, a perfect way to experience both the mountains and the water. Using the cable car, we ascended to the Santuario della Madonna del Sasso and were absolutely mesmerized by the sweeping views. I can honestly say they're some of the most beautiful I've ever seen over the lake. After soaking it all in, we took the peaceful footpath back down to town, surrounded by silence and nature.

Sanctuary of the Madonna of the Rock, Locarno

Varese Festivals and Sagre Throughout the Year

Carnevale Varesino

February

Varese's carnival transforms the historic center into a lively stage of color and noise. Costumed parades wind past the city's elegant piazzas, while marching bands and street performers keep the crowds entertained. Children dart about with paper streamers and brightly painted masks, joining in playful games organized in the squares. The highlight is the procession of floats, some satirical, others whimsical, crafted by local associations who compete for the most creative display.

Settimana del Sacro Monte

Last Weekend of June / Early July

This unique celebration honors the UNESCO-listed Sacro Monte di Varese, a sacred site that has drawn pilgrims for centuries. The week features evening torchlight processions along the cobbled via sacra that leads past fourteen Renaissance chapels to the sanctuary at the summit, creating an evocative atmosphere that recalls the journeys of medieval pilgrims.

Sacred music concerts echo inside the sanctuary and in the chapels, while guided tours reveal the frescoes, sculptures, and spiritual symbolism of the complex. Beyond its devotional character, the event highlights the cultural value of Sacro Monte, often pairing spiritual reflection with conferences, art exhibitions, and local food tastings in the surrounding hillside village of Santa Maria del Monte.

Festa di Ferragosto sul Lago di Varese

August 15

On the Feast of the Assumption, the shores of Lake Varese become the stage for one of the city's most anticipated summer celebrations. From early afternoon, rowing regattas and boat parades glide across the water, often with vessels adorned in lights and flags that add a festive splash of color.

Autunno Gastronomico Varesino

September to October

This beloved food and wine festival turns the entire province of Varese into a culinary journey. Dozens of restaurants, trattorie, and agriturismi join in by offering seasonal menus designed to showcase the region's best products. Diners can savor creamy risottos made with mushrooms from the surrounding woods, freshwater fish such as perch and pike prepared according to traditional recipes, and local cheeses paired with honey or mountain polenta.

Mercatini di Natale

December

Varese glows with holiday charm as Christmas markets fill Piazza Monte Grappa and the streets around the basilica. Wooden stalls sell crafts, ornaments, and festive treats, while choirs sing carols and mulled wine warms the winter evenings.

CHAPTER EIGHT

Villimpenta's Risotto Festival

Rice and Rural Traditions

Festa del Risotto di Villimpenta

Where: Villimpenta

When: Last weekend of May through the second weekend of June.

Average Festival Temperatures: High 26°C (79°F). Low 15°C (59°F).

Event Website: https://www.mantovanotizie.com/feste-sagre

Villimpenta: A Rice-Growing Village of the Mantuan Plain

Golden rice fields stretch endlessly across the fertile Po Valley, where ancient irrigation canals follow the lines first traced by Roman engineers and still feed the emerald paddies that have sustained northern Italy for centuries. Here, where the morning mist rises from the flooded plain and medieval towers rise along the horizon, stands Villimpenta, a village whose story reaches deep into the past.

The earliest traces of settlement date to Roman times, when this area lay along the routes connecting Mantua and Verona, part of the impressive network of roads that carried legions, merchants, and ideas across the Empire. Centuries later, as empires crumbled and the Middle Ages dawned, new powers rose to defend and control these fertile lands. Among them were the Scaligeri of Verona, who in the fourteenth century built the mighty castle that still dominates the heart of Villimpenta. Its square towers and thick walls recall an age when border wars swept across the plains, yet within those walls, life endured in the rhythm of the fields.

Over time, as feudal lords yielded to farmers and poets, the wealth of Villimpenta came not from conquest but from the careful marriage of water and grain. Today, the village preserves this legacy with quiet pride, its landscape a living testament to centuries of ingenuity and cultivation, an enduring symbol of the Mantuan plain's authentic rural soul.

Festa del Risotto

Rice has been cultivated in the Mantuan plains since the fifteenth century, when the Gonzaga family, rulers of Mantua, expanded irrigation networks to harness the waters of the Po and Mincio rivers. The flat, marshy terrain around Villimpenta proved ideal for growing rice, and over the centuries it became a staple of the local diet. The ritual of cooking risotto, a short-grain rice, in enormous copper cauldrons over an open fire developed naturally in farming communities, where meals were shared at harvest and on feast days.

The modern festival began in the late 1960s, when the town decided to highlight its agricultural roots with a community event. Volunteers organized the first risotto feasts using enormous paioli (cauldrons), stirring rice with long wooden paddles in view of the public. The recipe was simple and true to tradition: creamy Vialone Nano rice slowly transformed with golden butter, sweet onions, rich meat broth simmered for hours, and generous snowfalls of aged Grana Padano cheese, all sourced from the surrounding countryside and stirred into liquid perfection.

What started as a modest village celebration quickly grew in popularity. By the 1980s, Villimpenta's risotto sagra had become a regional attraction, known not only for its food but also for its warm community spirit. Today, over 80,000 portions of risotto are served during the festival's run, making it one of the largest food events in Lombardy.

More than just Rice

While risotto remains the star, the festival has expanded into a broader showcase of rural culture. Food stalls overflow with silky tortelli di zucca stuffed with sweet butternut squash and bathed in sage butter, succulent grilled meats that crackle over open flames, and local wines that capture the essence of the Po Valley terroir.

Folk musicians fill the air with traditional melodies while children chase through medieval castle grounds, and exhibitions showcase antique farming tools and sepia photographs that tell the story of generations who bent their backs in flooded fields. Every bite connects visitors to centuries of agricultural devotion, transforming a simple meal into a celebration of the land itself.

Evenings conclude with raffles, performances, or special events that vary each year. The atmosphere is one of abundance and community spirit, with risotto at the center of it all. Visitors often linger long after their meal, enjoying music, conversation, and the warm hospitality that defines this sagra.

Walking Tour of Villimpenta

#1. Scaligeri Castle

Begin at the imposing fourteenth-century Scaligeri Castle, the most prominent landmark in Villimpenta. Built during the era of the Scaliger family of Verona, the castle was part of a defensive network guarding the Mantuan plain. Its square towers and stone walls remain striking, offering a reminder of the town's medieval role as a frontier outpost. During the festival, the castle courtyard often serves as a gathering place for cultural events.

#2. Parish Church of San Michele Arcangelo

A short walk from the castle brings you to the Parish Church of San Michele Arcangelo, Villimpenta's religious cornerstone. The church's façade is simple, reflecting the agricultural character of the town, but inside you will find devotional altars and frescoes that speak to centuries of faith. The church is active during the festival period, with special Masses that connect the sagra to the town's religious traditions.

#3. Piazza San Michele

The central square of Villimpenta becomes the hub of festival life. Food stalls, exhibitions, and communal dining tents are set up here, filling the piazza with music, conversation, and the aroma of risotto. Even outside festival days, it is a pleasant spot to sit at a café and watch the slow rhythms of local life unfold.

#4. Rural Landscapes and Canals

From the town center, stroll along the small roads that lead into the surrounding countryside. Here you will see the network of irrigation canals that made rice cultivation possible, their waters reflecting the fields that stretch into the horizon. In late spring, the flooded paddies glisten in the sun, creating a landscape that has defined Villimpenta's economy and identity for centuries.

Logistics

Train: Villimpenta does not have its own train station. The nearest stations are Mantua (Mantova), about 20 kilometers (12 miles) away, and Verona Porta Nuova, about 35 kilometers (22 miles) away. Both are served by regional and high-speed trains from Milan, Brescia, and Venice. From either station, Villimpenta can be reached by taxi, local bus, or rental car.

Car: Driving is the most convenient way to reach Villimpenta, especially during the festival. From Mantua, take the provincial road SP30 east toward Nogara. From Verona, drive south on SR62 and connect through Nogara. The drive from Mantua takes around 25 minutes, while Verona is about 40 minutes.

Parking: Villimpenta is a small town, and much of the historic center is pedestrian-friendly. There is no permanent ZTL (limited traffic zone) as in larger cities, but access to the central piazzas is often restricted during major events. Visitors can normally find parking along the streets just outside the center or in small public lots near the main roads leading into town.

Restaurant Recommendation

Trattoria Da Gian. Via Mantova 42, Nogara (7 kilometers / 4 miles from Villimpenta)

A favorite among locals for its generous portions of risotto, tortelli di zucca, and grilled specialties. The relaxed, family-style atmosphere makes it an excellent stop before or after visiting the sagra.

Day Trip Options: Nearby Cities and Towns

Ferrara. 50 kilometers (31 miles) from Villimpenta. A Renaissance city and UNESCO World Heritage Site, Ferrara is celebrated for its harmonious blend of medieval streets and Renaissance planning. Once ruled by the Este family, it became a flourishing center of art and culture.

The city is enclosed by nearly 9 kilometers (5.5 miles) of well-preserved walls, perfect for walking or cycling. Key sites include the imposing Castello Estense, with its moat and towers, and the Palazzo dei Diamanti, famed for its diamond-shaped façade and prestigious art exhibitions.

Nogara. 7 kilometers (4 miles) from Villimpenta. A small town with deep agricultural roots, Nogara offers a quieter excursion that reflects the traditions of the Veronese plain. Its parish church of San Pietro holds medieval origins, while its weekly markets highlight local produce and cheeses. The town is also a practical stop for dining or accommodation if Villimpenta is fully booked during the sagra.

*Villimpenta does not have any other Festivals or Sagra throughout the year.

CHAPTER NINE

Legnano: Knights and the Battle of Legnano

Pageantry, Pride, & Palio

P alio di Legnano

Where: Legnano

When: Final Sunday of May.

Average Festival Temperatures: High 23°C (73°F). Low 14°C (57°F).

Legnano: A Town of Battles and Brotherhood

The thunder of hooves still seems to echo through the streets of Legnano, where cobblestones remember the clash of medieval armies and church bells once rang out in victory over an emperor. Just 20 kilometers (12 miles) northwest of Milan, this Lombard town carries the weight of a moment that changed Italian history forever.

Picture May 29, 1176: the green, white, and red banners of the Lombard League snapping in the wind as northern cities united against Frederick Barbarossa's imperial forces. Around a sacred war chariot called the Carroccio, citizens who had never wielded swords stood shoulder to shoulder with seasoned knights. When the dust settled, they had achieved something extraordinary, a victory so profound that Italy's national anthem still sings of *"il Carroccio di Legnano"* centuries later.

Walk through modern Legnano today, past its bustling factories and contemporary neighborhoods home to 60,000 residents, and you'll discover a town that refuses to let that glory fade. The towering bronze figure of Alberto da Giussano rises above the cityscape, the legendary commander's stance as defiant as the day he led those citizen militias to triumph.

Today, Legnano is a close-knit community where medieval memory and modern life still walk hand in hand.

The Palio of Legnano

A moment so powerful it refuses to stay buried in history books. For eight centuries, the echo of that May day in 1176, when ordinary citizens stood against an emperor, has lived on in whispered stories and faded chronicles.

That victory inspired one of Italy's most stirring traditions: the Palio di Legnano, a historic horse race that commemorates the city's triumph over Frederick Barbarossa. What began as a simple desire to honor their ancestors' courage has blossomed into something magical, a festival where an entire city steps backward through time.

The Palio di Legnano emerged from that peculiarly Italian genius for transforming memory into spectacle, fueled by a community's unshakeable pride in its defining moment. The world wars interrupted the celebration, as wars do, but when peace returned to Lombardy, so did the Palio.

Since 1945, every spring has brought the same intoxicating ritual: eight neighborhoods, called contrade, each spending months in secret preparation. Behind closed doors, seamstresses bend over silk and velvet, flag throwers practice their ancient choreography until their arms ache, and horses learn to dance to the rhythm of medieval drums.

When the last Sunday of May arrives, Legnano explodes into color and sound. Thousands of costumed citizens pour through streets that suddenly belong to the twelfth century. Solemn masses give way to thunderous parades, and the air crackles with the electricity that only comes when an entire community shares the same impossible dream: to make the past live again.

Festival Traditions

Morning

Religious Ceremonies

The Palio begins with a solemn Mass in the Basilica of San Magno, the spiritual heart of Legnano. Representatives from each contrada (neighborhood) attend in full medieval costume, carrying banners and standards. The highlight is the blessing of the palio, the painted banner that serves as the prize for the horse race and a symbol of civic unity.

Procession Preparations

From early morning, the streets fill with the sounds of drums and trumpets as thousands of participants gather for the grand historical parade. Each of the eight contrade brings out knights, nobles, pages, and townsfolk in elaborate costumes inspired by the Middle Ages. Horses are groomed and riders prepare, while families line the streets to secure the best viewing spots.

Afternoon

Historical Parade

The parade is the most spectacular part of the Palio, with more than 1,000 costumed participants. Richly embroidered gowns, gleaming armor, colorful flags, and traditional music transform the city into a living history tableau.

Each team tells a story through its procession, recalling medieval life with pageantry and pride. At the center marches the Carroccio, the great war chariot of the Lombard League, pulled by oxen and bearing the city's banner; a direct link to the Battle of 1176.

Arrival at the Stadium

The procession winds its way to the Stadio Giovanni Mari, where the horse race will be held. Crowds gather as dignitaries, flag-throwers, and musicians take their places. The atmosphere builds with chants, songs, and displays of neighborhood rivalry.

Evening

The Horse Race

Four contrade (neighborhoods) compete in a preliminary heat, followed by a second heat and then the final. Riders race without saddles, clinging only to the manes of their horses as they thunder around the track. The stadium roars with emotion as supporters cheer in their neighborhood colors. Victory brings immense prestige, and the winning team carries the palio banner home in triumph.

Victory Celebrations

After the race, the celebrations continue late into the night. The winners parade their banner through the streets, bells ring out, and neighborhoods host banquets and parties. For one year, the victors enjoy bragging rights and the honor of having their names inscribed in the long tradition of the Palio di Legnano.

Walking Tour of Legnano

#1. Basilica di San Magno

Begin at the Basilica di San Magno, the city's most important church. Built in the sixteenth century on the site of an earlier medieval church, it is dedicated to Saint Magnus of Anagni, one of Legnano's patron saints. Inside, the frescoes by Bernardino Luini, a pupil of Leonardo da Vinci, glow with Renaissance artistry. During Palio week, the basilica hosts the blessing of the palio banner, one of the festival's most solemn moments.

#2. Monument to Alberto da Giussano

A short walk brings you to the bronze equestrian statue of Alberto da Giussano, the legendary hero of the Battle of Legnano. Erected in 1900, the statue depicts the commander brandishing his sword and has become the enduring symbol of the city. It is a powerful reminder of the courage and independence that the Palio celebrates each year.

#3. Palazzo Malinverni

Next, visit Palazzo Malinverni, Legnano's elegant town hall, built in the early twentieth century with a striking neo-medieval design. The façade is decorated with coats of arms representing the Lombard League cities that fought at Legnano. Inside, the council chambers and frescoes evoke the civic pride of the city's past and present.

#4. Castello Visconteo (Castle of Legnano)

Continue to the Castello Visconteo, a brooding medieval fortress whose thick walls and corner towers once commanded the strategic Olona River crossing. Built as a defensive outpost, the castle gained prominence when the powerful Visconti family of Milan expanded it in the fourteenth century, transforming it into a symbol of their growing dominance over the Lombard plain. The fortress witnessed centuries of warfare, political intrigue, and shifting allegiances as various noble families vied for control of this vital trade route.

Medieval Castle of Legnano

Today, the castle's ancient chambers have been transformed into atmospheric exhibition spaces where medieval armor gleams under soft lighting and Palio banners hang from stone walls. Interactive displays bring to life the thunder of hoofbeats and clash of weapons from the historic Battle of Legnano, while period artifacts and illuminated manuscripts reveal the daily life of medieval warriors and nobles who once walked these very corridors.

The castle courtyard, enclosed by weathered battlements, provides a dramatic backdrop for cultural events and serves as a tangible link between Legnano's legendary past and its vibrant present-day celebrations. Surrounded by a leafy park, the castle is a favorite gathering spot for families and offers a sense of how Legnano balanced defense and community life in the Middle Ages.

#5. Piazza San Magno and Corso Garibaldi

Return to Piazza San Magno, the lively square in front of the basilica, where cafés and gelaterie spill out onto the cobblestones, creating a welcoming atmosphere perfect for a quick break. This central piazza has long been a gathering place for locals and visitors alike. From here, take a leisurely stroll down Corso Garibaldi, the city's principal shopping street. Lined with boutiques, elegant storefronts, and charming cafés, it's an ideal spot to soak in the daily rhythm of Legnano while browsing for local products or simply enjoying the vibrant street life.

#6. Museo Civico Guido Sutermeister

Finish the walk at the Museo Civico Guido Sutermeister, housed in a historic villa surrounded by gardens. The museum offers a fascinating journey through Legnano's past, with archaeological finds from prehistoric and Roman times, medieval artifacts, and rotating exhibitions that highlight various aspects of the city's cultural and artistic heritage. It provides a deeper perspective on Legnano's evolution through the centuries and makes for a thoughtful and engaging conclusion to your visit.

Logistics

Train: Legnano is easily reached from Milan by frequent regional trains. The journey is 30 minutes from Milano Porta Garibaldi or Milano Centrale. The train station is a short 15-minute walk from the Basilica di San Magno and the historic center.

Bus: Local bus routes connect the train station with key parts of the city, including the castle and stadium. During Palio week, additional services may operate to handle the influx of visitors.

Car: From Milan, take the A8 Autostrada dei Laghi toward Varese and exit at Legnano. The drive is about 30 minutes depending on traffic.

Parking: Much of central Legnano restricts traffic during festival days, so plan to park outside the historic core. Paid parking lots are available near the train station and at Piazza del Popolo, both within walking distance of the Palio events and city sites.

Restaurant Recommendations

Viro Steak Restaurant. Corso Magenta 48

A modern and inviting steakhouse in the heart of Legnano, celebrated for its wide selection of dry-aged cuts and premium meats like Fiorentina and Japanese Wagyu.

Villa ReNoir Ristorante. Via delle Robinie

Villa ReNoir Ristorante on Via delle Robinie is a grand venue that specializes in festive events and dinner-show experiences rather than traditional dining. The restaurant features expansive gardens and theatrical settings that create a dramatic backdrop for celebrations.

Day Trips: Nearby Sites, Cities and Towns

Novara. About 40 kilometers (25 miles) west of Legnano, Novara is a city with a distinctly Piedmontese character. Its skyline is dominated by the soaring dome of the Basilica of San Gaudenzio, designed by Alessandro Antonelli, the same architect behind Turin's Mole Antonelliana. Novara's historic center is a pleasure to explore, with elegant arcades, Romanesque churches, and the lively Piazza delle Erbe.

The Broletto complex, a medieval civic palace with a courtyard surrounded by frescoed walls, is one of the city's architectural jewels. Novara is also known for its rice fields in the surrounding countryside, which supply the Arborio rice essential for northern Italy's risottos. From Legnano, the city is easily reached by car in less than an hour or by regional train.

Arona. 45 kilometers (28 miles) northwest of Legnano on the southern shore of Lake Maggiore. Arona is a charming lakeside town perfect for a leisurely day trip. Its main promenade stretches along the water, lined with cafés, boutiques, and gelaterie, offering beautiful views across the lake. Above the town stands the colossal statue of San Carlo Borromeo, affectionately called the "Sancarlone."

Visitors can climb inside the statue for panoramic views over Lake Maggiore and the Alps. Ferries connect Arona with other lakeside destinations such as Angera and Stresa, making it an ideal base for exploring the lake. The journey from Legnano takes about 50 minutes by car or just over an hour by train.

Asti. About 115 kilometers (71 miles) southwest of Legnano, Asti is a historic city in the Piedmont region, best known for its wines and medieval towers. Once a wealthy banking center in the Middle Ages, Asti still displays its legacy in palaces and Gothic churches. The Cathedral of Santa Maria Assunta is a fine example of Lombard Gothic architecture, while the Torre Troyana offers sweeping views over the rooftops.

Asti is also home to the famous Palio di Asti, one of the oldest horse races in Italy, held every September. Visitors can enjoy tastings of Moscato d'Asti and Barbera wines in enoteche (wine shops) throughout the city. From Legnano, Asti can be reached in under two hours by car or via train connections through Milan.

Legnano Festivals and Sagre Throughout the Year

Carnevale Legnanese

February or March

A lively pre-Lenten celebration with parades, costumed processions, and music fills the streets. Children enjoy traditional sweets such as chiacchiere and tortelli, while floats decorated by local groups bring color and humor to the city.

Festa di San Giovanni

June 24

One of the city's traditional summer feasts, held with open-air concerts, food stalls, and a festive market. Neighborhood associations set up tables serving local dishes, and the evening often concludes with fireworks.

Estate Legnanese

June to September

A summer cultural program that fills Legnano with concerts, outdoor cinema, theater, and exhibitions. Events are hosted in piazzas, parks, and at the Castello Visconteo, creating a season-long celebration of the arts. Locals and visitors alike gather under the warm evening skies to enjoy performances that range from classical music to contemporary theater, making it one of the most anticipated times of the year. The festival gives Legnano a vibrant, festive atmosphere that lasts all summer long.

Festa di San Magno

November 5

Dedicated to Legnano's patron saint, San Magno, this feast day is celebrated with solemn Masses in the basilica and civic ceremonies in the piazza. Religious devotion blends with community spirit, and the basilica glows with candles and floral offerings. The celebration honors centuries-old traditions, bringing the community together in a shared expression of faith and civic pride. It's a day when Legnano's spiritual heart is fully on display.

Mercatini di Natale

December

Legnano's Christmas markets bring wooden stalls, holiday crafts, and festive foods to the historic center. Families gather for lights, music, and mulled wine, with Piazza San Magno transformed into a winter wonderland. Twinkling lights illuminate the square, the scent of roasted chestnuts fills the air, and live performances create a warm, joyful ambiance. It's the perfect setting to experience the magic of the season and pick up unique gifts from local artisans.

CHAPTER TEN

Polpenazze del Garda's Wine Festival

Hillside Charm & Valtenesi Wine

Festa del Vino di Polpenazze

Where: Polpenazze del Garda

When: Late May to early June (dates very).

Average Festival Temperatures: High: 26°C (79°F). Low: 14°C (57°F).

Event and Ticket Website:

https://www.oltrebrescia.it/en/articles/polpenazze-wine-festival

Polpenazze del Garda: A Hilltop Haven Over Lake Garda

Gracing the gentle, vineyard-covered hills of the Valtenesi region, Polpenazze del Garda is one of the most picturesque villages overlooking the western shores of Lake Garda. Its medieval core, crowned by a historic church and flanked by stone archways and narrow lanes, has the timeless atmosphere of a Lombard hill town that has seen centuries of agricultural prosperity. The surrounding landscape is a patchwork of olive groves, rolling vineyards, and cypress-lined lanes leading down toward the sparkling waters of the lake.

I visited Polpenazze del Garda on a day trip with a few girlfriends, and we loved exploring the remnants of its ancient walls and quiet stone alleys. The village feels frozen in time, yet alive with the scent of wine and olive oil from nearby estates. We lingered on the panoramic terrace near the parish church of Santa Maria, soaking in views that seemed to stretch endlessly across the Valtenesi hills to the lake below. It was one of the most breathtaking scenes we experienced during our trip.

Today, Polpenazze is best known for its connection to the surrounding vineyards, producing exceptional DOC[1] wines such as Groppello, Chiaretto, and Garda Classico. This deep-rooted viticultural tradition finds its greatest expression in the annual wine event.

Polpenazze Wine Festival

Every summer, the medieval streets and sunlit piazzas of Polpenazze del Garda come alive with the aromas of freshly uncorked bottles and sizzling local dishes. The Festa del Vino is the village's signature celebration, attracting thousands of visitors eager to sample the rich winemaking heritage of the Valtenesi hills. For decades, this festival has served as both a showcase for local producers and a joyful gathering of community and visitors.

The event began in the late 1940s as a small-town fair where vintners would bring their best wines to be tasted and judged. Over time, it developed into one of the most anticipated wine events on Lake Garda's western shore, now featuring dozens of wineries, guided tastings, music performances, and food stands highlighting traditional Lombard cuisine.

---

1. DOC stands for Denominazione di Origine Controllata ("Controlled Designation of Origin"), an Italian quality label that certifies a wine comes from a specific region and meets strict production standards for grape varieties, methods, and quality.

At its heart, the festival is a tribute to the Garda Classico DOC wines, crafted from native grape varieties such as Groppello, Marzemino, Sangiovese, and Barbera. Chiaretto, the pale rosé with delicate floral notes, is especially beloved, symbolizing the easygoing elegance of Garda summers. Olive oil, cheeses, cured meats, and artisanal breads from the region add layers of flavor to the experience.

Beyond the tasting booths, the Festa del Vino offers exhibitions about the Valtenesi's history, from Roman-era viticulture to modern sustainability in winemaking. Evening concerts fill the air with music as the sunset bathes the vineyards in warm light, and the cobbled streets buzz with the mingling of locals, wine enthusiasts, and travelers discovering Polpenazze for the first time.

Festival Traditions

Afternoon

The afternoon sees the highest flow of visitors. Crowds wander from stall to stall, glasses in hand, sampling different wines while chatting with producers. This is also the time for the much-anticipated wine competition awards, where expert judges announce the best wines of the year in several categories. The winners proudly display award ribbons, and visitors often line up to taste these distinguished bottles.

Street performers, including musicians and jugglers, add to the atmosphere, while guided tours of the town offer insight into Polpenazze's medieval architecture and panoramic viewpoints.

Evening

As the sun sets over the Valtenesi hills, the festival takes on a magical glow. String lights illuminate the piazzas, and the music shifts to evening concerts ranging from local bands to jazz ensembles. Couples and friends gather at long communal tables to enjoy wine and late-night snacks under the stars. The mood is celebratory yet relaxed, making it easy to linger until the final glasses are poured.

Walking Tour of Polpenazze del Garda

#1. Piazza Roma

Begin the tour in the charming Piazza Roma, the heart of Polpenazze. This small but lively square is framed by pastel-colored buildings, cafés with outdoor tables, and the local town hall. During the wine festival, it becomes a hub of activity, lined with stalls and alive with music. Even outside festival days, it is the perfect place to enjoy a morning espresso while watching village life unfold.

#2. Parish Church of Santa Maria

From the square, walk uphill to the Parish Church of Santa Maria, perched on the site of an earlier medieval church. Its neoclassical façade is elegant yet understated, while inside you will find frescoes and altarpieces that reflect centuries of devotion. Step outside onto the panoramic terrace, where the view sweeps across the Valtenesi vineyards toward the glittering waters of Lake Garda.

Parish Church and Lake Garda Views

#3. Porta San Marco and Medieval Walls

Continue through the historic streets to find remnants of Polpenazze's medieval fortifications. The Porta San Marco, a restored stone gateway, recalls the town's strategic past as a fortified settlement. Traces of ancient walls still line parts of the village, and the narrow lanes here are perfect for slow exploration.

#4. Belvedere Viewpoint

A short walk from the old gate brings you to a belvedere overlooking the hills and vineyards. On clear days, you can see the blue expanse of Lake Garda framed by the mountains beyond. Benches here invite you to pause and take in the timeless landscape that defines the Valtenesi.

Logistics

Train: Polpenazze del Garda does not have its own train station. The closest stations are Desenzano del Garda-Sirmione (about 12 kilometers / 7.5 miles away) and Lonato del Garda (about 14 kilometers / 8.7 miles away). Both are on the main Milan–Venice railway line, with frequent regional and high-speed train connections to Milan (around 1 hour) and Verona (about 30 minutes). From these stations, you can reach Polpenazze by local bus, taxi, or rental car.

Bus: The Arriva Italia bus network connects Polpenazze with nearby towns such as Desenzano del Garda, Salò, and other Valtenesi villages.

Car: Driving is the easiest way to reach Polpenazze, especially if you plan to explore the surrounding vineyards and countryside. From the A4 Autostrada, take the Desenzano del Garda exit and follow signs toward Salò and Polpenazze. The drive from Desenzano takes about 15 minutes, from Salò about 20 minutes, and from Brescia about 35 minutes.

Parking: During regular visits, street parking and small public lots are available near the town center. However, during the Festa del Vino, parking inside the historic core is restricted, and designated festival parking areas are set up on the outskirts with shuttle buses or a short walk into town. Arriving early is highly recommended to secure a convenient spot.

Restaurant Recommendations

Antica Trattoria Miravalle. Via Roma, 34

Situated in the heart of the village, this historic trattoria pairs rustic charm with panoramic views of the surrounding hills. Known for its casoncelli pasta, slow-cooked stews, and generous wine list featuring Valtenesi DOC selections, it's a favorite with both locals and visitors.

Agriturismo La Guarda. Via della Selva, 14

Set among the vineyards just outside Polpenazze, this agriturismo offers farm-to-table dining with dishes prepared from its own produce and meats. Seasonal menus feature fresh vegetables, homemade pasta, and locally raised meats, all paired with house wines.

Day Trip Options: Nearby Sites, Cities, and Towns

Desenzano del Garda. 12 kilometers (7.5 miles) from Polpenazze. The largest town on Lake Garda's southern shore, Desenzano blends lively lakeside energy with historical charm. The waterfront promenade is lined with cafés, gelaterie, and shops, while the historic center offers elegant piazzas, boutique shopping, and vibrant markets.

Key sights include the Roman Villa, with its beautifully preserved mosaics, the Cathedral of Santa Maria Maddalena with Baroque paintings by Andrea Celesti, and the hilltop Desenzano Castle, offering panoramic views over the lake. Ferries depart regularly from Desenzano's port, making it a hub for exploring other Lake Garda destinations.

Castello di Padenghe sul Garda. 7 kilometers (4.3 miles) from Polpenazze. Just a short drive away, this 10th-century hilltop fortress is one of the best-preserved medieval fortifications in the area, offering sweeping views over Lake Garda and the surrounding countryside. Inside, you can explore the interior courtyard and admire the sturdy stone walls that have withstood centuries of history. The village of Padenghe sul Garda itself is equally charming, with cobbled streets lined with small cafés, wine bars, and artisan shops.

Notable sights include the Romanesque Church of Sant'Emiliano, set amidst olive groves and offering peaceful lake views. Wandering through the historic center, visitors will also find boutique stores, family-run bakeries, and spots to enjoy local specialties like fresh focaccia and artisanal gelato.

Festivals and Sagre in Nearby Towns Throughout the Year

Moniga del Garda Chiaretto Festival (Italia in Rosa Wine Festival)

Early June

Held in neighboring Moniga del Garda, this festival is dedicated entirely to rosé wines, with a special emphasis on the local Chiaretto. Visitors can sample dozens of rosés from across Italy and abroad, enjoy live music, and relax by the lakefront.

Desenzano del Garda Summer Festival

July and August

A series of concerts, markets, and cultural events spread throughout the summer months in Desenzano. Performances range from classical music in historic piazzas to contemporary bands along the waterfront, often paired with local food and wine stalls.

Festa dell'Uva di Puegnago del Garda (Grape Harvest Festival)

Early September

Just a few kilometers from Polpenazze, the hilltop village of Puegnago hosts this lively grape festival. Events include grape pressing demonstrations, wine tastings, food stands, and music, all set against panoramic views of the Valtenesi hills and Lake Garda.

Mercatini di Natale di Desenzano del Garda (Christmas Market)

December

Desenzano's Christmas market transforms its historic center into a festive wonderland. Stalls sell artisan crafts, seasonal treats such as mulled wine and roasted chestnuts, and holiday decorations. The lakeside promenade sparkles with lights, making for a magical winter visit.

CHAPTER ELEVEN

Milan's Summer Celebrations

Nightly Open Air Events

E state Sforzesca at Castello Sforzesco

Where: Milan

When: Annually, from June through September.

Average Festival Temperatures: High 30°C (86°F). Low 23°C (73°F).

A Fortress Through the Ages

The Castello Sforzesco is one of Milan's most iconic landmarks. Its red brick walls and towers stand as symbols of both medieval might and Renaissance ambition. I first visited the Castello Sforzesco in 2023 for the summer music festival, and I was completely captivated. Since then, I have always tried to book an Airbnb close to the castle. It is stunning, and the park behind it is one of my favorite places in Milan to walk. We enjoyed strolling through the shaded paths, listening to street musicians, and watching locals gather on the open lawns as the sun set behind the towers.

The fortress was originally built in 1368 by Galeazzo II Visconti. After years of political upheaval in the fifteenth century, it was nearly destroyed. Francesco Sforza later rebuilt and transformed it after becoming Duke of Milan in 1450, giving the castle its name. The castle reached its height of splendor under Ludovico Sforza, known as il Moro, who turned it into a lavish Renaissance court. During his reign, some of the greatest artists of the age, including Leonardo da Vinci and Donato Bramante, worked here designing and decorating its halls. Over the centuries, the castle endured foreign domination, partial demolition, and neglect. Extensive restorations in the nineteenth and twentieth centuries revived it as a cultural center.

Today, the Castello houses Milan's Civic Museums, where visitors can discover everything from musical instruments and ancient arms to Renaissance masterpieces. The highlight is Michelangelo's Rondanini Pietà, the sculptor's final unfinished work. Its raw, elongated figures of Mary supporting the body of Christ are profoundly moving, and the castle's simple setting allows its spiritual intensity to shine.

Estate Sforzesca

Every summer, the Castello Sforzesco is reborn as Milan's largest open-air cultural stage during Estate Sforzesca. For nearly three months, the castle's spacious courtyards host an eclectic program of concerts, theater, dance, and film screenings. Both international stars and local ensembles perform here, offering everything from jazz and classical to pop and contemporary music. Theater troupes and dance companies bring the historic courtyards alive with dramatic energy, while film nights invite audiences to enjoy cinema beneath the stars.

One of the unique joys of the event is the setting itself. The concerts unfold against the backdrop of massive medieval walls and Renaissance towers, creating a magical blend of history and modern creativity. www.milanocastello.it

Milan's Other Summer Festivals

Milano Monza Open-Air Motor Show (MIMO)

June

An innovative auto show where the latest cars and prototypes are displayed outdoors in Milan and Monza. Visitors can see cutting-edge automotive design in historic piazzas and along elegant streets.

Milano Pride

Late June

A vibrant week of cultural events, debates, and performances culminating in a massive parade through central Milan. Rainbow flags, music, and festivities highlight the city's spirit of inclusion.

Estate all'Umanitaria (Summer Cultural Program)

July–September

Hosted at the Società Umanitaria, this long-running series features open-air concerts, theater, and film screenings in a beautiful cloister setting. A cultural oasis in the heart of Milan.

AriAnteo (Cinema Festival)

July–September

A beloved summer cinema festival with outdoor screenings in historic courtyards and piazzas. Classic films and new releases are projected under the stars, creating a magical atmosphere.

Festival Latinoamericano (Latin American Festival)

July–August

One of Europe's largest Latin American festivals. Concerts, dance, food, and cultural performances bring Latin rhythms and flavors to Milan's summer nights.

Sagra di San Cristoforo (Feast of St. Christopher)

July 25

Celebrated in the picturesque Naviglio district, this traditional festival honors Saint Christopher, patron saint of travelers. A religious procession is paired with music, food stalls, and community gatherings along the canal.

CHAPTER TWELVE

Brescia: Classic Cars & Timeless Elegance

Celebration of Speed and Style

Mille Miglia: Brescia's Legendary Vintage Car Rally

Where: Brescia (start and finish, with routes across Italy).

When: Mid-June, four days (Wednesday–Saturday).

Average Festival Temperatures: High 27°C (81°F). Low 17°C (63°F).

Brescia: City of Stone and Spirit

Brescia, known as "La Leonessa d'Italia" (The Lioness of Italy) for its proud role in the Risorgimento, is a captivating city in the Lombardy region of northern Italy. During the 19th-century struggle that united the Italian states, Brescia became a symbol of courage when its citizens rose against foreign rule. Their defiance and sacrifice during those turbulent years embody the spirit that earned the city its celebrated title. Set between the towering foothills of the Alps and the gentle shores of Lake Garda, it occupies a strategic location in the fertile Po Valley. The city lies about 90 kilometers (56 miles) east of Milan and 50 kilometers (31 miles) west of Verona, with the River Mella flowing through its western districts. Today, Brescia is home to 200,000 residents, making it the second-largest city in Lombardy after Milan.

The cityscape blends ancient history with urban elegance. Brescia's roots run deep into Roman times, when it was known as Brixia, an important settlement along key trade and military routes. Evidence of its Roman past still graces the city in the form of a forum, theater, and temple ruins, earning the area UNESCO World Heritage status alongside nearby monumental sites. In the Middle Ages, Brescia developed into a powerful commune and later came under Venetian rule, which enriched its architecture and fortified its defenses.

I first visited Brescia on a day trip with my family from Bergamo, and we were immediately enchanted by its beauty. The city feels intimate yet filled with grandeur, a place where history and elegance coexist effortlessly. We explored with a local guide, who brought the cathedrals and Roman ruins to life through stories that made the city's past feel tangible. We lingered in a lively café for cappuccinos, watched daily life unfold around us, and later walked up to the castle for breathtaking views over the rooftops and distant mountains. Brescia's compact size made it easy to see so much in one day, yet it left us eager to return.

Brescia's centro storico invites leisurely exploration, from its stately Renaissance squares to narrow lanes that suddenly open to reveal churches adorned with masterful frescoes. Roman ruins sit comfortably beside elegant palazzi, while modern boutiques and cafés add a lively pulse. The city's efficient and conveniently located train station makes arrival and onward travel easy, making Brescia an ideal base for day trips around Lombardy.

Mille Miglia

The Mille Miglia began in 1927, conceived by two young Brescian counts, Aymo Maggi and Franco Mazzotti, who wanted to elevate their hometown's prestige with an epic road race. The original course was a grueling loop from Brescia to Rome and back, covering roughly 1,600 kilometers (1,000 miles).

From 1927 to 1957, the Mille Miglia was held twenty-four times, becoming a proving ground for Italy's most prestigious automotive brands such as Ferrari, Alfa Romeo, Maserati, Porsche, and Mercedes-Benz, and a symbol of daring speed. Legendary drivers including Tazio Nuvolari and Stirling Moss cemented their reputations here, with Moss's 1955 victory in just over ten hours remaining one of the great moments in racing history.

The race came to an abrupt and tragic end in 1957 after a devastating accident near Guidizzolo, when a Ferrari crashed into spectators, claiming multiple lives. The tragedy brought an immediate halt to the competitive era of the Mille Miglia, but its spirit endured. In 1977, the event was reborn as a historic rally, limited to cars that had participated or could have taken part in the original race. Today it combines sporting rigor with cultural celebration, attracting participants and admirers from around the world.

The events of 1957 and their impact on Enzo Ferrari's life were later portrayed in the 2023 film *Ferrari*, directed by Michael Mann, which captured both the glory and the human cost of this legendary race.

Festival Traditions

Wednesday: Arrival & Exhibition

Wednesday marks the official arrival and exhibition day of the Mille Miglia in Brescia. Throughout the morning and afternoon, Piazza della Vittoria comes alive with the sound of engines and excited conversation as cars undergo scrutineering, the official inspection that ensures each vehicle meets the race's eligibility standards. Crowds gather to admire the gleaming vintage models up close, while civic leaders, car clubs, and international delegations join the opening ceremonies.

As evening falls, anticipation builds for the parade that signals the start of the legendary journey, when the first cars roll out from Brescia's historic center to the cheers of spectators lining the streets.

Thursday & Friday: The Race Across Italy

On Thursday and Friday, the Mille Miglia rally unfolds across some of Italy's most scenic roads, winding through Renaissance cities, charming villages, and rolling countryside. Spectators gather along the routes to watch priceless vintage cars roar past, escorted by motorcycles and police convoys that add to the sense of excitement. Along the way, local piazzas transform into festive hubs filled with food stalls, music, and small exhibitions celebrating regional traditions, turning the race into a moving celebration of Italian culture as much as a test of endurance and elegance.

Saturday: Return to Brescia

By Saturday afternoon, the Mille Miglia returns to Brescia in a scene of triumph and celebration. Crowds fill Viale Venezia to welcome the drivers back, cheering as engines roar and competitors wave proudly from their cockpits. The atmosphere is electric as the city once again becomes the heart of the rally. Later, in the elegant Piazza della Loggia, the awards ceremony honors the top performers, judged on precision and timing rather than speed.

As night falls, music drifts through the streets, fireworks light up the sky, and Brescia celebrates with style and joy, bringing the legendary event to a dazzling close.

Walking Tour of Brescia

#1. Piazza della Loggia

Begin your exploration in Piazza della Loggia, one of the most elegant squares in Lombardy. Surrounded by graceful Renaissance buildings, the square reflects Brescia's period under Venetian rule. The Loggia, an impressive white-marble palace that gives the square its name, houses the city hall and displays exquisite decorative details. A clock tower with an astronomical dial marks the hours over the bustling scene below.

#2. Duomo Vecchio and Duomo Nuovo

Just a short walk from Piazza della Loggia stands one of Brescia's most striking sights. The Old and New Cathedrals share the same piazza.

The Duomo Vecchio, also called the Rotonda, is a circular Romanesque masterpiece built in the 11th century. Its stone exterior may appear austere, but once inside, the dim light reveals a world of quiet beauty. Ancient columns support the heavy dome, and faint frescoes of saints still cling to the curved walls, their colors softened by time. Descending into the crypt, visitors find traces of even earlier churches, offering a tangible connection to Brescia's medieval past.

I remember stepping inside and being struck by the profound silence, a stillness that seemed to hold centuries of prayer.

11th Century Duomo Vecchio

Beside it, the Duomo Nuovo rises in Baroque grandeur, its gleaming marble façade and soaring dome dominating the skyline. Construction began in the early 17th century and continued for nearly two hundred years, resulting in one of the tallest domes in Italy. The interior dazzles with light and ornamentation, stucco angels, gilded altars, and expansive frescoes celebrating divine triumph.

Standing between the two cathedrals, you can feel the evolution of style and spirit, from the Romanesque simplicity of the Rotonda to the confident exuberance of the Baroque age. The contrast offers a vivid journey through architectural history in a single glance, perfectly capturing Brescia's layered identity.

#3. Piazza del Foro and the Capitolium

Walk toward Piazza del Foro to encounter the archaeological heart of ancient Brixia. Here stand the remains of the Roman Capitolium Temple, built in 73 AD under Emperor Vespasian. The surviving columns and reconstructed sections give a sense of the temple's former grandeur, while the nearby Roman theater hints at the city's cultural life nearly two thousand years ago. The site, part of a UNESCO World Heritage designation, is complemented by a small museum displaying artifacts found during excavations.

#4. Santa Giulia Museum

Continue to the Santa Giulia Museum, housed in a former Benedictine monastery founded in the 8th century. This vast complex leads visitors through more than a thousand years of Brescia's history, from Roman mosaics to medieval relics and Renaissance art. The museum's setting, with cloisters, chapels, and underground archaeological remains, makes it as much an architectural treasure as a cultural one. Highlights include the Desiderius Cross, an ornate masterpiece of Lombard goldsmithing.

Interior of the Duomo Nuovo

#5. Castello di Brescia

No visit to Brescia is complete without ascending to the Castello di Brescia on Cidneo Hill. This medieval fortress, expanded over centuries by both Visconti and Venetian rulers, offers sweeping views of the city and surrounding hills. Visitors can explore the ramparts, towers, and gardens, as well as museums dedicated to arms and the Risorgimento. The castle's stone walls and leafy pathways make it an inviting retreat for history lovers and photographers alike.

https://www.bresciamusei.com/en/museums-and-venues/the-castle/

#6. Corso Zanardelli and Teatro Grande

Descend from the castle and stroll along Corso Zanardelli, Brescia's elegant main street lined with shops, cafés, and theaters. Stop at the Teatro Grande, an opulent

18th-century theater with gilded interiors and a rich cultural program. Even if you do not attend a performance, guided tours reveal its ornate architecture and storied past. We paused here for coffee at a nearby café, where the lively hum of conversation and the clinking of porcelain cups felt like a scene from another era. The street exudes old-world charm and remains one of my favorite spots in the city for people-watching.

#7. Church of San Francesco d'Assisi

A short walk away lies the Church of San Francesco d'Assisi, a Gothic gem dating to the 13th century. Its façade combines brick and stone in harmonious simplicity, while the interior houses delicate frescoes and wooden choir stalls. The tranquil atmosphere offers a reflective pause before continuing the tour. I found this church especially peaceful, its quiet interior offering a moment to rest and take in the gentle scent of incense mixed with the cool air of centuries-old stone.

Castello di Brescia

#8. Via dei Musei

Conclude the walking tour along Via dei Musei, a historic thoroughfare that links many of Brescia's archaeological and artistic treasures. Lined with shops and cafés, it invites visitors to linger for an espresso or an aperitivo while reflecting on the city's layered history. We ended our visit here, sitting at an outdoor café as the afternoon light turned golden, watching the rhythm of local life flow by and feeling that familiar sense of contentment that comes after a day well spent exploring Italy.

Logistics

Train: Brescia is a major stop on the Milan–Venice railway line, making it easily accessible from multiple Lombard and northern Italian cities. High-speed Frecciarossa and Italo trains connect Brescia to Milan in about 45 minutes and to Verona in around 35 minutes, with frequent departures throughout the day. Regional trains link Brescia to Bergamo, Cremona, and Lake Garda towns such as Desenzano del Garda and Peschiera del Garda. The train station is conveniently about a 15-minute walk from the historic center, or a short bus ride if carrying luggage.

Bus: The city is served by the Brescia Trasporti network, which provides frequent bus services within the city and to nearby towns. Regional and long-distance buses connect Brescia with other destinations in Lombardy, Trentino, and Veneto. The main bus terminal is near the train station. During the Festa di San Faustino, extra bus services are scheduled to accommodate the sizeable crowds attending the fair.

Car: Brescia is located along the A4 Autostrada between Milan and Venice, making it straightforward to reach by car. From Milan, the journey takes about one hour, while Verona is roughly 45 minutes away. Roads are well maintained, and the signage is clear. However, driving into the historic center is restricted because of the ZTL (Zona a Traffico Limitato). Visitors arriving by car should use one of the designated parking areas outside the ZTL and continue on foot or by public transport.

Parking: Several parking garages and open-air lots are available close to the city center, including Parcheggio Stazione, Parcheggio Vittoria, and Parcheggio Arnaldo. Rates are reasonable, and many are within a short walk of major sites. During major events such as the Festa di San Faustino, parking fills quickly, so early arrival is recommended.

Restaurant Recommendations

Osteria al Bianchi. Via Gasparo da Salò, 32

A historic osteria with a warm, casual atmosphere, beloved by locals for generations. Known for traditional Lombard fare, it serves specialties such as casoncelli pasta, slow-cooked meats, and polenta. The setting, with wood-beamed ceilings and simple furnishings, adds to its timeless charm.

Antica Osteria del Borgo. Contrada del Borgo San Giovanni, 1

In the centro storico, this osteria pairs a rustic setting with a refined menu. Guests can enjoy regional cured meats, fresh lake fish, and house-made desserts. The wine list includes excellent Franciacorta selections from nearby vineyards.

Trattoria G.A. Porteri. Via Giuseppe Garibaldi, 18

One of Brescia's oldest trattorias, G.A. Porteri has been serving local recipes for over a century. Known for its spit-roasted meats and hearty pasta dishes, it is a favorite for those seeking authentic flavors in a cozy environment.

Day Trip Options: Nearby Sites, Cities, and Towns

Moniga del Garda. 45 kilometers (28 miles) from Brescia. Perched on the southwestern shore of Lake Garda, Moniga del Garda combines the charm of a small lakeside village with a touch of elegance. Its historic center is crowned by a medieval castle that once served as refuge for local residents during times of conflict. From its ancient walls, visitors can enjoy panoramic views of the lake and surrounding vineyards.

Down by the water, a scenic promenade leads to the marina, where cafés and restaurants invite visitors to linger over a leisurely lunch with lake views. Moniga is also known as the birthplace of *Chiaretto*, a delicate rosé wine made from local grapes, which pairs beautifully with the area's light summer cuisine. Nearby trails and cycling routes connect to neighboring lakeside towns, making Moniga an ideal destination for travelers seeking both relaxation and gentle exploration along the shores of Lake Garda.

Salò (Lago di Garda). 35 kilometers (22 miles) from Brescia. On the western shore of Lake Garda, Salò combines natural beauty with historic elegance. The town boasts one of the longest lakeside promenades in Italy, lined with palm trees, historic villas, and inviting cafés. Its centro storico is a maze of narrow streets and small squares filled with boutiques, gelaterie, and restaurants.

Key sights include the Gothic-Renaissance Duomo di Santa Maria Annunziata and the Palazzo della Magnifica Patria, which houses a civic museum. Salò also holds a unique place in history as the capital of the Italian Social Republic during World War II. Its serene setting and vibrant cultural life make it an excellent day trip for those seeking both history and lakeside charm.

Bolzano 200 kilometers (124 miles) from Brescia, offers a rewarding change of scenery and culture, blending Italian and Austrian influences in the heart of South Tyrol. I stayed here with my family for five nights in 2021, and it remains one of the most beautiful towns I have ever visited.

We arrived late in the evening, unaware of the view that awaited us. The next morning, when I stepped out onto our Airbnb balcony, I was completely stunned. Below us stretched a picture-perfect scene of pastel-colored rooftops, arcaded streets, and church spires, all set against the dramatic backdrop of the mountains glowing in the morning light.

Surrounded by the Dolomites, this alpine city enchants visitors with its harmonious blend of cultures and its colorful, flower-filled streets. Piazza Walther serves as the city's lively gathering spot, while the South Tyrol Museum of Archaeology houses the world-famous Ötzi the Iceman. Bolzano's medieval center is filled with shops selling Tyrolean crafts, artisanal chocolate, and cured meats. The city is also a gateway to scenic drives and cable car rides into the surrounding mountains, making it a perfect choice for travelers who wish to experience a different side of northern Italy in a single day.

Festivals and Sagre in Brescia Throughout the Year

Brescia Summer Music

July and August

A series of open-air concerts and cultural events held in piazzas, courtyards, and historic venues across the city. The program ranges from classical music to jazz and contemporary performances, often accompanied by food and wine tastings. The combination of warm summer nights and live music makes this a favorite among locals. During our visit, we wandered into one of the evening performances in Piazza della Loggia and stayed far longer than planned, swept up in the music and the glow of lights reflecting off the old stone buildings. The atmosphere felt both elegant and effortlessly joyful.

Notte Bianca di Brescia

Late June or early July

Brescia stays awake until dawn during this lively summer night festival. Shops remain open late, street performers fill the squares, and music stages offer entertainment from rock bands to folk ensembles. Food stalls and pop-up bars ensure that the city's energy never dips. I remember the excitement in the air as we strolled through the illuminated streets, the scent of sweets and roasted nuts drifting through the crowd, and the laughter of families mingling with live music well past midnight. It is one of those nights that perfectly capture the spirit of an Italian summer.

Festa dell'Uva di Puegnago (Wine Festival)

Early September

Just outside Brescia in the hilltop village of Puegnago, this grape festival celebrates the winemaking heritage of the Valtenesi area near Lake Garda. The event features wine tastings, local food stands, music, and contests. It is a great opportunity to explore the surrounding countryside while enjoying regional flavors.

Mercatini di Natale di Brescia (Christmas Markets)

December

Brescia's Christmas markets transform the historic center into a festive wonderland. Stalls sell artisan crafts, holiday decorations, and seasonal treats such as roasted chestnuts, mulled wine, and panettone. Lights and decorations brighten the streets, and music from choirs and bands adds to the holiday atmosphere.

CHAPTER THIRTEEN

Sondrio: Faith in the Valtellina

Saint, Procession & Alpine Pride

Festa di San Gervasio

Where: Sondrio

When: June 19

Average Festival Temperatures: High 25°C (77°F). Low 14°C (57°F).

Sondrio: Alpine Crossroads in the Heart of Valtellina

Sondrio is the principal city of the Valtellina Valley. The town sits in a dramatic Alpine landscape where terraced vineyards climb the snow-capped mountain slopes. This city of 20,000 stands at the crossroads of empires, where Roman legions once marched toward distant Alpine passes and medieval merchants counted coins earned from the precious cargo that flowed between Milan and the Swiss cantons beyond.

Long before its wines conquered tables across Europe, Sondrio's story was written in stone and struggle. Renaissance palaces with frescoed facades line cobbled streets that echo with the footsteps of traders, pilgrims, and conquerors who understood that whoever controlled this valley commanded the keys to the Alps. Above the bustling piazzas and wine cellars, the ancient Castello Masegra still keeps its silent vigil, its weathered walls remembering the clash of armies and the whispered negotiations that shaped the destiny of northern Italy.

Walk through Sondrio's historic center today and you'll find wine pressed from grapes that have absorbed centuries of Alpine sunshine and mountain air perfumed with the scent of aging Bitto cheese. It is a city that has mastered the art of honoring its past while embracing the future. Here, where church bells mingle with the laughter spilling from osterie (locally owned restaurants) and the distant whistle of trains carrying travelers toward Switzerland.

The Feast of Saint Gervasio

When June 19th dawns over the Valtellina, Sondrio awakens to its most sacred and spirited celebration, the Festa di San Gervasio. For centuries, this mountain town has placed its fate in the hands of the twin martyrs Gervasio and Protasius, those early Christian brothers whose devotion proved stronger than Roman steel. What began in medieval times as desperate prayers for protection against plague, invasion, and the harsh realities of mountain life has blossomed into a festival that captures the spirit and enduring character of Sondrio.

The day begins in hushed reverence within the Cathedral of Saints Gervasio and Protasius, where golden morning light filters through ancient windows and the baroque dome seems to lift prayers toward heaven itself. The Pontifical Mass fills the sacred space with Gregorian chant and the sweet smoke of incense, as the faithful gather to honor saints who understood that true strength lies not in conquest, but in unwavering faith. But when the cathedral doors swing open and San Gervasio's statue emerges into the mountain air, carried by locals as the celebration transforms into something magnificent and alive.

Who was Saint Gervasio?

Saint Gervasio is venerated as one of the earliest Christian martyrs of northern Italy, along with his brother Protasius. Tradition holds that they were the sons of Saints Vitalis and Valeria of Milan, martyred around AD 304 during the persecutions under Emperor Diocletian.

Their cult spread rapidly in Lombardy, especially after Saint Ambrose of Milan discovered their relics in AD 386. Ambrose himself testified to their miraculous intercession, which cemented their place in the spiritual life of Milan and beyond. Sondrio adopted Gervasio as its protector, enshrining him in the city's cathedral and dedicating its annual patronal feast to his memory.

Festival Traditions

Novena to San Gervasio

In the days leading up to June 19, parish groups and confraternities gather nightly for prayers, special liturgies, and offerings inside the Cathedral.

June 19: Feast Day

Morning

The Bishop of Sondrio presides over the main liturgy, joined by clergy and civic leaders. Hymns and incense fill the cathedral as the saint's relics are honored.

Children's Procession

Schoolchildren in white carry banners of their parishes through Piazza Garibaldi, symbolizing the passing of faith to the next generation.

Evening

Solemn Procession & Fireworks

Solemn Procession & Fireworks

As twilight paints the Alpine peaks in shades of rose and gold, the statue of San Gervasio emerges from the cathedral like a vision from another age, draped in cascades of mountain wildflowers and Alpine roses that seem to capture the very essence of the Valtellina summer. Members of ancient confraternities, resplendent in ceremonial robes that their grandfathers wore before them, bear the sacred figure through streets transformed into rivers of golden lantern light.

From every balcony and window, oil lamps flicker like earthbound stars while Renaissance palaces glow with the warm embrace of centuries-old devotion.

The procession moves festively through cobbled lanes, where voices rise in litanies that echo off stone walls and seem to call the very saints down from heaven. Children scatter rose petals in the statue's path while grandmothers clutch rosaries worn smooth by generations of faithful hands, and the air fills with the intoxicating blend of incense, mountain flowers, and the sweet anticipation of celebration.

When San Gervasio finally returns to his cathedral home, the night sky above the Valtellina explodes in cascades of brilliant fire. Fireworks burst like celestial flowers against the backdrop of ancient peaks, their colors dancing on the dark waters of the Adda and Mallero Rivers below.

Walking Tour of Sondrio

#1. Cathedral of Saints Gervasius and Protasius

Step inside and prepare to be enchanted by centuries of accumulated beauty. The ceilings are covered with frescoes of angels and martyrs. The paintings still glow with bright, vivid colors. Below them, white marble altars catch the soft light that streams through stained glass windows.

The gilded chapels contain priceless Renaissance treasures. But the city's most sacred object isn't made of gold. It's the statue of San Gervasio, carved with incredible skill and care. The statue looks so lifelike that locals believe his marble eyes follow them when they pray.

#2. Piazza Garibaldi

A short walk from the cathedral brings you to Piazza Garibaldi, the main square and civic hub of Sondrio. Surrounded by elegant nineteenth-century buildings and lively cafés, the piazza often hosts concerts, markets, and cultural events during festival week. It is the perfect spot to pause for a coffee and watch the rhythms of daily life in the Valtellina unfold.

#3. Mallero River Promenade

Flowing directly through Sondrio, the Mallero River is spanned by graceful bridges that offer some of the most iconic views of the town. From here you can see the Alps rising dramatically behind the city, the stone embankments lined with lampposts, and flower boxes that brighten the scene in summer. The riverside is a favorite spot for strolls, photographs, and appreciating how Sondrio balances its alpine landscape with its urban center. Crossing the Mallero also links the bustling Piazza Garibaldi to the path leading toward Castello Masegra.

#4. Castello Masegra

Perched above the old town, Castello Masegra is a medieval fortress that has guarded Sondrio since the fourteenth century. Today it houses the Valtellina Museum of History and Art, where exhibits recount the valley's Alpine culture, traditional crafts, and wine heritage. Sweeping views of the city and Sondrio's vineyards await at the top of the hill.

#5. Via Scarpatetti

Descending from the castle, wander into Via Scarpatetti, Sondrio's most atmospheric street. Narrow cobbled lanes twist between stone houses, many adorned with wooden balconies and flowers. Artisans and wine shops line the route, inviting visitors to experience the traditions of the Valtellina. This district offers an intimate sense of how medieval Sondrio once looked and provides a charming contrast to the grand piazzas.

Logistics

Train: Sondrio is served by regional trains on the Milano–Tirano line. The journey from Milano Centrale takes about two and a half hours, passing through Lecco and Lake Como before entering the Valtellina valley. From the station, it is a ten-minute walk to Piazza Garibaldi and the cathedral.

Bus: Local bus services connect the train station with outlying neighborhoods, nearby villages, and the terraced vineyards. During the festival week, additional routes often run to accommodate visitors attending evening processions and concerts.

Car: From Milan take the SS36 north along Lake Como and then follow the SS38 into the Valtellina. The drive to Sondrio takes about two and a half hours depending on traffic. The scenic route passes alpine lakes, mountain tunnels, and vineyards, making it one of the most beautiful drives in Lombardy.

Parking: The historic center of Sondrio has restricted traffic zones. Visitors should plan to park in designated lots on the edge of the old town. Large parking areas are available near Piazza Garibaldi and at the train station, both within easy walking distance of festival sites.

Restaurant Recommendations

Trattoria Olmo. Piazza Cavour, 13

A rustic trattoria in the heart of the historic center. Known for traditional Valtellina dishes such as pizzoccheri, sciatt cheese fritters, and hearty stews, all paired with local wines. The wood-paneled dining room provides a warm and authentic mountain atmosphere.

Ristorante 1862 Ristorante della Posta. Piazza Garibaldi, 19

An elegant choice near the main square with refined Lombard and Italian cuisine. Seasonal menus highlight local produce and wines, presented with modern flair. Ideal for a celebratory dinner after the fireworks of San Gervasio.

Day Trips from Sondrio

Morbegno. 26 kilometers (16 miles) west of Sondrio. Morbegno is a lively market town at the entrance to the Bitto Valley. It is known for its wine cellars and as the home of Bitto cheese, one of Valtellina's most prized products. Exploring the historic core, you'll discover fancy palaces, stone bridges spanning the Adda, and streets with local shops. It's also a gateway to the nearby Orobie Alps, perfect for a scenic drive or hike.

Chiavenna. 35 kilometers (22 miles) northwest. Chiavenna is a historic town where the Mera River cuts through dramatic gorges. The town is celebrated for its crotti, natural rock cellars where cured meats, cheeses, and wines are stored and served.

Sondrio Festivals and Sagre Throughout the Year

Carnevale di Sondrio

February or March

The historic center fills with costumed parades, children's games, and confetti showers. Floats created by local associations wind through the streets, while pastry stalls sell traditional lattughe (the Lombard name for chiacchiere) and tortelli di Carnevale filled with custard or jam.

La Valtellina in Festa

September

A celebration of the valley's harvest traditions, held throughout Sondrio and neighboring villages. Markets feature wines made from Nebbiolo grapes, cheeses from the Alpine pastures, and local specialties like pizzoccheri and bresaola. Folk music, dance performances, and artisan crafts add to the festive atmosphere.

Sondrio Festival

November

An international documentary film festival dedicated to nature and the environment. Screenings, talks, and exhibitions take place across the city's theaters and cultural centers, attracting filmmakers and audiences from around the world. The festival highlights Sondrio as a hub of Alpine culture and ecological awareness.

Mercatini di Natale

December

Sondrio's Christmas markets transform Piazza Garibaldi and the surrounding streets with wooden stalls selling crafts, ornaments, and festive treats. Choirs sing carols, children ride the holiday carousel, and mulled wine warms visitors as the mountains glow with snow.

CHAPTER FOURTEEN

FestaFusion Luino, Lago Maggiore

Where Italy Meets Switzerland

FestaFusion Luino

#1. Festa Patronale di Santi Pietro e Paolo. Luino's grand patronal feast blends solemn liturgy, processions, music, and fireworks on June 29.

#2. Palio Remiero. A spirited rowing competition among Luino's nine districts on Lake Maggiore is a highlight of the patronal festivities each year on June 28, when colorful boats glide across the water to the cheers of locals gathered along the shore.

Where: Luino

When: June 27–29

Average Festival Temperatures: High 26°C (79°F). Low 17°C (63°F).

Luino: A Borderland Jewel on Lake Maggiore

Perched on the eastern shore of Lake Maggiore, only a few kilometers from the Swiss border, Luino has long been a crossroads of cultures, trade, and travel. Its picturesque lakeside promenade is framed by the jagged silhouettes of Alpine foothills, while ferries and boats trace lines across the deep blue waters, connecting the town to Italy and Switzerland alike.

Luino's story stretches back to Roman times, when its strategic position on the lake made it an important trading stop. During the Middle Ages it was contested by noble families and regional powers, including the Visconti and Borromeo, each leaving their mark in fortifications and civic structures. By the nineteenth century, Luino had transformed into a lively market town, and today its Wednesday market remains one of the most famous in northern Italy, drawing visitors from both sides of the border.

Lago Maggiore, Key Cities and Islands

The town also holds a place in modern history. In 1848, Luino was the site of a clash between Austrian troops and Italian patriots led by Giuseppe Garibaldi, a skirmish that still resonates in the local memory of the Risorgimento. Strolling through its streets, visitors encounter elegant nineteenth-century palazzi, tree-lined squares, and a waterfront where cafés invite you to linger over a cappuccino as the ferries dock and depart.

With a population of about 14,000 residents, Luino blends the intimacy of a small town with the vibrancy of a border city. Its proximity to Switzerland and the surrounding valleys has given it a cosmopolitan character, while the surrounding landscape, from wooded hills to the expansive lake, ensures that nature is never far from view.

#1. The Patronal Feast of Saints Peter and Paul

For centuries, Luino has looked to Saints Peter and Paul as its protectors, celebrating their feast day on June 29 with devotion and community pride. Records trace the origins of the festa to the early modern era, when lakeside towns wove religious observance together with civic celebrations. Over time, solemn Masses and processions grew into larger gatherings, enriched by fireworks, music, and the rowing tradition of the Palio Remiero, where Luino's neighborhoods compete on the waters of Lake Maggiore.

Today, the festival remains one of the highlights of the town's cultural calendar, drawing not only Luinesi but also visitors from neighboring valleys and Switzerland.

Who Was Saint Peter?

Saint Peter, originally named Simon, was a fisherman from Galilee and one of the Twelve Apostles chosen by Jesus. According to the Gospels, Christ gave him the name "Peter" (from the Greek petros, meaning rock) and entrusted him with a foundational role in the early Church: "You are Peter, and on this rock I will build my church" (Matthew 16:18). Peter became the first leader of the Christian community in Rome and is venerated as the first pope. Tradition holds that he was martyred in Rome during the reign of Emperor Nero around AD 64, crucified upside down at his own request. His courage, faith, and leadership made him one of the pillars of Christianity.

Who Was Saint Paul?

Saint Paul, once known as Saul of Tarsus, began as a persecutor of Christians before experiencing a dramatic conversion on the road to Damascus. Thereafter, he became one of the most influential figures in spreading Christianity across the Roman Empire, writing letters that form a large part of the New Testament. Paul's missions carried him across Asia Minor, Greece, and Rome, where he was ultimately martyred, likely by beheading, also under Nero around AD 67. Celebrated as the "Apostle to the Gentiles," Paul's writings continue to shape Christian theology and inspire believers worldwide.

Festival Traditions

June 27

The festivities open with Luino Fashion Night, a stylish evening filled with fashion shows, music, and creativity that transforms the town center into a vibrant runway. The excitement continues as the rioni (districts) of Luino gather for the draw for the Palio, where race pairings are announced, setting the stage for the thrilling rowing competitions to come..

June 29

Feast of Saints Peter and Paul

The day begins with a solemn Mass in Luino's main parish church, attended by clergy, civic leaders, and townspeople, setting a reverent tone for the festivities. As evening falls, the statues of Saints Peter and Paul are carried through the historic center in a moving procession accompanied by confraternities, choirs, and banners. Streets and balconies are beautifully decorated, and the scent of incense drifts through the piazzas as the faithful follow the saints' images in a timeless display of devotion. The celebration continues into the night with lively music and performances in the piazzas, filling the town with joy and a strong sense of community.

#2. Palio Remiero

Each summer, Luino bursts to life for the Palio Remiero, a spectacular rowing festival that unites the community in friendly rivalry and celebration. The competition takes place on the shimmering waters of Lake Maggiore, where rowing crews from Luino's nine historic neighborhoods, known as rioni, face off in an afternoon of thrilling races. What began in 1994 as a local regatta organized by the town and the Canottieri Luino rowing club has grown into one of the area's most anticipated events, returning triumphantly in recent years after a long pause.

The day begins with a colorful parade as each rione marches through the streets, proudly carrying its banners toward the lakefront. Crowds gather along the shore as the elimination heats begin, with boats racing in tight lanes, circling buoys, and sprinting toward the finish. Cheers rise with every stroke as the best crews advance to the final round, held in the golden light of early evening. When the last race ends, the winning district claims the coveted Palio trophy and earns a year of local pride and celebration.

As night falls, the festivities reach their grand finale with a magnificent fireworks display over Lake Maggiore. The reflections shimmer across the water and illuminate the faces of spectators who have spent the day celebrating sport, tradition, and unity.

Walking Tour of Luino

#1. Piazza Libertà and the Town Hall

Begin at Piazza Libertà, the civic heart of Luino. The square is framed by the elegant façade of the Town Hall, a nineteenth-century building that reflects Luino's role as a market and administrative center during the years of Italian unification. The square is also the traditional gathering place during public events and remains one of the best spots to feel the town's daily rhythm.

#2. Chiesa di Santi Pietro e Paolo

A short walk uphill brings you to the parish church dedicated to Luino's patron saints. The current structure reflects later Baroque and neoclassical influences, though its roots stretch deeper into medieval history. Inside, the church houses altarpieces and devotional works that honor the saints, along with side chapels that serve as focal points during the June procession.

#3. Palazzo Verbania

Head toward the lakefront to discover Palazzo Verbania, an Art Nouveau jewel built in 1904. Once a luxury hotel, it now serves as a cultural hub hosting exhibitions, conferences, and a public library. Its lakeside terrace offers sweeping views of Lake Maggiore, and its architectural details recall the elegance of the Belle Époque era.

#4. The Lungolago (Lakeside Promenade)

Continue along the waterfront, where plane trees cast a dappled shade across the promenade. Cafés and gelaterie line the path, offering perfect pauses for coffee or a refreshing scoop of gelato. From here, ferries depart for other towns on Lake Maggiore, and the sweeping panorama extends toward the Borromean Gulf and the Swiss shore.

#5. Wednesday Market

If your visit falls on a Wednesday, no walk through Luino is complete without experiencing its famed market. Stretching along the streets and lakefront, it is one of the largest in northern Italy, with hundreds of stalls offering everything from fresh cheeses and cured meats to clothing, household goods, and antiques. The market has been a tradition since the sixteenth century and still draws crowds from both Italy and Switzerland.

#6. Porto Vecchio

Finish the walk in the Porto Vecchio, the old harbor area where colorful boats bob in the water and stone houses cluster around narrow lanes. This is one of the oldest quarters of Luino, a reminder of its fishing and trading past. In the evening, the setting sun paints the lake in gold and violet hues, providing a perfect close to your exploration.

Logistics

Train: Luino is well connected by regional trains from Milan and Varese. The journey from Milan's Porta Garibaldi or Centrale stations takes about 1 hour and 30 minutes, with frequent stops along the eastern shore of Lake Maggiore. From Varese, the ride is about 45 minutes. The train station sits close to the lakefront and is within a short walk of the historic center.

Car: From Milan, take the A8 Autostrada dei Laghi north, exiting at Sesto Calende and following the SS629 and SS394 along Lake Maggiore's eastern shore. The drive takes about 90 minutes depending on traffic and offers beautiful lake views.

Parking: Much of central Luino is accessible to cars, though traffic is heavy on Wednesdays during the market and during the patronal festival. Several paid parking areas are available along the lakefront and on the edges of the historic center. During major festivals, temporary lots and shuttle services are often arranged.

Boat: Passenger ferries connect Luino with towns along Lake Maggiore, including Cannobio, Cannero, and Verbania across the water. Seasonal services make it easy to combine a visit with other lakeside destinations.

Restaurant Recommendations

Ristorante Tiffany. Via Voldomino 6

A refined restaurant blending traditional Lombard flavors with contemporary presentation. Known for risotto, fresh lake fish, and a strong regional wine list.

Osteria del Castagno. Via XXV Aprile 38

A cozy osteria favored by locals, offering homemade pastas, polenta dishes, and hearty stews. The setting, with rustic wood beams and warm service, feels authentically Lombard.

Trattoria Pizzeria Al Cantinone. Via Cavallotti 2

Near the historic center, this trattoria is casual and lively, with wood-fired pizza, generous pasta portions, and a relaxed, family-friendly atmosphere.

Day Trips from Luino

Locarno and Ascona, Switzerland. 25 kilometers (15 miles) north of Luino, across the Swiss border, Locarno and neighboring Ascona are two of the most beautiful towns on Lake Maggiore's northern shore. Locarno is famed for its palm-lined promenades, medieval Castello Visconteo, and the Sanctuary of Madonna del Sasso, perched dramatically on a rocky hill with sweeping views.

Each August, the town hosts the Locarno Film Festival, when its main piazza becomes an open-air cinema. Just to the west, Ascona charms visitors with pastel-colored houses, cobbled alleys, and a lively lakefront dotted with cafés and galleries. Both towns are reachable in less than an hour by car or train from Luino, and ferries also link them seasonally, making for an easy and rewarding cross-border excursion.

On one of my own visits, however, we learned the hard way that "easy" is relative when it comes to ferries across the Swiss–Italian border. We had happily driven into Locarno with a driver our hotel organized, assuming we could simply float our way back to Italy by ferry. To our surprise, the Swiss–Italian ferry connections were not nearly as frequent as those on the Italian side of the lake. We found ourselves somewhat stranded, with taxis reluctant to take us back across the border because of the time and paperwork involved.

It was one of those moments where travel teaches you perseverance, and that phoning a friend for help may be needed! In the end, we managed to get back, but it taught us a valuable lesson: if you plan to cross between Switzerland and Italy on Lake Maggiore, check the official ferry schedules in advance. A little online planning can save you from an impromptu "adventure" like ours!

Caslano, Switzerland. A short drive west of Luino brings you to Caslano, a small Swiss town nestled on the shores of Lake Lugano. Known for its lakeside walks and peaceful atmosphere, Caslano is also home to the Alprose Chocolate Museum, a delight for families and sweet-toothed travelers. The town sits beneath Monte Caslano, a green promontory ideal for gentle hikes with panoramic views of Lake Lugano. With its mix of natural beauty and Swiss charm, Caslano offers a contrasting flavor to the Italian lake towns, and its proximity makes it an easy half-day trip.

Luino Festivals and Sagre Throughout the Year

Carnevale Luinese

February or March

In the weeks before Lent, Luino's streets burst with color as children and families don costumes and masks. Parades weave through the historic center with floats and marching bands, while piazzas fill with confetti and laughter. Local bakeries prepare traditional carnival sweets such as chiacchiere (crispy strips of fried dough covered in sugar) and tortelli di Carnevale (fried pastries filled with custard or chocolate), ensuring the air is sweet and festive.

Settimana del Santuario

Late June to Early July

In the days surrounding the Feast of Saints Peter and Paul, Luino also honors its Sanctuary with special liturgies and gatherings. The celebrations extend into early July, with concerts, open-air prayers, and moments of reflection that complement the civic festivities.

Natale a Luino

December

In December, Luino's lakefront and historic center are illuminated with festive lights and decorations. A Christmas market fills the piazzas with wooden stalls selling ornaments, crafts, and seasonal delicacies such as roasted chestnuts and mulled wine.

Enhance Your Journey with the Immersion Travel Podcast

To deepen your exploration of Lago Maggiore, I invite you to experience my Immersion Travel Podcast, which features an exclusive five part series dedicated to this enchanting Italian lake region. Each episode reveals hidden gems, local traditions, and insider perspectives that bring the magic of Lago Maggiore to life through audio storytelling.

Visit **katerinaferrara.com/video-podcast/** to access direct links to all episodes and enjoy this complimentary podcast series designed specifically to accompany this chapter. Let the sounds, stories, and spirit of Lago Maggiore transport you as you continue your journey through these pages and beyond.

Buon ascolto!

CHAPTER FIFTEEN

Peghera: Heart of the Taleggio Valley

Mountain Charm & Cheese

FestaFusion: Sagra del Taleggio and Festunt

#1. Sagra del Taleggio. A celebration of the famed Lombard cheese held in the Taleggio Valley, featuring tastings, traditional dishes, mountain markets, and cultural events that honor the region's pastoral heritage.

#2. Festunt. Treviglio's summer festival of beer, food, and live music, bringing together local breweries, international flavors, and lively performances in a vibrant open-air atmosphere.

Where: Peghera and Val Taleggio

When: Late June to early July (dates vary).

Average Festival Temperatures: High: 21°C (70°F). Low: 9°C (48°F).

#FestaFusion: When two festivals converge in the same town around the same time, your journey becomes twice as magical.

Event Website:

https://www.strachitunt.it/festunt-la-festa-della-terra-dello-strachitunt/

Peghera, the gateway to the Val Taleggio

Breathe in the mountain air thick with the scent of wild herbs and alpine flowers. Cowbells echo off limestone cliffs, and the rushing Enna River carves its ancient path through emerald pastures. Peghera is a tiny village tucked into Val Taleggio's alpine valleys. Despite its small size, it has a rich history, with families who have lived in these mountains for generations.

This is cheese country. Morning mist hangs over meadows where cattle graze. In rock cellars below, locals age wheels of Taleggio cheese and the rare blue-marbled Strachitunt, which Slow Food advocates work to preserve.

The village square is tiny, about the size of a courtyard, but it's the center of daily life. Villagers gather here over espresso, their conversations flowing easily as they catch up on local news.

Peghera's 200 citizens move to rhythms unchanged by centuries; the twice-daily procession of cows to pasture, the patient turning of cheese wheels in stone caves, the gathering of wild herbs from slopes that blaze with Alpine roses and gentians. Beyond the village, ancient mule tracks wind through forests of chestnut and beech toward peaks where eagles soar and wildflowers carpet meadows that seem to touch the sky.

Scattered across this enchanted valley, the communes of Taleggio, Vedeseta, and Morterone shelter barely a thousand residents total, each village a precious keeper of traditions that transform simple milk into liquid gold and simple living into something approaching the sacred. This is Lombardy's alpine heartland at its most authentic.

#1. Taleggio Cheese Festival

The Sagra del Taleggio celebrates one of Lombardy's most iconic cheeses in the very valley where it originated. First organized by local producers and the community of Peghera to showcase the area's rich dairy heritage, the festival has grown into a beloved annual tradition that draws visitors from across the region.

What is Taleggio?

Taleggio is a semi-soft, washed-rind cheese with a thin, edible crust and a pale, creamy interior. It has a distinctive aroma, earthy and tangy, yet its flavor is surprisingly mild and buttery with a slight fruity tang. The cheese dates back to at least the 10th century, when mountain herders in the Taleggio Valley developed it as a way to preserve surplus milk during the colder months. Wheels were aged in the region's natural caves, where the high humidity and mild temperatures created the ideal environment for their development.

The process, involving regular washing of the rind with brine, encourages the growth of the unique bacteria that give Taleggio its characteristic flavor and texture. Today, it holds a prestigious PDO (Protected Designation of Origin) status, ensuring that only cheese produced in the designated areas of Lombardy, using traditional methods, can bear the name.

The event is as much a cultural celebration as a culinary one, with cooking demonstrations, tastings, and educational exhibits about the valley's cheese-making history. Local farmers and artisans set up stalls, turning the village into an open-air market filled with the scents of aging cheese, freshly baked focaccia, and seasonal mountain dishes.

Festival Events

Afternoon

In the afternoon, cultural activities take center stage. Storytellers share the history of Val Taleggio's cheese-making traditions, while artisans demonstrate woodcarving, basket weaving, and other alpine crafts. Cheese-tasting workshops allow guests to compare Taleggio from different dairies, noting the subtle differences in flavor depending on the season and aging time. Families stroll through the festival area, children enjoy games and craft stations, and photographers capture the dramatic mountain scenery surrounding the village.

Evening

As evening falls, the golden light softens over the valley, and the pace of the festival becomes more relaxed. Visitors gather once more in the piazza for a final round of tastings, enjoying warm plates of melted cheese over crusty bread or sweet local desserts.

The last musical performances, traditional folk dances, bring the day to a joyful close. For those staying overnight, the quiet of the mountain night is accompanied by the lingering scent of wood smoke and the memory of the valley's rich flavors.

#2. Festunt, the Festival of the Land, Language and People

Festunt is a month-long celebration of Val Taleggio's cultural soul, uniting the valley's villages in a tribute to its land, language, and people. First launched by the Consorzio per la Tutela dello Strachítunt DOP, the festival was born out of a desire to preserve and promote the region's rural traditions, especially those tied to its unique cheese-making heritage.

Festunt takes place each summer between late June and mid-July. The festival celebrates local Lombard culture with puppet shows performed in ancient dialects, folk music concerts in the meadows, and traditional dishes served alongside stories passed down through families. This event is held in three towns: Peghera, Vedesta and Val Brembilla.

What is Strachítunt?

Strachítunt is a raw-milk, blue-veined cheese made using a rare double-curd technique that dates back to medieval times. Produced exclusively in Val Taleggio, it combines evening and morning milk curds layered together, then aged in natural caves where the cool, humid conditions foster the growth of Penicillium molds. The result is a cheese with a marbled interior, a rustic rind, and a flavor that's bold, earthy, and slightly spicy. Recognized with PDO status and protected by the Slow Food Presidium[1], Strachítunt is a symbol of the valley's resilience and artisanal pride.

---

1. This is a global initiative by the Slow Food movement to protect endangered foods, traditional production methods, and small-scale producers. When a cheese like Strachítunt is part of a Presidium, it means it's recognized as culturally and gastronomically important, and efforts are made to preserve its heritage and support the artisans who make it.

Festunt showcases this cheese alongside Taleggio and other mountain specialties, pairing them with local wines, honeys, and breads in open-air tastings and guided culinary walks. But the festival goes beyond food; it's a cultural immersion.

Visitors can attend theater performances in Bergamasque dialect, explore frescoed churches and alpine trails, and join workshops on traditional crafts and farming techniques. Each village contributes its own flavor to the celebration, from Peghera's cheese market to Vedeseta's musical parades.

At its heart, Festunt is a celebration of belonging. It honors the rhythms of mountain life, the wisdom of its elders, and the creativity of its youth. Whether you come for the cheese or stay for the stories, Festunt offers a rare chance to experience Val Taleggio not just as a destination, but as a community rooted in centuries of tradition.

Walking Tour of Peghera

#1. Piazza Centrale

Begin the exploration in the heart of Peghera at the main piazza, where village life unfolds at a gentle pace. The square is framed by stone houses with wooden balconies and dotted with small cafés where locals gather over espresso.

#2. Chiesa Parrocchiale di San Giovanni Battista

A short walk from the piazza brings you to the Parish Church of Saint John the Baptist, Peghera's spiritual center. The simple yet graceful façade opens into a warm interior with wooden pews, painted ceilings, and devotional artworks that reflect the faith of this mountain community.

#3. The Old Dairy (Caseificio Storico)

Head along a quiet lane to the historic dairy building, where generations of cheese-makers once transformed fresh milk into Taleggio and Strachitunt. While no longer in full production, the site occasionally opens for guided tours during the festival, giving visitors a close look at the tools and techniques used in traditional cheese-making.

#4. Via degli Artigiani

Stroll down this charming street known for its artisan workshops. Here, local craftspeople create handwoven textiles, carved wooden kitchenware, and traditional baskets. It's an ideal place to pick up a handmade souvenir that reflects Val Taleggio's rural heritage.

#5. Scenic Viewpoint over Val Taleggio

Continue uphill toward a small overlook that offers sweeping views across the valley. From here, you can see terraced meadows, forested slopes, and the dramatic limestone cliffs that define the landscape. In the distance, alpine pastures hint at the grazing grounds where the milk for Taleggio is still sourced.

#6. The Enna River Path

End the walking tour with a tranquil stroll along the Enna River, whose clear waters run through the village. The gentle trail is lined with wildflowers in spring and summer, and the sound of rushing water is a peaceful backdrop to your visit. In fall, the surrounding hills are painted in gold and amber, making this a beautiful spot for photographs.

Logistics

Train: Peghera does not have its own train station. The nearest major rail connection is in Bergamo, about 40 kilometers or 25 miles away, which is served by Trenitalia and Trenord regional trains from Milan, Lecco, and other Lombard cities. From Bergamo, visitors can continue by bus or car into Val Taleggio.

Bus: Regular bus services connect Bergamo with San Giovanni Bianco, the gateway to Val Taleggio. From there, a local bus or shuttle runs to Peghera, though schedules are limited, especially on weekends, so it is advisable to check ahead when planning your visit during the festival.

Car: Driving is the most convenient way to reach Peghera, particularly for those coming from outside the immediate area. From Bergamo, take the SP25 road through the Brembana Valley to San Giovanni Bianco, then follow the scenic SP24 into Val Taleggio. The route winds through narrow mountain roads and past dramatic limestone gorges, offering a beautiful introduction to the area. The travel time from Bergamo is about one hour.

Parking: Limited parking is available in and around the village, with additional spaces opened in nearby fields during the Sagra del Taleggio. Festival signage directs visitors to designated lots, from which it is a short walk to the main piazza. Arriving early is recommended, as spaces fill quickly on peak festival days.

Restaurant Recommendations

Agriturismo La Piana. Località La Piana, Val Taleggio

This working farm and agriturismo serves meals prepared with its own produce, fresh milk, and cheeses. Visitors can enjoy multi-course lunches that feature Taleggio in different preparations, from starters to desserts. The setting is peaceful, surrounded by meadows and pastures, and the hosts often share stories about the history of cheese-making in the valley.

Ristorante Moderno. Piazza Zignoni, San Giovanni Bianco

About 15 minutes from Peghera, this restaurant blends traditional Lombard cooking with a refined presentation. Known for its risottos, cheese-based antipasti, and homemade desserts, it is a good choice for those who want to combine a meal with a visit to San Giovanni Bianco's historic center.

Day Trip Options: Nearby Sites, Cities, and Towns

San Giovanni Bianco. 8 kilometers (5 miles) from Peghera. This charming town on the Brembo River is the gateway to Val Taleggio and an excellent stop for history and local culture. Its medieval bridge, the Ponte Vecchio, is steeped in legend and offers beautiful river views. The town's historic center is a pleasant place to stroll, with narrow lanes, small piazzas, and artisan shops selling local cheeses and cured meats.

The Parish Church of San Giovanni Battista contains notable frescoes, and the town often hosts smaller food markets and events throughout the year.

Valtorta. 10 kilometers (6 miles) from Peghera. Nestled in the heart of the Orobie Alps, Valtorta offers a peaceful gateway into the Orobie Bergamasche Regional Park. This alpine village is ideal for nature lovers and cultural explorers alike. Hiking trails wind through forests and meadows, leading to panoramic viewpoints and rustic mountain huts.

The historic Church of San Lorenzo and the Ethnographic Museum provide insight into local traditions and crafts. In summer, the area is perfect for trekking and picnicking; in winter, it transforms into a ski resort with cozy lodges and well-maintained slopes.

Piazza Brembana. 15 kilometers (9 miles) from Peghera. Serving as the main commercial center of the upper Brembana Valley, Piazza Brembana offers a mix of mountain charm and convenient services. Its lively weekly market draws vendors from across the region, selling fresh produce, cheeses, and handmade goods.

The town is surrounded by hiking trails that lead to alpine pastures and panoramic viewpoints. Key sights include the Parish Church of San Martino and the scenic riverside promenade.

Festivals and Sagre in the Val Taleggio Throughout the Year

Festa Patronale di San Giovanni Battista in Peghera

June 24

This religious celebration honors the village's patron saint with a special Mass, a procession through the streets, and community gatherings in the piazza. Local food stands serve traditional dishes, and the evening ends with music and dancing.

Sagra dello Strachitunt in Vedeseta

October (second weekend)

Just a short drive from Peghera, the nearby village of Vedeseta hosts a festival dedicated to Strachitunt, a rare blue-veined cheese produced in the valley. Visitors can enjoy tastings, see cheese-making demonstrations, and learn about the centuries-old techniques behind this Slow Food protected specialty.

Festa di San Martino in Piazza Brembana (St. Martin)

November 11

This annual celebration honors Saint Martin of Tours, a patron saint known for his compassion and generosity. Held in mid-November, the festival blends religious devotion with seasonal festivity. The day typically begins with a mass and procession through the town, followed by a lively autumn market featuring local produce, cheeses, handmade crafts, and mountain specialties.

Visitors can enjoy roasted chestnuts, polenta taragna, mulled wine, and other cold-weather treats while listening to live folk music and watching performances by local bands and school groups. Children often take part in games and workshops, and some years include storytelling or puppet shows inspired by Saint Martin's legendary act of charity, cutting his cloak in half to share with a beggar.

The event draws residents from across the Upper Brembana Valley, offering a warm, communal atmosphere that reflects the spirit of Saint Martin and the changing season. It's a perfect opportunity to experience the local culture, sample traditional foods, and enjoy the crisp mountain air before winter sets in.

Mercatini di Natale in San Giovanni Bianco

December

The Christmas market in San Giovanni Bianco fills the streets with stalls selling handcrafted gifts, holiday decorations, and festive foods. The atmosphere is made even more magical by carol singers, twinkling lights, and a backdrop of snow-covered mountains.

Chapter Sixteen

Lake Iseo Illuminated: Fire and Faith

Processions & Fireworks

F esta di San Fermo

Where: Monte Isola, Lake Iseo

When: Weekend closest to August 9.

Average Festival Temperatures: High 29°C (84°F). Low 18°C (64°F).

Monte Isola: A Timeless Island in the Heart of the Lake

Discover an island rising from silk-smooth waters where morning mist clings to olive groves and the gentle splash of fishing boats replaces the roar of engines. Here, on Europe's largest inhabited lake island, time moves to the rhythm of bicycle wheels on stone paths and the ancient art of weaving fishing nets beneath centuries-old plane trees. This is Monte Isola, a 4.5-square-kilometer (1.7 square mile) jewel floating in the sapphire embrace of Lake Iseo, where 1,700 locals live as their ancestors did, in harmony with water, wind, and the turning seasons.

No private cars disturb the island's medieval tranquility. Instead, life flows along cobbled lanes that wind past stone houses draped in bougainvillea (colorful flowering vines), where the scent of wood-fired ovens mingles with the fresh lake breeze and the silver flash of sardines drying in the sun creates an edible constellation along weathered dock posts. From Roman times, when legions recognized this strategic crossroads between the Alps and Po Valley, to the medieval centuries when the Oldofredi family crowned its heights with fortress walls, Monte Isola has remained a place apart.

Village by village, from Peschiera Maraglio's harbor bustle to Siviano's hilltop serenity, the island unfolds like a living museum where olive presses still turn and fishing nets emerge from skilled hands as they have for generations. The prized sardines, smoke-cured to amber perfection, speak of traditions that transform the lake's bounty into liquid gold, while ancient olive groves produce oil so fine it carries the very essence of the Mediterranean sun distilled by Alpine waters.

Lago d'Iseo and Surrounding Towns

The Feast of San Fermo

Who Was Saint Firmus?

Saint Firmus lived in the third century when the Roman Empire was persecuting Christians. He and his companion Rusticus were from Bergamo and traveled through Lombardy spreading Christianity. They continued their mission despite knowing they risked execution for their faith.

The empire's answer was swift and brutal. Dragged before Roman magistrates who demanded they abandon their God, both men stood unmoved as stone, Firmus meeting the executioner's blade with prayers on his lips, while Rusticus faced his own martyrdom in Verona's dusty streets. Yet death could not extinguish what they had kindled. Their sacrifice blazed across Lombardy and the Veneto like wildfire, transforming two humble preachers into legends that would outlive emperors.

From the fishing boats of Lake Iseo to the mountain villages of the Alps, Firmus's name became a shield against the storms that batter both soul and body. When lightning splits the sky and waves turn to fury, fishermen still whisper his name, trusting that a martyr who faced imperial wrath with such calm might calm the tempests that rage across these ancient waters.

Festival Traditions

Procession to the Sanctuary

As afternoon shadows grow long on the cobblestones, devotion washes over the village. The crowned statue of San Fermo emerges from the church doors, draped in cascades of white roses and golden marigolds that seem to glow against the weathered wood. Strong shoulders bear the burden while voices rise in ancient hymns that echo off stone walls and float across the lake like prayers.

People wear traditional clothing for the procession. Women wear embroidered aprons, men wear white shirts, and children carry wildflowers they picked from nearby meadows. The clergy move like a gentle tide at the procession's heart, their Latin chants weaving through the mountain air while incense mingles with the scent of lake breeze and blooming linden trees.

People climb the old stone steps to the sanctuary. The path is steep, and everyone breathes heavily as they go up. From here, you can see the lake spread out far below. The climb is hard work. Many believe the difficulty is part of the pilgrimage. The physical effort connects them to San Fermo's story. This path has been used for centuries by people coming to pray.

Evening

Concerts and Lakefront Festivities

As the sun sets, music and entertainment take center stage. Local bands and choirs perform, and visitors gather along the lake to share food, drink, and fellowship. The island glows with lanterns and lights reflected in the water, creating a festive and welcoming atmosphere.

Fireworks over Lake Iseo

Brilliant colors explode across the night sky, mirrored in the dark waters surrounding Monte Isola. The sight of the island silhouetted against the shimmering bursts of light is one of the most unforgettable spectacles on Lake Iseo.

Festival Food

Lake Sardines and Polenta

No celebration on Monte Isola is complete without the island's most iconic dish: sardine essiccate. These small lake fish are cleaned, salted, and dried for several weeks on wooden racks before being grilled over open fires. At the Festa di San Fermo, villagers serve them sizzling hot alongside creamy polenta, often paired with local olive oil and a glass of crisp Franciacorta wine from the vineyards on the mainland.

Walking Tour of Monte Isola

#1. Peschiera Maraglio

Begin in the charming harbor village of Peschiera Maraglio, the main landing point for ferries from Sulzano. Narrow lanes wind between pastel-colored houses, artisan shops selling traditional fishing nets, and trattorias serving the island's famous sardines. The waterfront promenade offers lake views and is often the heart of the evening festivities during the festival.

#2. The Sanctuary of San Fermo

From Peschiera Maraglio, follow the uphill path through olive groves and chestnut trees to reach the Sanctuary of San Fermo. At the island's crown, the Sanctuary of the Madonna della Ceriola has stood sentinel since the eleventh century, its weathered stones witnessing a thousand sunrises reflected in the lake below. From this sacred peak, the panorama spreads; mountain ranges dissolving into morning haze, vineyards cascading toward water's edge, and the timeless dance of light on water that makes clear why pilgrims and poets alike have long considered Monte Isola a bridge between earth and heaven.

#3. The Sanctuary of the Madonna della Ceriola

For the most rewarding climb, head to the summit of Monte Isola at 600 meters (1,968 feet), where the Sanctuary of the Madonna della Ceriola has stood since the eleventh century. The church itself is simple, but the surrounding views are breathtaking, encompassing the entirety of Lake Iseo, the surrounding mountains, and the rolling hills of Franciacorta. On a clear day, you can see as far as the snow-capped Alps.

#4. Sensole and the Lakeside Path

Descend toward the lakeside hamlet of Sensole, where a peaceful path connects the village to Peschiera Maraglio. Along the way, you will pass olive groves and terraces with views across the lake to Monte Isola's two tiny satellite islands, Loreto and San Paolo. This is one of the most scenic stretches of the island, ideal for a leisurely walk or cycle.

Logistics

Train: The most convenient access point to Monte Isola is from the mainland town of Sulzano, which is directly linked to Brescia by the Trenord regional railway. The train ride from Brescia to Sulzano takes about 30 minutes. From Milan, take a train to Brescia (approximately 1 hour) and then transfer. The Sulzano station is just a short walk from the ferry dock.

Car: From Milan, take the A4 Autostrada toward Venice and exit at Rovato or Ospitaletto, following signs for Lake Iseo and Sulzano. From Verona, the A4 Autostrada connects you westward, with the same exits leading to the lake. Parking is available near the ferry port in Sulzano, but during the festival, spaces fill quickly. Arriving early in the day is recommended.

Ferry: Monte Isola is reached only by ferry. Services run regularly from Sulzano to Peschiera Maraglio and from Sale Marasino to Carzano. During festivals such as San Fermo, additional boats are scheduled, including evening sailings to allow visitors to return after the fireworks. The ferry ride takes only 5–10 minutes, offering beautiful first views of the island.

Getting Around the Island: Private cars are not permitted on Monte Isola. Transportation is by walking, bicycle, or the small island bus that connects the main villages. Many visitors enjoy renting bicycles to ride the 9-kilometer (5.6-mile) loop road that circles the island, stopping at fishing hamlets, chapels, and lakeside cafés. To reach the sanctuaries of San Fermo or the Madonna della Ceriola, expect uphill walking paths that reward the effort with spectacular views.

Restaurant Recommendations

Ristorante Locanda al Lago. Via Peschiera Maraglio 174, Monte Isola

Set directly on the waterfront in Peschiera Maraglio, this locanda is known for traditional lake dishes, especially the island's signature sardines preserved in olive oil. The outdoor terrace offers sweeping views of the lake, making it a wonderful place to dine during the festival evenings.

Trattoria Cacciatore. Località Cure 11, Monte Isola

Reached by a short uphill walk from Peschiera Maraglio, this rustic trattoria specializes in hearty island cuisine, from polenta with grilled meats to pasta dressed with local sauces. Its welcoming, family-run atmosphere makes it a favorite with locals.

Ristorante Vittoria da Rachì. Via Sensole 60, Monte Isola

In the lakeside hamlet of Sensole, this restaurant is famous for its grilled fish, risotto, and Franciacorta wines. The lakeside terrace offers romantic sunset views, ideal for a dinner after watching the procession or before the fireworks begin.

Day Trip Options

Endine Gaiano (Lago di Endine). Just a short drive east from Lake Iseo lies Lago di Endine, a smaller and more tranquil lake framed by forested hills. The town of Endine Gaiano sits along its shore and keeps the quiet charm of a traditional Lombard village.

The lake is especially known for its serenity, with opportunities for canoeing, fishing, or simply enjoying the reflections of the mountains in its still waters. Visiting Endine offers a chance to experience a different pace, away from the busier towns of Lake Iseo.

Iseo. On the southern shore of the lake, the town of Iseo gives its name to the entire region. Its lively historic center is filled with elegant piazzas, arcaded streets, and the twelfth-century Pieve di Sant'Andrea, one of the oldest Romanesque churches in the area. The lakeside promenade is ideal for a stroll, while cafés and gelaterie provide the perfect vantage point to watch ferries crisscrossing the water. Weekly markets and boutique shops make Iseo a delightful destination for a half-day excursion.

Lovere. On the northern tip of Lake Iseo, Lovere is officially recognized as one of "I Borghi più belli d'Italia," the most beautiful villages of Italy. The town's medieval core blends seamlessly with Renaissance palaces and neoclassical facades that line Piazza XIII Martiri, a lively square overlooking the lake.

View of Monte Isola from Lovere

Art lovers will enjoy the Accademia Tadini, which houses an important collection of paintings, sculptures, and ceramics. The scenic waterfront and surrounding hills offer plenty of opportunities for leisurely walks.

Festivals and Sagre Throughout the Year

Onde Musicali sul Lago d'Iseo (Waves of Music Festival)

June to July

This music festival features classical and contemporary performances staged in churches, villas, and piazzas around the lake. Each concert pairs the beauty of the music with the unique atmosphere of the setting, from medieval chapels to panoramic terraces.

Sagra delle Sardine, Peschiera Maraglio (Monte Isola)

July

This beloved food festival celebrates the island's age-old tradition of drying and grilling sardines over open fires. Locals serve the delicacy with polenta, accompanied by music, games, and lakeside merriment. It is one of the best opportunities to taste the culinary heritage of Monte Isola.

Iseo Jazz Festival

July

A long-standing cultural event, the Iseo Jazz Festival brings international musicians to the town of Iseo and surrounding villages. Open-air concerts in piazzas and historic venues blend world-class jazz with the relaxed ambiance of the lakeshore.

Festa di Santa Croce, Carzano (Monte Isola Feast of the Holy Cross)

Every five years in September (2030, 2035)

One of the most extraordinary festivals in northern Italy, Carzano's Festa di Santa Croce transforms the village into a floral wonderland. Thousands of handmade paper flowers and wooden arches adorn every street, creating an enchanting setting for religious processions and evening concerts.

Franciacorta in Cantina (Wine Festival)

Second weekend of September

Just south of the lake, the celebrated Franciacorta wine region hosts its signature event. Dozens of wineries open their doors for tastings, vineyard tours, and food pairings. It is the ideal occasion to discover Italy's finest sparkling wine while enjoying the rolling hills that frame the southern approach to Lake Iseo. See Chapter 28 for the wine region map and information.

Festa dell'Uva di Capriolo (Grape Harvest, Wine Festival)

Mid-September

In the town of Capriolo, near the western shore of Lake Iseo, this lively grape festival celebrates the harvest with wine tastings, parades, artisan markets, and music. It continues a tradition that has linked local life to the vineyards for generations.

CHAPTER SEVENTEEN

Pavia: Processions and Pageantry

Faith, Food, and Festive Streets

Festa di Sant'Agostino

Where: Pavia

When: August 28

Average Festival Temperatures: High 30°C (86°F). Low 16°C (61°F).

Pavia: A City of Ancient Kings and Timeless Faith

A city stands where the Ticino River winds through fertile Lombard plains, connecting past and present, that once echoed with kings' footsteps. This is Pavia, known as *la città dalle cento torri*, the city of 100 towers. Here, medieval towers rise through the morning mist like fingers reaching toward the sky, and smooth cobblestone streets, once crossed by kings and nobles, now lead students to classes at a university that has shaped minds since 1361.

Once the capital of the Lombard Kingdom, Pavia has never forgotten its regal birthright. Walk its ancient streets and you'll trace the same paths where Roman legions marched, where Lombard nobles plotted beneath soaring Romanesque arches, and where the Visconti and Sforza dynasties wove their ambitious dreams into stone and mortar. The city's 70,000 citizens live within walls that have witnessed the rise and fall of empires, yet pulse with the rhythm of university life and market day bustle thirty-five miles south of Milan.

Here, beneath the golden dome of San Pietro in Ciel d'Oro, lies one of Christianity's greatest minds. Saint Augustine of Hippo rests in marble splendor, his final earthly home drawing theologians and seekers from across the globe. The surrounding countryside unfolds in quilted patterns of vineyards and rice fields, where morning fog rises from paddies that feed Lombardy's most celebrated risottos, and ancient vines produce wines that taste of sunshine distilled by centuries of patient cultivation.

The Feast of Saint Augustine

When the August harvest moon rises over Pavia's old towers, the city comes alive with warm light and the sound of sacred music. Each year on the twenty-eighth day of the month, pilgrims pour through medieval gates, drawn by the same magnetic pull that has summoned the faithful for thirteen centuries. This is a celebration born from royal devotion when Lombard King Liutprand, moved by divine inspiration, enshrined Augustine's precious relics within the marble embrace of San Pietro in Ciel d'Oro on that same August day in 724.

The sacred drama unfolds as dawn breaks over the basilica's golden dome. Liturgical ceremonies fill the sanctuary with voices that seem to echo Augustine's own prayers, while candlelight dances across frescoed walls that have witnessed nearly a millennium of devotion. Music spills from every corner as church bells create symphonies that rise and fall like celestial breathing, while clouds of frankincense weave through the procession like visible prayers ascending toward heaven.

Who Was Saint Augustine?

From the sun-baked hills of North Africa emerged a soul so restless it would reshape the very foundations of Western thought. Augustine of Hippo was born in 354 into a world where the Roman Empire still cast its shadow across three continents, yet his true empire would be built not of stone and sword but of words that continue to illuminate minds sixteen centuries later.

As a young man, he was consumed by an intense hunger for knowledge. He immersed himself in rhetoric and philosophy, exploring the complex teachings of the Manicheans and Platonists, but found no lasting peace for his heart. The transformation came like lightning splitting a dark sky: in Milan's sacred gardens, beneath the patient guidance of Saint Ambrose, the restless seeker found his rest. Baptized in 387, Augustine returned to Africa a different man, leaving behind the ambitions of his youth and carrying with him a deep and fervent faith.

As Bishop of Hippo Regius, Augustine's pen became a powerful instrument, shaping ideas that would outlast empires. In *Confessions*, he explored the depths of the human soul with remarkable honesty, so that even today readers recognize their own struggles in his words. *The City of God* set human history against a vast, eternal backdrop, illuminating the unfolding drama between earthly kingdoms and divine purpose.

When the Vandals approached Hippo's walls in 430, Augustine breathed his last on August 28. He died as the world around him burned, yet his heart was at peace, fixed on the vision of the eternal city that no barbarian sword could destroy. His relics traveled across seas and centuries before finding their resting place in Pavia's marble sanctuary, where centuries of prayer have turned his tomb into a lasting symbol of faith.

Festival Traditions

Morning

From early morning, pilgrims arrive at the Basilica di San Pietro in Ciel d'Oro to pray before the saint's golden reliquary, located beneath the richly decorated apse. Many walk the final stretch through Pavia's historic center, joining informal processions of faithful carrying banners of their parish or religious community.

10:00 a.m.

Solemn Pontifical Mass

Pavia's bishop presides over the feast's central liturgy, frequently joined by visiting bishops or Augustinian representatives. The basilica is filled to capacity, with many following the service from the courtyard via loudspeakers.

11:30 a.m.

Veneration of the Relics

Following Mass, the reliquary of Saint Augustine, a masterpiece of medieval goldsmithing, is displayed for public veneration. Pilgrims approach in silence, some leaving written prayers or lighting candles in the side chapels.

5:45 p.m.

Solemn Vespers

Vespers at the Basilica di San Pietro in Ciel d'Oro, led by the Augustinian community, is the spiritual peak of the day, featuring a moving musical liturgy. The basilica fills with the scent of incense and the sound of ancient chants as the faithful gather for this final act of devotion before the evening celebrations.

Evening Mass and Return of the Relics

The Pontifical Mass is solemnly presided over by the Cardinal, in the presence of civic, military, and religious dignitaries. The liturgy reflects both the grandeur of the occasion and a deep reverence for the saint. Immediately following the Mass, the reliquary of Saint Augustine is reverently returned to its resting place in the Arca, the beautifully carved ark beneath the high altar.

Walking Tour of Pavia

#1. Basilica di San Pietro in Ciel d'Oro (Saint Peter in the Golden Sky)

Begin at the heart of the Sant'Agostino celebration. Inside the basilica, the golden ceiling is a sight to behold, especially with the Arca di Sant'Agostino, which holds the saint's remains. Admire the intricate carvings depicting scenes from his life, the Romanesque façade, and the luminous rose window.

#2. Piazza della Vittoria

A short walk brings you to Pavia's main square, a lively hub surrounded by elegant arcades. This is the perfect spot to soak in the city's atmosphere, enjoy a coffee, or browse the boutiques lining the piazza. Look for the 14th-century Broletto (Town Hall) with its harmonious blend of Gothic and Renaissance elements.

#3. Duomo di Pavia (Cattedrale di Santo Stefano e Santa Maria Assunta)

From Piazza della Vittoria, stroll to the imposing cathedral, whose massive dome dominates the skyline. Construction began in the late 15th century, and Leonardo da Vinci is believed to have contributed to its design. Inside, the airy nave leads the eye upward to the soaring cupola and down to the marble altars adorned with Baroque details.

#4. Covered Bridge (Ponte Coperto)

Head toward the Ticino River to see one of Pavia's most iconic landmarks. The current bridge, rebuilt after World War II, preserves the charm of its medieval predecessor. Its red-brick arcades frame sweeping views of the water and the city's towers. Pause midway for photos or to watch rowers glide along the river.

#5. Basilica di San Michele Maggiore

A short walk from the river takes you to this masterpiece of Lombard Romanesque architecture. Its honey-colored sandstone façade, detailed with sculpted reliefs, is especially striking in the afternoon light. Inside, admire the carved capitals and the beautiful mosaic floors. This basilica hosted the coronations of medieval kings, adding to its historic prestige.

#6. Strada Nuova & the University of Pavia

Return toward the center via Strada Nuova, the city's elegant principal thoroughfare. Along the way, visit the University of Pavia, one of the oldest in Europe, founded in 1361. Peek into its courtyards and arcades, where centuries of scholars have walked.

#7. Castello Visconteo & Gardens

End the tour at the 14th-century castle built by Galeazzo II Visconti. Once a lavish ducal residence, it now houses Pavia's Civic Museums, showcasing art, archaeology, and medieval artifacts. Behind the castle, the expansive gardens offer a peaceful green space for a relaxing conclusion to your walk.

Castello Visconteo

Logistics

Train: Pavia is easily reached from Milan by frequent regional trains. The journey takes about 30 minutes from Milano Centrale or Milano Porta Garibaldi, arriving at Pavia's principal station, which is a 15-minute walk from the historic center and the Basilica di San Pietro in Ciel d'Oro.

Bus: Local buses connect the train station with various points in the city. Line 3 stops near the basilica and main squares.

Car: From Milan, take the A7 Autostrada toward Genova and exit at Bereguardo/Pavia Nord. Follow the signs to the city center. Paid parking is available at Viale della Libertà and Piazza Castello, both within walking distance of the basilica.

Parking: The center has restricted traffic zones (ZTL), so be sure to park outside the designated areas.

Restaurant Recommendations

Antica Osteria del Previ. Vicolo del Previ, 4

A cozy, traditional osteria serving local specialties like Pavia-style agnolotti and slow-cooked meats. Warm atmosphere, ideal for a more intimate dinner.

Osteria della Madonna. Piazza della Madonna, 1

Historic eatery near the Duomo, popular for its homemade pasta and classic Lombard fare. Simple, hearty dishes in a setting full of old-world charm.

Day Trips: Nearby Sites, Cities, and Towns

Lodi. 45 kilometers (28 miles) east of Pavia. Founded by Frederick Barbarossa in 1158 after the destruction of the earlier settlement, Lodi is a graceful town along the Adda River. Its central Piazza della Vittoria, often called one of Italy's most beautiful squares, is framed by arcaded palaces and the Cathedral of the Assumption.

I have a friend, Irina, who lives in Lodi, and I love to visit the beautiful, compact historical center with her. There is often a lively market in the square, which adds to the town's warm and inviting atmosphere. The Tempio Civico dell'Incoronata, a Renaissance jewel adorned with frescoes by Lombard masters, is the town's artistic highlight. Visitors can also stroll along the Adda and sample the area's famous cheeses, especially mascarpone, which originated here.

Piacenza. 55 kilometers (34 miles) southeast of Pavia. Straddling the border of Lombardy and Emilia-Romagna, Piacenza is an ancient Roman colony that flourished as a medieval trade hub. A friend and I once visited Piacenza on a day trip from Milan, exploring its beautiful historic center. We visited the Cathedral and the Palazzo Farnese, both impressive landmarks that showcase the city's artistic and architectural richness.

The town's core is dominated by the Piazza dei Cavalli, framed by the Gothic Palazzo Gotico and equestrian statues of Farnese dukes. Richly decorated with frescoes, the Cathedral of Piacenza is a Romanesque masterpiece created by Guercino and Procaccini. The Palazzo Farnese, now a museum, houses works by Antonello da Messina and a rare 15th-century globe by Toscanelli. Piacenza's location on the Via Emilia makes it a cultural crossroads and an excellent gateway into Emilia.

Tortona. 60 kilometers (37 miles) southwest of Pavia. An ancient Roman settlement and later a Lombard stronghold, Tortona in Piedmont sits along the Via Emilia route toward Liguria. The town's historic heart is marked by the Cathedral of Santa Maria Assunta e San Lorenzo, rebuilt in the Baroque style.

The Pinacoteca Fondazione Cassa di Risparmio di Tortona preserves works by 19th–20th century Italian artists, including Divisionists like Pellizza da Volpedo. Rising above the town are the remains of the Castello di Tortona, offering panoramic views of the surrounding hills and vineyards. Tortona is also a center for fine wines, including the nearby Timorasso whites.

Pavia Festivals and Sagre Throughout the Year

Carnevale Pavese

February or March

Carnevale Pavese brings a burst of color and energy to the quiet winter months. This lively pre-Lenten celebration fills the historic center with parades, costumed processions, marching bands, and street performers who entertain crowds of all ages. Children dress up in traditional and fantastical costumes, while confetti rains down over Piazza della Vittoria and the surrounding streets. Food stalls offer local specialties, including sweet fritters such as chiacchiere and frittelle, which are a beloved part of Carnival celebrations across Lombardy.

Palio del Ticino (Rowing Race)

June

The Palio del Ticino is a spectacular historic regatta that blends medieval pageantry with athletic competition, bringing centuries-old traditions to life along the river. Through Pavia's historic center, the festivities start with processions. The highlight is the rowing race itself, held on the Ticino River, where crews representing different districts compete in long, elegant boats inspired by medieval designs.

Festa del Ticino (River Fest)

Early September

The Festa del Ticino is one of Pavia's signature annual celebrations, honoring the river that has shaped the city's history and identity. Over the course of a week, the banks of the Ticino come alive with a lively mix of cultural events, sports, music, and food. Traditional river regattas showcase local rowing teams competing in friendly but spirited races, while concerts and performances bring festive energy to the evenings. Open-air markets and food stalls line the riverfront, offering regional specialties and street food that draw both locals and visitors. Illuminated bridges and riverfront walks create a magical atmosphere after sunset, making this festival a highlight of late summer in Pavia.

Mercato Europeo di Pavia

Early September (often coinciding with Festa del Ticino)

Each September, Pavia welcomes the Mercato Europeo, a vibrant traveling market that brings together vendors from across Europe. Stalls line the streets and squares of the historic center, offering an enticing mix of international street food, artisanal crafts, clothing, and specialty products. It's a lively, cosmopolitan event that gives the city a festive, open-air market atmosphere. Visitors can wander from stall to stall sampling German sausages, Spanish churros, French cheeses, Belgian waffles, and other specialties, all while enjoying cultural performances and music.

Autunno Pavese

Late September to Early October

Autunno Pavese is one of the region's most anticipated annual events, celebrating the rich agricultural and culinary heritage of the province. Hosted in Pavia's exhibition spaces and often spilling into the streets, the fair highlights the best local products from the fertile lands of the Oltrepò Pavese. Visitors can taste DOC and DOCG wines, artisanal cheeses, cured meats, olive oils, breads, honey, and seasonal dishes prepared by local chefs.

Festa di San Siro

December 9

Pavia's year concludes with the Festa di San Siro, a celebration honoring the city's patron saint. The day begins with solemn religious services in the historic center, where the faithful gather to pay tribute to San Siro, the first bishop of Pavia. The streets surrounding the churches come alive with food stalls, artisan vendors, and a small winter fair that fills the squares with a festive yet intimate atmosphere. Visitors can sample seasonal specialties, warm drinks, and traditional sweets while enjoying the charm of Pavia's historic center in winter.

CHAPTER EIGHTEEN

Immersion Experience: Pilgrimage

Pilgrimage to Pavia

Immersion Experience: Cammino di Sant'Agostino

The Way of Saint Augustine connects two sacred places in Lombardy: Milan's Sant'Ambrogio, where Augustine was baptized in 387 AD, and Pavia's San Pietro in Ciel d'Oro, where his remains rest today. This pilgrimage route has drawn seekers for over a thousand years, each tracing the same path across the fertile Lombard countryside.

The journey unfolds through rice fields and along ancient canals, past medieval villages where church bells still mark the hours as they have for centuries. In August, when heat shimmers across the plains and morning mist rises from the fields, pilgrims time their arrival in Pavia to coincide with the feast day celebrations that transform the city into a center of devotion.

A Saint's Legacy in Stone and Story

In 723, Lombard King Liutprand brought Augustine's remains north from Sardinia to Pavia, creating one of medieval Europe's most important pilgrimage destinations. Augustine had a brilliant mind that reshaped Christian thought, and his Confessions spoke to anyone who had ever struggled with doubt and faith.

The tradition flourished when Europe was crisscrossed with sacred routes. Medieval pilgrims would begin at the Romanesque basilica of Sant'Ambrogio, where Bishop Ambrose had baptized the future saint, then journey south through countryside dotted with ancient Roman roads and medieval pathways.

Today, Italians embrace their many pilgrimage routes not only as spiritual journeys but as expressions of slow tourism, opportunities to commune with nature and fellow travelers. This route offers something profound: the chance to traverse literally Augustine's story of transformation, from his restless youth through his conversion, ending at the marble tomb where his legacy continues to inspire visitors from around the world.

Suggested Pilgrimage Route

Total Distance: 35 kilometers (22 miles) from Milan to Pavia.

The route can be completed in a single day by experienced walkers or split into two days for a more leisurely pilgrimage.

Start: Basilica di Sant'Ambrogio, Milan

Begin at one of Milan's most sacred churches, where Augustine received the sacrament of baptism. Admire the early Christian mosaics, the tomb of Saint Ambrose, and the atmosphere of quiet reverence before setting off.

Milan to Rozzano: 8 kilometers (5 miles)

Leaving the historic center, you follow quieter suburban streets toward Rozzano. This section of the walk offers glimpses of everyday Milanese life and small parish churches that welcome travelers.

Rozzano to Binasco: 10 kilometers (6.2 miles)

From Rozzano, follow the path along the Naviglio Pavese canal. This waterway has been an artery of commerce and travel for centuries, and its shaded paths make for pleasant walking.

Binasco to Certosa di Pavia: 10 kilometers (6.2 miles)

The monumental Certosa di Pavia, one of Italy's most extraordinary monastic complexes, is the next stop.

Certosa to Pavia: 7 kilometers (4.3 miles)

The Certosa di Pavia was founded in 1396 by Gian Galeazzo Visconti, the first Duke of Milan, as both a dynastic mausoleum and a spiritual sanctuary for the Carthusian order. Gian Galeazzo, who also commissioned the grand Duomo of Milan, envisioned the Certosa as a symbol of power, faith, and artistic patronage.

The decorated dome of the Certosa

Pilgrimage Resources and Practical Information

Certosa di Pavia Monastery. www.certosadipavia.com

Augustinian Order Italy. www.agostiniani.it

City of Pavia Tourism Office. www.visitpavia.com

CHAPTER NINETEEN

Festa Fusion on Lake Como

Saints Feast & the Emperor's Palio

FestaFusion Como

#1. Fiera di Sant'Abbondio. This centuries-old festival in honor of Como's patron saint combines religious ceremonies with lively markets, music, and food, creating a vibrant mix of devotion and community celebration.

#2. Palio del Baradello. A grand historical reenactment and medieval games event commemorating Emperor Frederick Barbarossa's visit to Como in 1159, featuring parades, competitions, and a medieval banquet.

Where: Como

When: Fiera di Sant'Abbondio August 31, Palio del Baradello two weeks in September.

Average Temperatures: High 25°C (77°F). Low 14°C (57°F).

#FestaFusion: When two festivals converge in the same town around the same time, your journey becomes twice as magical.

Event Website: https://www.paliodelbaradello.it/

Como, Jewel of Lake and History

Where the lake mirrors Alpine peaks and morning mist drifts over historic villas, you find Como, a city that has attracted visitors since Roman times. Known as the jewel of the lake, Como combines medieval squares, elegant streets, and a lively waterfront filled with history and charm. Over the centuries, it grew under the Lombards, the Visconti, and Spanish rule, each leaving a lasting mark on its architecture and culture.

Once called Novum Comum by Roman settlers who recognized paradise when they saw it, Como has gracefully weathered the rise and fall of empires. Lombard kings, Visconti nobles, and Spanish governors each left their mark on streets that still whisper with history, while master craftsmen wove silk so fine it adorned the courts of Europe.

One morning during the Fiera di Sant'Abbondio, I saw this stunning town come to life. We began the day with coffee and a warm cornetto at Bar Mariett Caffè, where locals chatted softly over their newspapers and the scent of espresso filled the air. The medieval streets soon filled with colorful market stalls, cheeses, handmade crafts, and the laughter of children. We wandered from the heart of town down to the lakefront, where the breeze carried the shimmer of water and the bells of nearby churches. Later, the funicular cable car lifted us high above the city, revealing Como from a new perspective: rooftops glowing in afternoon light, the basilica standing proud, and the lake stretching like a silver mirror toward the Alps.

Ancient streets wind between Romanesque churches and lively markets, where the smell of fresh bread mixes with the mountain air, and the sound of water against stone sets the rhythm of daily life. In this place where Italy meets Switzerland and the Alps meet the lake, Como continues to be a crossroads of beauty and history in perfect harmony.

#1. Fair of Saint Abundius (Sant'Abbondio)

In late summer, the sound of bells and laughter fills Como as the city prepares for its most time-honored celebration. The Fiera di Sant'Abbondio transforms the medieval streets into a vibrant festival that flows toward the ancient basilica, where the city's patron saint has been honored for fifteen centuries.

With roots stretching back to medieval times, when pilgrims gathered at Sant'Abbondio's walls to honor their bishop-saint on August 31st. What started as solemn worship and thanksgiving for the summer harvest has grown into days of celebration where religious devotion and community joy come together naturally.

The festival captures something essential about Como's character, blending the city's deep spiritual heritage with the simple pleasure of gathering together as summer reaches its peak.

Who is Saint Abundius?

Saint Abundius came to Como from Syria in the fifth century, bringing gentle strength that would guide the city through some of Christianity's most turbulent times. He arrived as Como's fourth bishop when theological disputes threatened to divide the early Church and Arian heresy was spreading across northern Italy. Yet this humble shepherd proved himself a skilled diplomat, earning Pope Leo's trust and traveling all the way to the Council of Chalcedon in 451, where his voice helped shape the foundations of the Christian faith.

Through Como's valleys and hillside villages he traveled, his sandaled feet wearing paths between scattered flocks, bringing comfort to the sick and hope to the weary. When death claimed him in 469, the faithful knew they had lost not just a bishop but a father, and the basilica that rose over his resting place became a beacon of devotion that still draws pilgrims today.

Festival Traditions

Morning

The day begins with the solemn celebration of Mass inside the Basilica di Sant'Abbondio. The service, presided over by the Bishop of Como, includes prayers for the city, the presentation of the saint's relics, and the blessing of the faithful. Bells ring from the basilica's twin Romanesque towers, announcing the feast day to all. After Mass, the outdoor fair begins in the surrounding piazza and streets. Merchants open their stalls, displaying artisanal crafts, fresh cheeses from local dairies, seasonal produce, and handmade sweets.

Afternoon

The afternoon features a mix of entertainment and devotion. A highlight is the procession of the relics of Saint Abundius, carried through the streets by clergy, altar servers, and townspeople dressed in traditional attire. The route winds through Como's historic center, with residents lining the streets to watch and join in the prayers.

Procession in Medieval Costume in Como

Evening

As the sun sets, the pace of the fair slows to a relaxed rhythm. Visitors linger over coffee or a final plate of sweets, while musicians perform in the piazza. The evening concludes with a small fireworks display or a concert in honor of the patron saint. The lights of the market stalls glow against the night sky, and the celebration ends in a spirit of gratitude and community.

#2. The Palio del Bardello

The Palio del Baradello is Como's most spectacular historical reenactment, created to commemorate the visit of Holy Roman Emperor Frederick I, known as Barbarossa, to the city in 1159. The event recalls the medieval alliance between Como and the Emperor, forged after the city's victory over Milan in the long and bloody wars of the 12th century. According to tradition, Barbarossa's arrival was marked by grand celebrations, tournaments, and the strengthening of fortifications, including work on the imposing Castello Baradello that still dominates the skyline.

First organized in modern times in 1981, the Palio has grown into a multi-week festival held each September, transforming Como into a living medieval city. Neighborhoods and surrounding towns compete in games and contests, each vying for the honor of winning the coveted Palio banner.

Beyond the pageantry, the Palio del Baradello features a range of medieval-themed competitions, from archery and tug-of-war to boat races on the lake. Markets offer food inspired by medieval recipes, and visitors can taste dishes such as spiced meats, rustic breads, and local wines. Cultural exhibitions, concerts, and storytelling sessions bring the history of Barbarossa's era to life, while guided tours lead to the Castello Baradello for panoramic views over the lake and city.

Festival Traditions

Afternoon: Cariolana Race

The highlight of the Palio is the grand historical parade, which winds through Como's streets from the city gates to the lakeside. Hundreds of participants march in authentic medieval attire: knights in chain mail, noble ladies in flowing gowns, monks, merchants, soldiers, and standard bearers. Drums and trumpets announce the arrival of each contrada, or neighborhood team, as crowds cheer.

Following the parade, the competitive games begin, with events such as archery, tug of war, and the lively Cariolana race, where one person pushes a cart while another rides. Some years also feature boat races on the lake, recalling Como's history as a strategic port.

Evening: Medieval Dinner

The evening brings the ceremonial awarding of the Palio banner to the winning team, often in a central piazza filled with cheering spectators. The festival's grand medieval dinner follows, usually staged under the arches. Guests dine on multi-course meals inspired by 12th-century recipes, while musicians, acrobats, and actors provide entertainment.

The celebration often continues late into the night, with music, dancing, and the warm glow of torches and lanterns lighting the medieval streets of Como.

Palio Procession

Walking Tour of Como

#1. Piazza Cavour

Begin the tour in the bustling Piazza Cavour, the main square on the lakefront. Once a harbor, it is now a lively gathering spot surrounded by cafés and shops, with beautiful views of the water and mountains. This is also a good place to orient yourself, as many of Como's main streets radiate from here.

#2. Duomo di Como (Cattedrale di Santa Maria Assunta)

A short walk from Piazza Cavour brings you to the magnificent Duomo, one of the last Gothic cathedrals built in Italy. The façade, with its intricate stonework and statues, transitions into Renaissance elements, reflecting its long construction period from the 14th to 18th centuries. Inside, admire the soaring nave, richly decorated side chapels, and remarkable tapestries.

#3. Broletto (Medieval Town Hall)

Next to the Duomo stands the Broletto, a striking 13th-century building made of alternating bands of white, gray, and pink stone. Once the seat of civic government, it now serves as an exhibition space. Its elegant arches and Gothic windows offer a striking contrast to the cathedral beside it.

#4. Piazza San Fedele

Continue into the medieval center of Como to reach Piazza San Fedele, a charming square surrounded by arcaded buildings and small shops. Here stands the Romanesque Basilica di San Fedele, built on the site of an early Christian church. The interior's stone columns and frescoes provide a sense of Como's spiritual history.

Duomo di Como

#5. Porta Torre

Walk along Via Vittorio Emanuele II toward Porta Torre, an imposing 12th-century gate built as part of Como's defensive walls. The massive stone structure, with its four tiers of open arches, is a reminder of the city's medieval strength and strategic importance.

#6. Tempio Voltiano

Head back toward the lake and stroll along the Lungolago (lakefront) promenade to the Tempio Voltiano, a neoclassical museum dedicated to Alessandro Volta, the Como-born inventor of the electric battery. The exhibits trace his life and groundbreaking experiments.

#7. Funicolare Como–Brunate

End the tour with a ride on the historic funicular railway to Brunate, a hilltop village overlooking Como. The quick trip offers panoramic views, and from Brunate you can take a brief walk to the Faro Voltiano lighthouse for even more breathtaking vistas of the lake and surrounding Alps.

Panoramic View from the Funicular Como

Logistics

Train: Como is easily reached by train from Milan in about 35 to 50 minutes, depending on the route. The city has two primary stations: Como San Giovanni, served by Trenitalia and long-distance trains, and Como Lago, served by Trenord regional trains. Both are within walking distance of the historic center and the lakefront.

Bus: The local bus network connects Como with surrounding towns and villages, including many along the lake. Regional buses also run to Lugano in Switzerland and to nearby mountain destinations. Tickets can be purchased at tabacchi shops, newsstands, or directly from the driver.

Boat: Navigazione Laghi operates frequent ferry, hydrofoil, and slow boat services from Como to other Lake Como towns such as Cernobbio, Menaggio, Bellagio, and Varenna. The ferry terminal is conveniently located next to Piazza Cavour.

Car: Driving into Como is possible, but much of the historic center is a limited traffic zone. Visitors are encouraged to park in designated lots outside the restricted area and explore on foot. From Milan, the journey by car takes about one hour along the A9 Autostrada.

Parking: Several parking garages are located close to the center, including Autosilo Valduce near the Duomo and Centro Lago Parking near the waterfront. Spaces can fill quickly during festivals, so early arrival is recommended.

Restaurant Recommendations

Ristorante Sociale. Via Rodari, 6

A refined yet welcoming restaurant offering traditional Lombard dishes such as risotto with perch from the lake and braised meats with polenta. The historic setting and attentive service make it ideal for a special evening.

Osteria del Gallo. Via Vitani, 16

A cozy osteria in the medieval quarter serving homemade pasta, local cheeses, and hearty meat dishes. The friendly atmosphere and rustic décor create a warm dining experience.

Gelateria Lariana. Viale Geno, 10

Perfect for a sweet treat by the lake, this gelateria offers a wide range of flavors made fresh daily. Their fruit sorbets are especially refreshing in the warmer months.

Day Trip Options: Nearby Sites, Cities, and Towns

Bellagio. A 45-minute ferry ride or 30 kilometers (19 miles) by car from Como. Often called the Pearl of Lake Como, Bellagio sits at the meeting point of the lake's three branches, offering postcard-perfect views in every direction. On my most recent visit, my friend Svetlana and I strolled through Bellagio beneath a bright morning sun, the air carrying the scent of blooming flowers and espresso. Often called the Pearl of Lake Como, Bellagio sits at the meeting point of the lake's three branches, offering postcard-perfect views in every direction. We explored Villa Melzi d'Eril, its neoclassical villa surrounded by peaceful gardens where camellias and azaleas framed the lake like a painting. At the edge of the town, the Punta Spartivento viewpoint offered one of the most unforgettable sights of the trip: the three branches of Lake Como meeting beneath a soft haze of light, the mountains rising beyond in quiet majesty. From here, it was easy to see why travelers have fallen in love with Bellagio for centuries. Before leaving, we boarded a ferry bound for Varenna, the short ride revealing yet another perspective of this timeless jewel on the lake.

Varenna. A 5-minute ferry ride from Como. 35 kilometers (22 miles) from Como. Varenna is a romantic village with pastel-colored houses that seem to tumble down toward the water. The lakeside Passeggiata degli Innamorati, or Lovers' Walk, is perfect for a slow stroll, especially at sunset when the lake glows gold. Visit Villa Monastero, once a Cistercian convent, whose long terraced gardens overlook the lake and feature Mediterranean and exotic plants. Climb up to Castello di Vezio for sweeping views and to see falconry demonstrations in summer. Varenna is well connected by train from Lecco and by ferry from Bellagio, making it easy to include in a day trip.

Menaggio. 33 kilometers (20 miles) from Como. One-hour ferry ride from Como. Menaggio combines a charming lakeside atmosphere with an active town center. The wide promenade is ideal for walking and has benches where you can pause to watch the ferries glide by. Piazza Garibaldi, the main square, is filled with cafés that spill onto the pavement, inviting visitors to sit with a cappuccino and soak in the lake view. Menaggio is also a gateway to the Val Menaggio and other mountain trails, making it a good starting point for scenic hikes. Its location in the center of the lake makes it a practical hub for exploring Bellagio, Varenna, and other towns by ferry, with travel times of only a few minutes.

Cernobbio. A 10-minute ferry ride from Como. 7 kilometers (4 miles) by car from Como. Just a short boat or bus ride away, Cernobbio is a refined lakeside town known for its historic villas and tranquil atmosphere. Villa Erba, a 19th-century estate, hosts cultural events and exhibitions throughout the year, while the world-famous Villa d'Este operates as a luxury hotel with magnificent gardens and a floating pool on the lake. The town's lakeside promenade is lined with trees and elegant cafés, perfect for a leisurely walk. Cernobbio is also the starting point for the Strada Regia, an old mule track turned hiking path with views of the lake and mountains.

Como Festivals Throughout the Year

Sant'Agostino Fair (Como or Senigallia)

August 28

In late summer, the Sant'Agostino district comes alive with this traditional fair, which has roots stretching back centuries. Located near the lakeshore at the foot of the funicular to Brunate, the fair transforms the neighborhood streets into a lively open-air market. Stalls are filled with local products, handmade crafts, toys, and sweets, creating a cheerful, family-friendly atmosphere. The evenings feature live music ranging from folk groups to local bands, adding to the festive mood.

Food stands serve regional specialties such as polenta, local cheeses, and fresh lake fish, offering visitors a chance to taste Como's culinary traditions. Unlike the larger citywide events, the Sant'Agostino Fair is more intimate, giving travelers a chance to mingle with locals, shop for unique souvenirs, and enjoy the slower pace of a community celebration.

Natale a Como: Città dei Balocchi (Christmas Market)

Late November to early January

During the holiday season, Como transforms into a magical Christmas wonderland. The historic center is illuminated with spectacular light projections that cover the façades of churches and palaces, turning the city into an enchanting open-air gallery. A lively Christmas market fills the squares with wooden chalets selling artisanal gifts, ornaments, local products, and festive treats like mulled wine, roasted chestnuts, and sweets. Families flock to the open-air ice skating rink, while concerts and performances add music and cheer to the winter air.

Known as the *Città dei Balocchi* (City of Toys), the event delights children with activities, workshops, and visits from Santa Claus, while adults enjoy the romantic atmosphere and seasonal flavors.

CHAPTER TWENTY

Monza's Amazing Race

Racing, Roars, and Royal Gardens

Gran Premio di Monza

Where: Monza

When: Typically first weekend of September.

Average Festival Temperatures: High 25°C (77°F). Low 16°C (61°F).

Event Website: https://monzagpf1.ticketone.it/

Monza: The Royal Park Meets Racing Glory

Imagine a city where the roar of Formula 1 engines echoes through ancient royal parklands, where sleek race cars blur past neoclassical villas, and where the energy of modern sport collides with centuries of aristocratic heritage. This is Monza, a Lombardy town of about 120,000 residents, located just 15 kilometers (9 miles) northeast of Milan.

Built in 1922, the Autodromo Nazionale Monza is located in the Parco di Monza, which is one of Europe's largest parks. Known as the "Temple of Speed," the circuit has hosted legendary races and immortalized champions from Fangio to Schumacher. The Grand Prix each September transforms Monza into a global stage, drawing tens of thousands of fans draped in Ferrari red.

However, Monza offers more than just racing. The historic center boasts elegant piazzas, stylish cafés, and the Gothic Duomo of Monza, where the Iron Crown of Lombardy, once used to crown kings and emperors, is preserved. The Royal Villa of Monza, built in the 18th century for the Habsburgs, anchors the city's cultural life with gardens, exhibitions, and concerts.

Balancing regal heritage with high-octane thrills, Monza offers a rare dual identity: a place where visitors can trace royal footsteps in the morning and feel the ground shake with Formula 1 in the afternoon.

The Italian Grand Prix at Monza

Few sporting events in the world carry the prestige and passion of the Gran Premio d'Italia. First held in 1921 near Brescia and permanently moved to Monza in 1922, the race is one of the oldest on the Formula 1 calendar and the only event, besides the British Grand Prix, to be held every year since the championship's founding in 1950. The Autodromo Nazionale Monza, built in just 110 days in the royal park, instantly became a temple of speed and innovation, boasting high-speed straights and challenging curves that tested the limits of both man and machine.

Over the decades, Monza has been the stage of triumph and tragedy, with legendary names like Juan Manuel Fangio, Jim Clark, Ayrton Senna, and Michael Schumacher securing their place in history here. The tifosi, Ferrari's devoted fans, transform the event into a national celebration, waving scarlet flags and filling the grandstands with chants that echo across the park. The image of the track's final podium, crowded with thousands of jubilant fans surging beneath it, has become an enduring symbol of Italian motorsport passion.

Today, Monza's Grand Prix week is a festival in every sense: concerts, fan zones, exhibitions, and street parties spill from the racetrack into the city, ensuring that both seasoned fans and first-time visitors are swept up in the excitement. Each September, Monza is the place to be for a weekend of Formula 1 action.

Festival Events

Thursday

Pit Walks and Fan Festival

Grand Prix week begins on Thursday with the official F1 Fan Festival. The Autodromo opens its gates for pit lane walks, giving visitors the rare chance to see mechanics at work, cars being prepared, and drivers signing autographs. In Monza's historic center, fan zones come alive with simulators, live music, and pop-up shops filled with Ferrari red merchandise.

Friday

Practice Sessions

The first roar of engines fills the Royal Park as the morning and afternoon practice sessions begin. Fans take their seats in the grandstands along the Curva Parabolica, Rettifilo Tribune, and Ascari Chicane to watch drivers fine-tune their cars. Food stalls and sponsor villages around the circuit serve Italian street foods, from panini to gelato, keeping the atmosphere festive throughout the day.

Saturday

Qualifying Day

Saturday morning features the final practice session, while the afternoon brings the high drama of qualifying. The three-part knockout format sees cars eliminated until the final ten battle for pole position.

The fan chants reach a fever pitch when Ferrari takes to the track, and the entire circuit reverberates with excitement. In the evening, concerts and light shows take place both in the fan zones and in Piazza Trento e Trieste in the city center.

Sunday

Race Day

Race day is the pinnacle of the festival. Gates open early as fans flood into the park, picnic blankets in hand. The buildup includes a drivers' parade, national anthem, and spectacular flyovers by the Italian Air Force's Frecce Tricolori. At 3:00 p.m., the lights go out and the Italian Grand Prix begins, cars reaching speeds of over 350 km/h (217 mph) on the straights. The winner's podium celebration is legendary, with fans swarming and flags waving.

Evening Celebrations

After the race, Monza continues the party. Restaurants and bars spill into the piazzas with celebratory meals and music, and the city hums late into the night as fans share stories of the day's race. Whether Ferrari triumphs or not, the spirit of the tifosi (Ferrari fan base) ensures an unforgettable finale to the weekend.

Ticket and Hotel Experience

We included Monza on a September festival-focused trip. Knowing that the Italian Grand Prix takes place the first Sunday of September, we started our planning around September 15 a year before, only to discover just how quickly the city transforms for race week. Every hotel nearby was either completely sold out or asking jaw-dropping prices, some as high as €10,000 per night.

At one point, I seriously thought about dropping this chapter from the book altogether. The combination of sold-out tickets and astronomical hotel rates made it feel impossible to experience firsthand. But the Monza Grand Prix is one of Italy's most prestigious and historic sporting events, and ultimately, it was too important to leave out. The truth is, I was simply a week too late with my planning.

We searched for alternatives in Como, Lecco, and other towns, but ultimately found our best option in Milan, near Castello Sforzesco. From there, frequent trains to Monza made the commute manageable and stress-free, turning Milan into the most practical base for race weekend.

Tickets proved to be just as elusive. They had officially gone on sale September 9, and by the time we checked a week later, everything was gone. The lesson is simple: if you want to include this legendary race in your itinerary; you need to plan well in advance. Expect tickets to be released about a year before the event and be ready to purchase as soon as sales open. The same goes for hotels; book as soon as reservations become available. By September 1, you should already know the race date, have your tickets secured, and have your hotel booked. Anything less, and you risk missing out on one of Italy's most exhilarating sporting experiences. Our solution was third-party ticket seller StubHub.

Walking Tour of Monza

#1. Duomo di Monza (Cathedral of Saint John the Baptist)

Begin at the Gothic Duomo, the spiritual and historic heart of Monza. Its marble façade hides a treasury of art, including the legendary Iron Crown of Lombardy, once used to crown kings and emperors. Step inside to admire the soaring nave and the frescoes of the Theodelinda Chapel, celebrating the Lombard queen who made Monza her home in the 6th century.

#2. Arengario (Medieval Town Hall)

A quick stroll leads to the Arengario, Monza's 13th-century town hall. With its brick arches and bell tower, it recalls the city's medieval civic pride. The loggia beneath is often filled with markets or small exhibitions, linking Monza's past role as a civic hub with its lively present.

#3. Piazza Trento e Trieste

This large square is Monza's modern gathering place. During Grand Prix week, it becomes an extension of the festival, with open-air concerts, fan zones, and street performances. On non-race days, cafés and gelaterie line the square, making it a pleasant stop for people-watching.

#4. Villa Reale di Monza (Royal Villa of Monza)

Continue toward the neoclassical Royal Villa, built in the 1770s for Archduke Ferdinand of Austria, son of Empress Maria Theresa. Designed by architect Giuseppe Piermarini, who also created Milan's Teatro alla Scala, the villa was modeled after Vienna's Schönbrunn, embodying the grandeur of Habsburg power in Lombardy. Inside, grand salons, sweeping staircases, and lavishly decorated apartments reflect 18th- and 19th-century court life. The villa later became a royal residence for the Italian Savoy kings, and its rooms still echo with the elegance of that era.

Aerial View of the Palace of Monza

Behind the palace lie extensive Italian and English-style gardens, with fountains, statues, and tree-lined avenues that lead into the vast Parco di Monza. Today, the villa serves as a cultural hub, hosting art exhibitions, concerts, and special events, making it a living monument rather than a relic. Strolling through the villa and its gardens provides a striking contrast to the noise and speed of the racetrack just beyond the park walls.

#5. Parco di Monza

One of Europe's biggest walled parks, Parco di Monza, is beyond the villa. Created in 1805 under Napoleon's reign, the park was designed to complement the villa and provide hunting grounds, agricultural estates, and leisure spaces. Today, it encompasses forests, rivers, meadows, and historic farmsteads such as Cascina San Fedele, along with bridges and mills that reveal its layered past.

#6. Autodromo Nazionale Monza

Conclude the tour at the legendary racetrack itself, built in 1922 and forever known as the "Temple of Speed." Even outside race weekend, visitors can book guided tours of the pits, podium, and circuit. Standing at the old banked oval or on the starting grid, you can almost hear the echoes of past races and the cheers of generations of tifosi.

Logistics

Train: Monza is easily reached from Milan by frequent regional trains departing from Milano Centrale, Milano Porta Garibaldi, and Milano Lambrate. The journey takes about 15–20 minutes, making rail the most convenient option during Grand Prix week. From Monza station, shuttle buses run directly to the Autodromo Nazionale Monza and Parco di Monza.

Bus: Local bus services operate from Monza station into the park and city center, though during the race weekend, special shuttles and dedicated routes are added to handle the surge of visitors. Fan zone buses often extend into the late evening after concerts and events.

Car: From Milan, take the A4 autostrada east toward Venice and exit at Monza. The drive takes around 30 minutes depending on traffic. During the Grand Prix, however, congestion is intense, and many streets near the park are closed to non-resident traffic. Visitors are strongly advised to use trains and shuttles instead of driving.

Parking: If traveling by car is unavoidable, large temporary parking areas are established outside Monza and Lissone, with shuttle services into the park. Parking inside Parco di Monza is strictly prohibited during race weekend. Advance booking for official parking lots is highly recommended.

Restaurant Recommendations

Ristorante Derby Grill. Viale Regina Margherita di Savoia, 15

Located inside the Hotel de la Ville across from the Royal Villa, Derby Grill is Monza's most refined dining experience. Known for Lombard classics elevated with contemporary flair, it is an elegant choice for celebrating after a day at the Grand Prix.

Osteria del Cavolo. Via Carlo Alberto, 8

In the historic center, this cozy osteria offers homemade pastas, risotti, and seasonal dishes. The rustic décor and welcoming staff make it a favorite for both locals and visitors. Perfect for a relaxed evening meal after exploring the city's piazzas.

Trattoria Caprese Monza. Via Bergamo, 37

A lively trattoria with a southern Italian flair, specializing in Neapolitan pizzas, seafood pastas, and generous antipasti. Its casual vibe and hearty portions make it popular with groups of racing fans.

Il Moderno. Piazza Trento e Trieste, 6

Overlooking Monza's main square, Il Moderno blends a stylish café with a contemporary restaurant. It is ideal for lunch during fan zone events or aperitivo (happy) hour, with a menu that ranges from light bites to classic Lombard dishes.

Day Trips from Monza

Brianza Hills. 30 kilometers (18 miles) north of Monza. This scenic area is dotted with vineyards, historic villas, and small villages such as Villasanta and Biassono. Visitors can explore villa gardens, sample regional wines, or enjoy a leisurely lunch in a countryside trattoria. The rolling landscape provides a serene contrast to the high-octane excitement of the Grand Prix.

Lake Pusiano. 35 kilometers (22 miles) northeast of Monza. Lake Pusiano is a small glacial lake nestled at the foothills of the Alps. The lake is known for its tranquil beauty, birdlife, and recreational opportunities. Visitors can walk or cycle along the shoreline, rent a small boat, or simply relax in the village of Pusiano with its lakeside promenade and cafés. Far less crowded than Lake Como, it offers an authentic and quiet retreat.

Crespi d'Adda. 40 kilometers (25 miles) east of Monza, Crespi d'Adda is a UNESCO World Heritage Site and one of Italy's most unusual destinations. This perfectly preserved 19th-century workers' village was built by the Crespi family as part of a visionary industrial project along the Adda River. Guided tours reveal the town's harmonious layout of workers' houses, the Crespi family villa, and the old textile mill.

Festivals and Sagre Throughout the Year

Carnevale Monzese

February or March

Monza celebrates Carnival with lively parades through the historic center. Costumed children, floats, and brass bands fill Piazza Trento e Trieste, while local bakeries serve traditional sweets such as chiacchiere and tortelli di Carnevale.

Festa di San Gerardo dei Tintori (Patron Saint Festival)

June 6

Honoring Monza's co-patron saint, this local celebration includes religious ceremonies, a solemn procession, and community gatherings. San Gerardo is remembered for his charitable works in medieval Monza, and the feast emphasizes the city's deep historical roots.

Festa di San Giovanni Battista (St. John the Baptist)

June 24

Dedicated to Monza's patron saint, this feast day centers on the Duomo, where solemn Mass is followed by processions through the city streets. The celebration also includes markets, concerts, and fireworks over the Lambro River.

Estate Monzese (Summer Festival)

June to September

Throughout the summer, Monza hosts open-air concerts, theater performances, and cultural events in its piazzas, parks, and the Royal Villa gardens. The program ranges from classical music to modern shows, attracting audiences of all ages.

Mercatini di Natale (Christmas Market)

December

In the weeks before Christmas, Monza's historic center is filled with holiday charm. Wooden stalls line the streets with ornaments, crafts, and festive foods.

CHAPTER TWENTY-ONE

Cremona: Strings of History and Harmony

From Stradivari to the Stage

Cremona Musica International Exhibition

Where: Cremona

When: Late September

Average Festival Temperatures: High: 24°C (75°F). Low: 12°C (54°F).

Event Website: https://cremonamusica.com/en/

Cremona: City of Violins and Timeless Harmony

Cremona, set gracefully along the banks of the Po River in southern Lombardy, is a city whose very name resonates with music. Known worldwide as the birthplace of the violin, it was home to master luthiers (stringed instrument makers) such as Antonio Stradivari, Andrea Amati, and Giuseppe Guarneri, whose instruments remain legendary for their beauty, craftsmanship, and unmatched sound. The city lies about 100 kilometers (62 miles) southeast of Milan, surrounded by fertile plains that have supported its agricultural and cultural life for centuries.

Founded by the Romans in 218 BC as a military outpost, Cremona grew into a prosperous trading center in the Middle Ages and Renaissance. The city flourished under various rulers, including the Visconti, Sforza, and Spanish Habsburgs, each leaving their mark on its architecture and urban design. Today, its historic core is a harmonious blend of medieval towers, Renaissance palaces, and graceful piazzas, anchored by the magnificent Piazza del Comune.

When I visited Cremona, I was instantly charmed by its warm, inviting atmosphere. The skyline is dominated by the soaring Torrazzo, one of the tallest brick bell towers in Europe, offering sweeping views over the Po Valley. Below, narrow streets lead to artisan workshops where luthiers still craft violins using centuries-old techniques. I lingered at the violin museum, mesmerized by the artistry and history behind these exquisite instruments.

Cremona's rhythm is unhurried, its beauty revealed in details: the intricate carvings of the cathedral's façade, the elegant arcades that shade its streets, and the hum of conversation drifting from cafés. Its location and excellent train connections make it a calm day trip from Milan, but staying longer rewards visitors with evenings of music, fine dining, and the quiet magic of a city deeply in tune with its heritage.

Cremona Musica International Exhibition

Cremona's most prestigious cultural event, the Cremona Musica International Exhibition, is a celebration of sound, craftsmanship, and the enduring legacy of the city's world-famous luthiers. Held each year in late September, it transforms Cremona into the global capital of music-making, attracting instrument makers, musicians, collectors, and enthusiasts from every continent.

The event's origins are rooted in Cremona's centuries-old reputation for excellence in stringed instrument making. Over the years, this musical heritage inspired the creation of a dedicated fair that would not only showcase the artistry of violin-making but also embrace the wider world of music. Today, the exhibition is the largest of its kind in the world, welcoming hundreds of exhibitors and thousands of visitors.

Hosted at the modern Cremona Exhibition Centre, the festival features a dazzling array of instruments: violins, violas, cellos, double basses, guitars, pianos, accordions, and wind instruments, as well as sheet music, accessories, and audio equipment. Visitors can meet master artisans at their benches, watch demonstrations of traditional techniques, and learn how centuries-old methods are preserved while adapting to contemporary needs. The air is filled with music from every corner; recitals, impromptu performances, and rehearsals spill into the piazzas and courtyards of the historic center.

Beyond the exhibition halls, the event includes a rich program of concerts, masterclasses, and workshops. Renowned soloists and chamber groups perform in Cremona's churches, theaters, and open-air venues, while international competitions bring together emerging talents from around the world. For many musicians, performing in Cremona is a dream fulfilled, a connection to the city that shaped the very sound of classical music.

The Cremona Musica International Exhibition is a bridge between past and present, where centuries-old craftsmanship meets the artistry of today's performers. Whether you are a professional musician, a collector, or simply someone who loves the beauty of music, the festival offers a rare chance to immerse yourself in the heart of Cremona's cultural identity.

Walking Tour of Cremona

#1. Piazza del Comune

Exploration begins in Piazza del Comune, the heart of Cremona and one of the most beautiful main squares in Lombardy. Here, the city's most important landmarks stand shoulder to shoulder: the Cathedral of Santa Maria Assunta, the Baptistery, the Torrazzo bell tower, and the elegant Palazzo Comunale.

The square is paved with stone and framed by graceful arcades, offering a perfect starting point for appreciating Cremona's harmonious mix of medieval and Renaissance architecture.

#2. Cathedral of Santa Maria Assunta

The cathedral's façade is a masterpiece of Lombard Romanesque with later Gothic and Renaissance additions. Marble columns, rose windows, and intricate sculptures adorn the exterior, while the interior reveals richly frescoed vaults and chapels. Highlights include 16th-century fresco cycles depicting the life of Christ, painted by masters such as Boccaccio Boccaccino and Girolamo Romanino. The cathedral's harmonious blend of art and architecture reflects Cremona's prosperity during the Renaissance.

Cathedral and Torrazzo Bell Tower

#3. Torrazzo di Cremona (Bell Tower)

Adjacent to the cathedral stands the iconic Torrazzo, rising over 112 meters (367 feet), making it one of the tallest brick bell towers in Europe. Climb its 500 steps to enjoy panoramic views of the city and surrounding Po Valley. Along the ascent, the vertical museum displays historical clocks, bells, and the story of the tower's construction. The astronomical clock on the tower's façade is a marvel of medieval engineering, depicting lunar phases and zodiac signs.

#4. Baptistery of Cremona

Next to the Torrazzo, the octagonal Baptistery dates to the 12th century and is built of warm red brick, softened by centuries of sunlight. Inside, its simple yet imposing space amplifies sound, a reminder of the city's devotion to harmony in both music and architecture. The marble baptismal font is a striking centerpiece, and the acoustics often draw musicians for special performances.

#5. Palazzo Comunale

On the opposite side of the square, the Palazzo Comunale has served as the seat of city government since the 13th century. Its graceful loggia and arched windows reflect Lombard civic architecture at its best. The building houses a collection of historic paintings and artifacts, including valuable musical instruments crafted by Cremona's legendary luthiers (violin builders).

#6. Museo del Violino (Violin Museum)

A short walk from the piazza is the violin museum, the city's premier cultural treasure. Here, visitors can see instruments by Stradivari, Amati, and Guarneri, preserved in glass cases like works of fine art. Interactive exhibits explain the meticulous process of violin-making, and the museum's auditorium hosts regular concerts, allowing guests to hear these masterpieces played as they were meant to be.

#7. Via Solferino and Artisan Workshops

Continue to Via Solferino and nearby streets, where small artisan workshops keep Cremona's luthier tradition alive. Craftsmen can often be seen planing wood, shaping scrolls, and varnishing violins, their techniques passed down through generations. Many are happy to explain their craft and show works in progress, making this a fascinating stop for anyone interested in the artistry behind the music.

#8. Chiesa di Sant'Agostino

Venture a little further to the Church of Sant'Agostino, a Gothic gem with a façade of alternating red and white marble. Inside are notable frescoes, including a depiction of the Madonna and Child by Perugino, adding another layer of Renaissance artistry to the city's offerings.

#9. Teatro Ponchielli

End the tour at Teatro Ponchielli, Cremona's elegant 19th-century opera house. With its horseshoe-shaped auditorium, gilded balconies, and plush red seating, it embodies the grandeur of Italian musical tradition. If your visit coincides with a performance, attending a concert or opera here is a fitting finale to your Cremona experience. Consider attending a show: https://www.teatroponchielli.it/en/

Logistics

Train: Cremona is well-connected by regional trains, making it an easy destination from cities across Lombardy and Emilia-Romagna. From Milan, direct regional trains take around 1 hour 15 minutes, while from Brescia the journey is about 1 hour. There are also regular services from Piacenza, Parma, and Mantua. The train station is about a 15-minute walk from the historic center, or a short local bus ride if you have luggage.

Bus: Local buses operated by KM S.p.A. connect the train station, city center, and surrounding neighborhoods, with extra services often scheduled during major events such as the Cremona Musica International Exhibition. Regional buses link Cremona to nearby towns including Casalmaggiore, Soresina, and Crema, providing alternative transport options for day trips.

Car: Cremona is accessible via the A21 Autostrada (Turin–Piacenza–Brescia), with exits clearly marked for the city. From Milan, the drive takes about 1 hour 20 minutes, and from Parma just under 1 hour. Roads in the region are well-maintained, but the centro storico is subject to a ZTL (Zona a Traffico Limitato), restricting access for non-residents. Visitors arriving by car should park outside the restricted zone and walk or use public transportation into the historic center.

Parking: Convenient parking areas include Parcheggio Massarotti (near the station), Parcheggio Santa Monica (a short walk to Piazza del Comune), and Parcheggio Porta Venezia (close to the ZTL boundary). During the Cremona Musica International Exhibition, parking spaces fill quickly, so early arrival is advised.

Restaurant Recommendations

Osteria del Melograno. Via Sicardo, 3

A cozy, family-run osteria known for its warm atmosphere and traditional Cremonese cuisine. Specialties include marubini pasta in broth, pumpkin tortelli, and bollito misto served with mostarda di Cremona, the city's signature candied fruit condiment.

Trattoria Cerri. Via Francesco Arisi, 3

Beloved by locals for hearty portions and authentic flavors, this trattoria offers dishes such as risotto alla zucca, braised beef, and local cheeses. Simple décor and friendly service make it a welcoming stop for lunch or dinner.

Il Violino. Vicolo Raimondi, 4

One of Cremona's most refined dining experiences, Il Violino serves elevated interpretations of Lombard cuisine in an elegant setting. The menu features fresh pasta, seasonal game, and carefully selected wines, with attentive service befitting its reputation.

Locanda Torriani. Via Janello Torriani, 7

A charming inn and restaurant near the Museo del Violino, offering a seasonal menu with dishes like guinea fowl, slow-cooked pork, and artisanal desserts. The intimate dining room and curated wine list make it ideal for a relaxed evening meal.

Enoteca Cremona. Via Platina, 66

Part wine bar, part deli, this spot is perfect for a lighter meal or aperitivo. Guests can enjoy platters of local cured meats, cheeses, and fresh bread paired with wines from Lombardy and beyond.

Day Trip Options: Nearby Sites, Cities, and Towns

Piacenza. 37 kilometers (23 miles) from Cremona. Situated just across the Po River in Emilia-Romagna, Piacenza is a city of elegant squares, Romanesque churches, and fine palaces. Begin at Piazza Cavalli, where two striking bronze equestrian statues of Farnese dukes dominate the scene. The nearby Palazzo Gotico, with its distinctive red brick and white marble façade, is a masterpiece of Gothic civic architecture.

The Cathedral of Piacenza, dating to the 12th century, features magnificent frescoes by Guercino and Morazzone. Piacenza is also known for its hearty cuisine. Try pisarei e fasö (pasta with beans) or coppa piacentina (cured pork) paired with local Gutturnio wine.

Parma. 55 kilometers (34 miles) from Cremona. Parma is a cultural and culinary gem, celebrated for its opera heritage, Renaissance art, and world-famous food. This is the home of Parmigiano Reggiano cheese and Prosciutto di Parma, both of which can be sampled at local shops or enjoyed in a traditional trattoria. Highlights include the pink marble Baptistery, the frescoed dome of the Cathedral by Correggio, and the elegant Teatro Regio, one of Italy's most important opera houses. Art lovers should visit the Galleria Nazionale in the Palazzo della Pilotta, home to works by Leonardo da Vinci, Parmigianino, and Canaletto.

In September, I went with two girlfriends to the Palio di Parma, a beautiful medieval celebration that fills the city with color, music, and pageantry. Costumed processions wind through the historic center, banners wave from every corner, and each district competes in traditional games and races, reviving centuries-old traditions in a joyful atmosphere. Parma's culinary reputation is legendary, making it the perfect place to pair history and culture with unforgettable food.

Crema. 42 kilometers (26 miles) from Cremona. A picturesque Lombard town with a charming historic center, Crema offers a relaxed, small-town atmosphere ideal for a leisurely day trip. The Cathedral of Santa Maria Assunta blends Gothic and Renaissance styles, while the nearby Torrazzo provides a focal point in the main square.

Stroll through cobblestone streets lined with pastel-colored palaces, stop for coffee in Piazza Duomo, and browse local boutiques. Crema is also known for its sweet specialty, tortelli cremaschi, pasta filled with an unusual mix of sweet and savory ingredients, including amaretti and candied fruit. The town's peaceful pace and friendly cafés make it a pleasant escape from busier destinations.

Festivals and Sagre in Cremona Throughout the Year

Palio del Po

June

A unique event on the River Po celebrating Cremona's maritime and sporting heritage. Rowing competitions, boat parades, and river-themed activities attract teams from across the region. Visitors can enjoy riverside picnics, food stalls serving local specialties, and evening fireworks over the water.

Settembre Cremonese

September

A month-long program of cultural events, concerts, theater performances, and markets that coincides with the city's late summer and early autumn festivals. Music plays a central role, often featuring classical performances, open-air jazz concerts, and folk music in the piazzas.

Festa di Sant'Omobono

November 13

Dedicated to the patron saint of Cremona, this feast day includes religious processions, special Masses, and a traditional fair. Sant'Omobono, a 12th-century merchant known for his charitable works, remains a symbol of civic pride. The celebration is an important day for the faithful and is often accompanied by markets selling local goods.

Festa del Torrone (Chapter 27)

Mid to Late November

Cremona's sweetest festival celebrates the city's claim to fame: torrone, the traditional nougat made with honey, sugar, egg whites, and almonds. Legend links its creation to the 1441 wedding of Bianca Maria Visconti and Francesco Sforza, where a nougat shaped like the Torrazzo was served.

https://www.festadeltorrone.com/

Chapter Twenty-Two

Immersion Experience: Gardaland Theme Park

Coasters & Kids Rides

Thrills and Fantasy at Gardaland

As you step through Gardaland's gates, a world of color, music, and imagination unfolds before you. The air carries a mix of popcorn sweetness and the faint scent of fresh-cut grass from the nearby shores of Lake Garda. Families chatter in a dozen languages, teens dart toward the latest thrill ride, and younger children tug at their parents' hands, eager to meet the park's friendly dragon mascot, Prezzemolo. I can't believe that just a short drive away lies the serene, sunlit beauty of Lake Garda because here, you have entered another universe.

Gardaland is Italy's largest and most famous theme park, a dazzling blend of adrenaline-pumping roller coasters, whimsical fantasy rides, and meticulously themed areas. It is the kind of place where you can soar above medieval castles one minute, dive into the depths of a submarine adventure the next, and then find yourself drifting lazily through a jungle river. Every turn of the path reveals a new scene: pirate ships anchored in crystal blue waters, dragons perched atop fortress walls, or lush tropical gardens hiding gentle family rides.

A Day of Adventure

Your day begins at the grand entrance plaza, where music builds anticipation and the first rides rise in the distance. Adrenaline seekers often head straight for Oblivion-The Black Hole, a vertical drop coaster that sends your stomach to your shoes in a matter of seconds, or Raptor, a winged coaster with heart-stopping inversions. For a smoother start, wander toward the Fantasy Kingdom, where Prezzemolo's treehouse offers panoramic views of the park and a sense of childlike wonder.

Midmorning is the perfect time to explore the Kung Fu Panda Academy or Peppa Pig Land, especially if you are visiting with younger travelers. Themed rides, gentle tracks, and colorful sets make these areas just as memorable as the high-speed coasters.

If water rides call your name, Fuga da Atlantide combines majestic ancient cityscapes with splashing descents, while Jungle Rapids sends you twisting through tropical vegetation. On warm summer days, these rides are not only thrilling, they are refreshing.

The Magic Continues

In the afternoon, the tempo can shift. Step into the Gardaland Theatre for a dazzling live show, or take a leisurely journey on the Transgardaland Express to rest your feet while you absorb the park's diverse landscapes. Children will be enchanted by character meet and greets, while adults can appreciate the craftsmanship of the park's design.

As the sun begins to set, the lights around the park flicker to life, turning castles and coasters into glowing silhouettes. The final parade sweeps through the streets, with dancers, illuminated floats, and music that lingers in your mind long after you leave.

Practical Tips for Your Visit

- **Best Time to Visit:** Late spring and early autumn offer pleasant weather and shorter lines. Summer brings longer opening hours and more evening shows, but also larger crowds. The park opens the first week of April and closes the first weekend in November.

- **Tickets:** Buy online in advance to save time and often money. Combo tickets with Sea Life Aquarium are available.

- **Location:** Castelnuovo del Garda, about 8 kilometers from Peschiera del Garda.

- **Getting There:** By train, Peschiera del Garda station is the closest; shuttle buses run from the station to the park during opening hours. By car, follow the A4 motorway to the Peschiera exit. Parking is plentiful but fills quickly in peak season.

- **Plan Ahead:** Start with the big thrill rides early in the day when lines are shortest. Reserve time for shows and parades, and remember that some attractions have height restrictions.

- **Stay Nearby:** Consider an overnight stay at one of the themed hotels, such as Gardaland Hotel or Gardaland Adventure Hotel, to extend the magic.

Why It Is Worth the Journey

With Lake Garda's natural beauty only minutes away, it offers the perfect pairing of adventure and relaxation. Whether you come for the roller coasters, the theatrical shows, or simply the joy on your children's faces, Gardaland will leave you with a head full of memories and a heart ready to return.

For tickets and information: www.gardaland.it

Fall Celebrations

September through November

CHAPTER TWENTY-THREE

Vigevano Renaissance Fair

A Sixteenth Century Spectacle

Palio delle Contrade di Vigevano

Where: Vigevano

When: Second weekend in October.

Average Festival Temperatures: High 19°C (66°F). Low 11°C (52°F).

Vigevano: A Town Shaped by Dukes, Designers, and Dreams

In the fertile embrace of Ticino's green plains, where rice fields stretch toward distant hills and ancient canals still carry the dreams of Renaissance visionaries, stands a town that has mastered the art of reinvention. This is Vigevano, just thirty-five kilometers (21 miles) southwest of Milan's bustling energy, where 60,000 residents live within walls that have witnessed the transformation of ducal ambitions into modern mastery.

Step into the historic center and time bends around you. The Piazza Ducale spreads out in perfect Renaissance symmetry, its frescoed facades and balanced proportions earning it a reputation as one of Italy's most stunning historic squares. Under the watchful eye of Ludovico il Moro in the late fifteenth century, master architects crafted these elegant arcades with the precision of jewelers, each column and arch calculated to capture light and shadow in perfect balance.

Yet Vigevano refused to remain frozen in Renaissance amber. As the centuries turned, the town's artisan spirit found new expression in leather and thread, transforming modest workshops into Italy's shoe capital. From cobblestone streets emerged footwear that would grace the runways of Paris and Milan, turning practical craft into high fashion. The castle's Shoe Museum now tells this remarkable story, displaying everything from delicate Renaissance slippers to the bold stilettos that conquered twentieth-century catwalks.

Here, within the protective embrace of the Parco del Ticino, Renaissance elegance meets industrial innovation. Cobblestone piazzas echo with five centuries of creativity, while modern ateliers continue traditions that began when dukes dreamed of perfect squares and artisans shaped leather with the same passion their ancestors carved stone. Vigevano stands as living proof that true beauty lies not in choosing between past and present, but in weaving them together with Italian genius.

Vigevano Renaissance Fair

When October arrives in Vigevano, the town steps backward through time. What began in the early 1980s as a modest tribute by local cultural groups has grown into the Rievocazione Storica Rinascimentale di Vigevano, one of Lombardy's most spectacular celebrations, drawing thousands who come to witness history. The event is also called the Palio delle Contrade di Vigevano.

Unlike typical festivals that celebrate a saint or commemorate a battle, Vigevano's festival recreates an entire historical period, bringing back the Renaissance era when the town was a major center of power. Under the rule of Ludovico il Moro and his brilliant wife Beatrice d'Este, these streets once echoed with the footsteps of genius as Donato Bramante sketched architectural dreams and Leonardo da Vinci walked these same cobblestones, his mind spinning with inventions that would reshape the world.

Every corner of the historic center comes alive with the sounds and sights that once defined Renaissance elegance: courtiers exchanging whispered secrets, craftsmen displaying their finest work, and common folk celebrating in ways their ancestors would recognize.

Festival Traditions

Saturday

Opening Parade in Piazza Ducale

The Renaissance awakens with the first blast of trumpets as hundreds of costumed participants begin their grand entrance into the piazza. The procession unfolds in careful formation: first come the herald trumpeters, their golden instruments catching the morning light, followed by the standard bearers whose colorful banners stream in the breeze like captured rainbows.

Behind them march the soldiers in gleaming armor, their measured steps creating a rhythmic thunder on ancient cobblestones. Musicians follow with lutes and drums, filling the air with melodies that once entertained real Renaissance courts. Then come the townsfolk in their finest period dress, merchants displaying their wares, and artisans carrying the tools of their medieval trades.

Flag-Throwing Performances

Contrade teams perform dazzling routines, filling the piazza with a whirl of colors and banners, a tradition rooted in Renaissance civic pride.

Renaissance Market

Artisans set up stalls offering jewelry, textiles, pottery, leatherwork, and handcrafted items inspired by sixteenth-century designs. Food vendors serve rustic Lombard dishes and treats.

Evening Banquet at the Castle

A Renaissance-style feast with long wooden tables, music, and entertainment unfolds in the castle courtyards. Guests enjoy hearty fare while jugglers, dancers, and musicians recreate the festive atmosphere of a ducal banquet.

Sunday

Courtly Pageants

The day opens with theatrical reenactments and dances recalling life at the Sforza court. Actors and musicians bring to life scenes of Renaissance ritual and splendor.

Falconry and Jousting Displays

Skilled falconers present birds of prey in flight, echoing noble pastimes of the Renaissance. Knights and riders stage equestrian games and jousts in the castle grounds, thrilling the crowd with their knightly skills.

Grand Parade Finale

As twilight falls on the Renaissance stones, Piazza Ducale is transformed into a vibrant scene. The grand parade begins, with silk banners fluttering in the evening breeze and torchlight flickering across the ancient arcades, casting moving shadows that recall the days of the Sforza court.

The procession moves with stately grace beneath the same arches where Ludovico il Moro once welcomed ambassadors and artists. As the last notes of Renaissance music fade, fireworks light up the sky above the castle towers in cascades of gold and silver, illuminating the square in a dazzling glow. In that moment, visitors feel suspended between past and present, as if touching something timeless at the heart of this remarkable town.

Walking Tour of Vigevano

#1. Piazza Ducale

Begin in the vast Renaissance square commissioned by Ludovico il Moro and designed by Bramante in 1492. Surrounded by arcaded palazzi and frescoed façades, it remains the historic core of the town.

#2. Castello Sforzesco

Walk up the grand staircase, once used by dukes, and see rooms that echo Renaissance ambition. Within these fortress walls, the Sforza court orchestrated alliances that shaped the fate of kingdoms, while lavish banquets unfolded in halls where every glance carried meaning and every toast sealed a destiny. The castle remembers the rustle of silk gowns and the clink of golden goblets as nobles danced the delicate steps of Renaissance diplomacy.

At the fortress's center stands the Torre del Bramante, designed by the same architect who would later create St. Peter's Basilica in Rome. From its heights, the view sweeps across the fertile Lombard plains like a map of history itself, where medieval armies once clashed and merchant caravans traced paths that connected empires.

#3. Leonardiana Museum

Located inside the castle, this fascinating museum explores Leonardo da Vinci's often-overlooked contributions to Lombardy, including his revolutionary designs for Vigevano's urban plan and ingenious waterworks that transformed the surrounding countryside into fertile farmland. Here you'll discover sketches and models showing how the Leonardo's engineering genius extended far beyond his famous paintings. His hydraulic innovations still influence the region's irrigation systems today, and his urban planning concepts helped create one of Italy's most perfectly proportioned piazzas.

#4. Cathedral of Sant'Ambrogio

Standing at the edge of Piazza Ducale, the cathedral presents one of architecture's most diplomatic achievements. In adding a Baroque church to Renaissance perfection, seventeenth-century builders created a remarkable façade.

Step through its doors and discover how Lombard craftsmen turned constraint into genius. Every curve and column was calculated to honor the piazza's Renaissance harmony while expressing Baroque grandeur, creating an interior that feels both intimate and majestic.

#5. Shoe Museum (Museo della Calzatura)

Vigevano is celebrated as Italy's "shoe capital," and this fascinating museum, located inside the castle complex, highlights the town's centuries-old shoemaking tradition. The collection begins with finely crafted Renaissance slippers and footwear once worn at the Sforza court, illustrating Vigevano's early role as a center of luxury craftsmanship. It then moves through the centuries, showcasing how the town became a hub for innovation and design in the twentieth century, producing elegant heels and stylish creations that were exported around the world.

Displays include shoes made for celebrities and fashion houses, as well as machinery, tools, and archival photographs that reveal the evolution of the industry. Interactive exhibits help visitors understand the artistry and technical skill behind Italian shoemaking. It's a unique museum that blends history, fashion, and craftsmanship, offering insight into how a small town became a global name in footwear.

Logistics

Train: Vigevano is well connected to Milan by frequent regional trains. Direct trains depart from Milano Porta Genova station and take about 35 minutes. From Pavia, the journey is around 25 minutes. Vigevano's train station is a short walk from Piazza Ducale and the castle.

Bus: Regional buses link Vigevano with nearby towns in Lomellina and Pavia province. During the Renaissance Fair, additional services are sometimes added to accommodate visitors, although trains remain the most convenient option from Milan.

Car: From Milan, take the A7 motorway toward Pavia and exit at Bereguardo, then follow signs to Vigevano. The drive takes about 45 minutes depending on traffic. From Pavia, the drive is about 30 minutes.

Parking: The historic center of Vigevano, including Piazza Ducale, is pedestrian-only and closed to traffic during the festival. Visitors should park in lots near the Castello Sforzesco.

Restaurant Recommendations

L'Oca Ciuca. Via XX Settembre, 34

A celebrated trattoria in the historic center known for refined Lombard cooking. Signature dishes include risotto, duck specialties, and traditional cured meats, paired with an extensive wine list. The elegant yet cozy setting makes it an excellent choice for a special dinner after the festival's evening events.

Antico Granaio. Via del Popolo, 17

Set in a charming rustic building with vaulted brick ceilings, this restaurant offers a menu rich in seasonal ingredients and regional flavors. Homemade pasta, braised meats, and hearty soups reflect the traditions of Lomellina. Ideal for those looking to enjoy authentic cuisine in a warm and historic atmosphere.

l'Toscanaccio. Corso della Repubblica, 9

A lively spot popular with locals, blending Tuscan specialties with Lombard favorites. Guests can savor ribollita, Florentine-style steaks, and robust regional wines in a welcoming trattoria setting. A perfect option for a relaxed lunch or informal dinner during the festival weekend.

Day Trips: Nearby Sites, Cities, and Towns

Mortara. 18 kilometers (11 miles) southwest of Vigevano. A small Lombard town known for its deep ties to rice cultivation in the fertile Lomellina plain. Mortara is famous for its Sagra del Salame d'Oca, a goose salami festival held each September, celebrating its historic Jewish and farming traditions. The town also features the Basilica di San Lorenzo, with origins tracing back to the Middle Ages, and makes a pleasant stop for food lovers exploring the rice fields and waterways of the region.

Novara. Only 40 kilometers (25 miles) northwest of Vigevano, Novara is a historic Piedmontese city with a distinctive skyline dominated by the soaring dome of the Basilica di San Gaudenzio, designed by Alessandro Antonelli. The heart of the city is Piazza delle Erbe, surrounded by arcades, cafés, and the elegant Broletto complex, which houses museums and cultural exhibitions.

Casale Monferrato. 55 kilometers (34 miles) west of Vigevano. Casale Monferrato is a jewel of the Piedmont region. The town is renowned for its elegant Baroque architecture, the seventeenth-century Synagogue with its ornate interior, and the imposing Castello dei Paleologi. Casale is also famous for Krumiri Rossi, buttery biscuits shaped like small mustaches, a perfect local souvenir.

Vigevano Festivals and Sagre Throughout the Year

Carnevale di Vigevano

February or March

Vigevano celebrates Carnival with parades of floats, children in costume, music, and games across the historic center. Confetti showers the streets, and traditional sweets such as chiacchiere (fried dough with sugar) and tortelli (fried dough balls filled with cream) are enjoyed at stalls throughout Piazza Ducale.

Festa di San Maiolo

May 10

This festival honors Saint Maiolus of Cluny, one of Vigevano's patron saints, who is celebrated with a religious procession through Piazza Ducale and Mass in the Cathedral of Sant'Ambrogio. The day includes community gatherings and cultural activities that highlight the town's spiritual heritage.

Estate in Piazza Ducale

June to July

During the summer months, Piazza Ducale transforms into a grand open-air stage for concerts, theater, and cultural events. The Renaissance square, with its arcades and elegant façades, becomes the heart of Vigevano's social life as locals and visitors gather under the warm evening sky.

Performances range from classical music to contemporary bands, dance, and community shows, creating a vibrant atmosphere that lingers well into the night. Sitting in the piazza as music fills the air is one of the most memorable ways to experience Vigevano in summer.

Festa di San Bernardo

August 20

Dedicated to Saint Bernard of Clairvaux, one of Vigevano's patron saints, this festival blends religious devotion with civic pride. The day begins with solemn religious services and a procession through the historic center, accompanied by banners and local confraternities. Civic events, traditional music, and gatherings in the piazza follow, honoring the saint's role as protector of the town. Food stands serve regional specialties, and the sense of community gives the celebration a warm, authentic atmosphere.

Fiera dell'Oca

November

This traditional fair celebrates the goose, an animal deeply tied to the agricultural heritage of Lomellina. Stalls offer a tempting array of goose-based specialties such as roasted goose, salumi d'oca, and hearty local rice dishes, all paired with regional wines. The streets fill with music, games, and artisan markets, drawing both locals and visitors. The fair recalls centuries of rural tradition, marking the arrival of autumn with lively community festivities and unforgettable flavors.

CHAPTER TWENTY-FOUR

Immersion Experience: Bernina Express

Historic Scenic Train Ride

Riding the Bernina Express from Tirano

Tucked into the Valtellina valley at the foot of the Alps, the small town of Tirano (Sondrio province) may look unassuming at first glance, but it holds one of Italy's most unforgettable travel experiences. Tirano is the Italian starting point of the Bernina Express, the scenic red train that climbs into Switzerland, crossing the Alps through spiraling viaducts, glaciers, and high mountain lakes.

Construction of the Bernina line began in 1906 and was completed in 1910 by the Bernina Railway Company. Engineers faced enormous challenges in carving a path through the high Alps without the use of cogwheel technology. Instead, they designed long loops, spiral tunnels, and the famous Brusio Circular Viaduct to manage the steep gradients. At the time, it was the highest mountain railway in Europe running without rack assistance, and it remains one of the steepest adhesion railways in the world.

In 1944, the line was taken over by the Rhaetian Railway (Rhätische Bahn), which also operates the Albula line. Together, these two Alpine railways form the heart of the Bernina Express route.

The line gained worldwide recognition when it was inscribed as a UNESCO World Heritage Site in 2008, praised for its outstanding combination of natural beauty and technical achievement. Today, the Bernina Express has become an icon of slow travel in the Alps, drawing visitors from across the globe.

Bernina Express Train in the Alpine snow

Walking Tour of Tirano

#1. Sanctuary of the Madonna di Tirano

Begin at the magnificent Sanctuary, built in the sixteenth century after the Virgin Mary appeared here in 1504. Admire the richly decorated interiors, gilded altars, and the remarkable wooden organ, one of the finest in Lombardy. This church remains the spiritual heart of Tirano and is considered a destination of pilgrimage.

#2. Walk to Piazza Cavour

From the Sanctuary, stroll toward the historic center and arrive at Piazza Cavour, the town's lively main square. Here you will find Renaissance façades, cafés with outdoor tables, and the Palazzo Marinoni, home to the town hall. This is an excellent place to pause for a coffee.

#3. Explore the Old Town Streets

Continue through the narrow cobblestone streets lined with stone houses and arcades. Notice the Renaissance palaces such as Palazzo Salis, which preserves frescoed rooms and a fine collection of historical furnishings. This area reflects Tirano's prosperity during the sixteenth and seventeenth centuries.

#4. Cross the Adda River

Follow the path toward the bridge that crosses the Adda River. From here, you will see the vineyards climbing the surrounding hillsides. These vineyards produce the prized Valtellina wines such as Sassella and Inferno, whose flavors are tied to the steep terraces and mountain climate.

Boarding the Bernina Express

From the Tirano station, step aboard the iconic red train. The route runs from Tirano to St. Moritz, climbing nearly two thousand meters with gradients so steep it is astonishing to think the train runs without a rack and pinion system.

Highlights of the journey include:

Brusio Spiral Viaduct. A remarkable circular stone viaduct where the train loops over itself.

Alp Grüm. A station perched high above the valley, offering sweeping views of the Palü Glacier.

Lago Bianco and Lago Nero. Twin mountain lakes shimmering against snow-capped peaks.

St. Moritz. The chic Swiss resort where the train journey ends, perfect for strolling by the lake or enjoying Swiss pastries.

Traveling on the Bernina Express is a journey across cultures and landscapes, linking Italian Tirano with the high Swiss Alps. The panoramic windows allow you to witness every curve, glacier, and village, making you feel part of the mountain world rather than just a visitor passing through.

Options for Boarding the Bernina Express

While Tirano is the official Italian gateway, travelers in northern Italy have several options for reaching the train:

Milan. Frequent Trenord and Trenitalia trains connect Milan Centrale with Tirano in about two hours and thirty minutes.

Lecco. Direct regional trains reach Tirano in about two hours and fifteen minutes, a convenient choice.

Varenna (Lake Como). Take the ferry across the lake, then connect by train through Lecco to Tirano in about two and a half hours.

This makes the Bernina Express a peaceful day trip from many northern Italian cities.

Best Time to Ride the Bernina Express

The Bernina Express operates year-round, and each season brings its own atmosphere:

Spring. Melting snow and alpine blooms brighten the valleys.

Summer. Lush meadows and long daylight hours, but also the busiest season.

Autumn. Glorious golden larch forests, vineyard harvests in Valtellina, and fewer crowds.

Winter. A snowy wonderland with frozen lakes and festive charm.

Recommendation: Autumn is the best season to ride. The combination of vibrant colors, cultural festivals, and relaxed crowds makes it the most rewarding time.

Itineraries

It is possible to experience the Bernina Express on a one-day trip from Milan. Travelers can take the morning train to Tirano, ride the Bernina Express to St. Moritz, and return in the evening. This is thrilling and convenient, but it can feel rushed.

For deeper immersion, consider:

Three Days. Spend the first day in Tirano with time to explore the sanctuary and enjoy local cuisine. On the second day, take the Bernina Express to St. Moritz, with an overnight stay in Switzerland. On the third day, return at a relaxed pace, stopping in Poschiavo or Pontresina.

Seven Days. Combine Tirano with hiking or wine tasting in the Valtellina, enjoy leisurely stops along the railway route, and use St. Moritz as a base to explore Engadin villages or ski areas. This turns the Bernina line into a full alpine holiday.

Recommendation: While a day trip is possible, travelers who allow three or more days will discover much more than the view from a window. They will immerse themselves in the food, wine, and mountain culture of both Lombardy and Switzerland.

Practical Notes for Riding the Bernina Express

Length of Journey

The full Bernina Express route from Tirano to St. Moritz takes about four hours one way. The train travels just over 60 miles but climbs nearly two thousand meters, which is why the pace is slow and scenic.

Hop On and Off

On the official Bernina Express panoramic train, you must stay in your reserved seat from start to finish. It is a point-to-point service with set timings. However, the same route is also served by regular regional trains run by the Rhaetian Railway. These trains follow the exact line and allow you to hop on and off at villages such as Poschiavo, Alp Grüm, or Pontresina with a standard ticket. If you want to explore along the way, the regional trains are more flexible, while the Bernina Express is about the uninterrupted panoramic ride.

Tickets

For the Bernina Express, the ticket and seat reservation are separate purchases. If you disembark mid-route, you will need to book another reservation to continue on a later Bernina Express service. With the regional trains, you can simply use a valid day ticket or point-to-point fare, so buying extra tickets is only required if you break your journey over multiple days.

CHAPTER TWENTY-FIVE

Milan's Protector Celebrated

The Legacy of St. Charles

Festa di San Carlo Borromeo

Where: Milan, Basilica di San Carlo al Corso

When: November 4

Average Festival Temperatures: High 15°C (59°F). Low 6°C (43°F).

Festival Website:

https://www.duomomilano.it/liturgical/solennita-di-san-carlo-borromeo/

Feast of Saint Charles Borromeo, Archbishop and Reformer

As autumn deepens and the last leaves fall across Milan's courtyards, the city turns its heart toward a man who chose compassion over comfort, walking among the sick when fear silenced others. Celebrated annually on November 4, the feast honors Milan's beloved 16th-century archbishop, canonized in 1610, whose leadership during the Counter-Reformation and selfless care for plague victims left an indelible mark on both Church and city.

The roots of the celebration reach back to the year of his canonization, when Milan began observing the day with solemn liturgies, processions, and charitable acts in his memory. The feast has always blended deep reverence with a civic sense of gratitude, a recognition of Borromeo not just as a saint, but as a moral guardian in one of Milan's most challenging eras.

Today, the central celebration takes place at the Basilica di San Carlo al Corso in Milan, while the town of Arona, his birthplace on Lake Maggiore, hosts an equally important pilgrimage and procession that draws crowds from across Lombardy.

Apse of the Basilica di San Carlo

Who Was St. Carles Borromeo?

Born in 1538 into the influential Borromeo family, Charles seemed destined for ecclesiastical prominence, ascending to Archbishop of Milan at just twenty-five. But his true calling revealed itself not in the comfortable halls of power, but in the plague-ravaged streets of his suffering city.

When the Protestant Reformation challenged Catholic authority across Europe, Borromeo answered with action rather than rhetoric. He traveled to remote mountain parishes that previous archbishops had never visited, insisted that priests actually know their theology, and implemented the Council of Trent's reforms with methodical determination. His was a revolution of competence and care in an age that desperately needed both.

The plague of 1576 became his defining moment. While city officials fled to safety and even some clergy abandoned their posts, Borromeo remained. Barefoot and carrying a simple wooden cross, he walked through streets where death lurked in every doorway, bringing last rites to the dying and organizing food for the starving. His courage wasn't in the dramatic gesture of a moment, but the steady resolve of months spent among Milan's most vulnerable citizens.

When death claimed him in 1584, Milan lost more than an archbishop. They mourned a shepherd who had proven that true leadership means staying closest to those who are in need, a lesson the city has never forgotten.

Festival Traditions

Novena (October 26 to November 3)

In the days leading up to the feast, a solemn novena is held at the Basilica di San Carlo al Corso. Evening Mass is followed by prayers recalling the saint's life, with themes of charity, reform, and steadfast faith.

Feast Day in Milan (November 4)

Morning Solemn Mass: At the Basilica di San Carlo al Corso, the Archbishop of Milan often presides over the liturgy, attended by civic leaders and the faithful.

Veneration of Relics: A reliquary containing a relic of the saint is placed for public veneration.

Charitable Works: Many parishes organize food and clothing drives, echoing Borromeo's dedication to the poor.

Pilgrimage and Procession in Arona

Arona, where Borromeo was born, holds a major procession through the town's historic streets. The relics of the saint are carried with solemnity, accompanied by clergy, lay confraternities, and local bands. Many pilgrims also visit the towering statue of San Carlo overlooking Lake Maggiore, one of the largest statues in the world, which symbolizes his protective presence over the region.

Cultural and Musical Tributes

Sacred concerts, lectures, and art exhibitions focused on the saint's legacy, providing a cultural dimension to the religious commemoration accompanying the festival.

Basilica di San Carlo al Corso

The Basilica di San Carlo al Corso stands prominently along Corso Vittorio Emanuele II, one of Milan's busiest thoroughfares, its neoclassical façade an imposing landmark in the city center. Built between 1838 and 1847, it was dedicated to Saint Charles Borromeo and intended as a monumental tribute to the city's archbishop and patron saint. The site previously housed the Church of San Maria dei Servi, but the new basilica reflected Milan's 19th-century ambition to honor San Carlo with a church worthy of his legacy.

Stepping inside, visitors are immediately struck by the sheer scale of the interior. The basilica's design was inspired by Rome's Pantheon, with a vast central nave crowned by one of the largest domes in Milan, soaring nearly 70 meters (229 feet) high. Light filters in through a ring of windows at the dome's base, casting a soft glow over the marble floor and Corinthian columns that line the nave.

At the far end, the main altar is dedicated to Saint Charles Borromeo, with a large altarpiece depicting him ministering to plague victims, a scene that captures the compassion and courage for which he is remembered. The altar is flanked by richly decorated chapels, each housing side altars dedicated to various saints.

One highlight is the Chapel of the Madonna of the Servants, which preserves the venerated image from the original church on this site. Another is the Sacristy, where portraits of Milan's archbishops line the walls, connecting the city's ecclesiastical history to Borromeo's enduring influence.

The basilica also contains several memorials and sculptures honoring key figures in Milanese religious life. Look upward to admire the coffered dome's painted decorations, which depict scenes from the life of Saint Charles and emphasize his role as reformer and protector of the faithful.

Walking Tour from the Basilica di San Carlo al Corso

#1. Chiesa di San Babila (2-minute walk)

Just steps away at Piazza San Babila, this church has ancient origins dating back to the 11th century, though its current form is largely 20th-century reconstruction. Dedicated to Saint Babylas of Antioch, it's known for its simple red-brick façade and peaceful interior. Inside, you'll find modern frescoes alongside relics of the saint, offering a quiet contrast to the grandeur of San Carlo.

#2. Chiesa di San Vito al Pasquirolo (5-minute walk)

Hidden just off Corso Europa, this small Baroque church from the early 17th century is a true gem. It once served as a meeting place for the Confraternity of the Blessed Sacrament. The ornate stucco work, gilded details, and intimate scale make it a lovely place for reflection.

#3. Chiesa di San Bernardino alle Ossa (10-minute walk)

Famous for its ossuary chapel, San Bernardino is near Piazza Santo Stefano. Originally built in the 13th century, then rebuilt after burning down, its walls are decorated with complex patterns made of skulls and bones, a stark symbol of death. Despite the macabre décor, the chapel has a strangely peaceful atmosphere.

Restaurant Recommendations Near the Basilica

Ristorante Valentino Legend. Corso Monforte, 16, about a 4-minute walk.

An elegant Milanese restaurant known for refined Italian classics with a focus on fresh pasta, high-quality meat, and seasonal ingredients. The interior is warm and sophisticated, making it a brilliant choice for a more formal dining experience. Signature dishes include risotto alla Milanese, ossobuco, and fresh seafood pasta.

Trattoria del Pescatore. Via Atto Vannucci, 5, about a 6-minute walk.

Though best known for its Sardinian-style lobster and seafood risotto, it also offers a variety of non-seafood Italian dishes in a cozy trattoria atmosphere. It's family-run, with an authentic feel, and has been a local favorite for decades.

CHAPTER TWENTY-SIX

Giro di Lombardia & Cycling in Lombardy

Cycling Mountains & Vineyards

Cycling Events in Lombardy

Where: Lombardy, with routes passing through towns such as Como, Bergamo, Lecco, and Milan. Key climbs include the Madonna del Ghisallo above Lake Como.

When: Early October

Average Festival Temperatures: Low 10°C (50°F). High 18°C (65°F).

Event Website: https://gfilombardia.it/en/

#1. Giro di Lombardia

Each October, Lombardy becomes the stage for one of cycling's greatest events: the Giro di Lombardia. Known as La Classica delle Foglie Morte (the Race of the Falling Leaves), this one-day competition is the final monument of the professional cycling season. Its winding route showcases Lombardy's beauty at fall's peak, passing through lakefront towns, alpine climbs, and historic piazzas filled with cheering spectators.

The Giro di Lombardia began in 1905. Originally called Milano–Milano, organized by journalist Tullio Morgagni. Over time, it grew into one of cycling's five "Monuments," legendary races that every champion aspires to win. Italian heroes like Fausto Coppi, who triumphed five times, and Gino Bartali forged their reputations here, while international stars continue to battle over its demanding climbs.

Central to the race is the ascent to the Sanctuary of the Madonna del Ghisallo, perched above Lake Como. Declared the patron saint of cyclists by Pope Pius XII in 1949, the chapel has become a pilgrimage site, housing jerseys, bicycles, and relics from cycling's greatest names. The combination of sacred devotion and sporting challenge gives the race a unique identity that blends tradition, culture, and athleticism.

Events

The Race: Covering 240–260 kilometers (149-162 miles), the course changes yearly but typically links Como, Bergamo, Lecco, and Milan. Riders face steep ascents and dramatic descents, with the Ghisallo climb as the symbolic highlight.

Village Atmosphere: Towns along the route host markets and food stands serving autumn specialties like roasted chestnuts, polenta, and local cheeses. Streets and piazzas fill with confetti, flags, and bands.

Spectator Gathering: The steep mountain roads, lakeside curves, and city finishes draw thousands of fans who create a festive, carnival-like atmosphere.

Pilgrim Cyclists: Before and after race day, amateur riders cycle sections of the course, turning Lombardy into a cycling festival. Guided tours and rentals often coincide with the event.

Awards Ceremony: The finish line, usually in Como or Bergamo, becomes a celebration with packed crowds, international media, and the crowning of the race winner.

#2. Gran Fondo Lombardia Felice Gimondi

https://gfilombardia.it/

The Gran Fondo Lombardia Felice Gimondi is one of Italy's premier amateur cycling events, created to honor Bergamo's legendary champion Felice Gimondi. A Giro d'Italia, Tour de France, and Vuelta a España winner, Gimondi is remembered not only for his victories but also for his grace, endurance, and deep connection to his hometown and the Lombardy region.

Each year thousands of cyclists from around the world gather to ride the same challenging routes that once tested the greatest professionals. The event winds through Lombardy's dramatic landscapes, from rolling hills to steep alpine climbs, offering participants both a demanding athletic challenge and breathtaking scenery. For many, riding the Gran Fondo is as much a pilgrimage as a race, a chance to celebrate the sport's history while pushing their own limits.

Spectators line the roads, cheering as riders stream through towns and villages, and the finish becomes a festival in itself.

#3. Milano Sanremo

https://milano-sanremo.org/en/

The Milano–Sanremo is the longest professional one-day cycling race in the world and one of the five legendary "Monuments" of the sport. First run in 1907, it stretches nearly 300 kilometers (186 miles) from the heart of Milan to the Ligurian coast at Sanremo. Known as *La Classicissima*, this springtime race traditionally marks the opening of the European cycling season and attracts the world's best riders.

The course begins in the bustling streets of Milan before crossing the Lombard and Piedmontese countryside and descending toward the sparkling Mediterranean. Its final kilometers are famous for the Cipressa and the Poggio, two climbs that often decide the race, followed by a thrilling sprint finish along Sanremo's Via Roma.

For cyclists and fans alike, Milano–Sanremo is a journey that captures Italy's diverse landscapes, from urban avenues to mountain passes and coastal roads. With its blend of distance, strategy, and spectacle, the Classicissima remains one of the most anticipated and prestigious events on the international cycling calendar.

Immersion Experience: Cycling Lombardy

Lombardy is a cyclist's paradise. With its mix of shimmering lakes, rolling vineyards, and Alpine foothills, the region offers some of the most varied and scenic cycle routes in Italy. Whether you prefer a gentle lakeside ride or a challenging mountain ascent, cycling provides an intimate way to discover Lombardy's landscapes and villages at your own pace. Most paths are also open to walkers and hikers, making them ideal for travelers who want to combine cycling with leisurely strolls.

Lake Circuits

Lago di Varese: Just 5 kilometers (3 miles) south of Varese lies one of Lombardy's most inviting cycling experiences. The 28-kilometer (17-mile) loop around Lake Varese is fully paved and largely flat, making it perfect for families, casual riders, and even walkers who want to take on shorter stretches. The trail winds through lush countryside and along the lake's edge, offering ever-changing views of Monte Rosa and the surrounding Prealps.

Along the way, you pass through sleepy fishing villages, wayside chapels, and stretches of reeds where herons and swans glide across the water. A highlight is the Brabbia Marsh Nature Reserve, a haven for birdwatchers and photographers. Small cafés and picnic spots dot the route, giving you plenty of chances to pause and soak in the scenery. Bicycles can be rented in Varese or at kiosks near the lake, and the circuit can be enjoyed in a leisurely half day.

Lago Maggiore: Cycling along the Lombard shore of Lake Maggiore feels like gliding through a postcard. From Laveno to Luino, the paths hug the water's edge, curving past pastel-colored harbors, sandy coves, and flower-filled promenades. The ride is gentle, with stretches open to both cyclists and walkers, and occasional sections of dedicated cycle lanes that allow you to relax and take in the views.

Stop in Luino for its famous Wednesday market, one of the largest in northern Italy, or in Laveno to sample a lakeside gelato before boarding a ferry. The beauty of cycling here is the possibility of combining routes: from Laveno, car ferries and passenger boats cross to Verbania and Intra on the opposite shore, opening a whole new world of two-wheeled exploration on the Piedmontese side. Each town along the way has its own character, from quiet fishing villages to lively piazzas with outdoor cafés, making the ride as much about culture as it is about scenery.

Lake Iseo: Lombardy's other great lakes also offer unforgettable rides. Around Lake Iseo, one of the most dramatic stretches is the Vello to Toline path, a 5-kilometer (3-mile) trail carved directly into the cliffs. Suspended above the deep blue water, it is closed to cars and perfect for both cyclists and walkers seeking a breathtaking experience. The views across the lake to Monte Isola, Europe's largest lake island, are mesmerizing.

Lake Como: Lake Como, meanwhile, rewards those who combine cycling with exploration of its villages. In Menaggio, a lakeside promenade shared by walkers and cyclists offers beautiful views across to Bellagio. In Colico at the lake's northern end, you can link up with mountain trails that descend to the water, blending gentle shoreline riding with more challenging Alpine terrain. Even short rides here feel like a journey through history, as villas, gardens, and medieval towers appear around every curve.

Mountain and Countryside Routes

Valtellina Trail (Sentiero Valtellina)

One of Lombardy's best-known long-distance routes, the Valtellina Trail runs for more than 110 kilometers (68 miles) from Colico on Lake Como through Sondrio and into the Alpine valley. The mostly paved path follows the Adda River, winding past vineyards, apple orchards, and medieval castles. Suitable for both cycling and walking, it is popular with families for shorter sections and with serious riders for multi-day journeys.

Adda River Cycle Path

South of Lecco, the Adda River path runs along the water toward Milan. This route is rich in scenery and history: cyclists pass Leonardo da Vinci's ferry at Imbersago, historic mills, and tranquil stretches of woodland. The path is flat and well maintained, making it a good option for leisurely rides and walking excursions.

Franciacorta Wine Hills

Between Brescia and Lake Iseo, Franciacorta's rolling vineyard landscape is laced with cycle trails that connect villages, wineries, and abbeys. These are ideal for e-bike tours or leisurely rides with wine tastings along the way. Walkers can also enjoy marked trails through the vineyards, especially during autumn harvest.

Mincio Cycle Path

Connecting Lake Garda with Mantua, the Mincio Cycle Path follows the course of the Mincio River for 45 kilometers (28 miles). It is one of the most beloved routes in Lombardy, almost entirely flat and separate from car traffic. The trail begins in Peschiera del Garda and passes through Borghetto sul Mincio, one of Italy's prettiest villages, before reaching Mantua's Renaissance squares. The path is open to both cyclists and walkers.

Alpine Challenges

For experienced cyclists, Lombardy's high mountain passes are the ultimate test of endurance and spirit. These climbs are not for the casual rider, but for those who attempt them, the effort is rewarded with some of the most breathtaking scenery in Europe and the chance to ride roads immortalized in the Giro d'Italia.

Stelvio Pass

At 2,758 meters (9,049 feet), the Stelvio is one of the highest paved mountain passes in the Alps and perhaps the most iconic in all of cycling. The northern ascent from Prato allo Stelvio features 48 tight hairpin bends that snake up the mountainside in dizzying succession. Riders gain nearly 1,800 meters of elevation over just 25 kilometers, with gradients often hovering around 7 to 8 percent.

The higher you climb, the more the view expands, glaciers glitter above, while meadows and valleys unfold far below. At the summit, marked by a cluster of cafés and souvenir stalls, cyclists pose for the obligatory photo at the sign that reads Passo dello Stelvio. Riding here places you in the company of legends: the Stelvio has been featured in the Giro d'Italia over 70 times since 1953.

Gavia Pass

Slightly lower but equally formidable, the Gavia rises to 2,621 meters (8,599 feet). It is infamous among cyclists for its remoteness and dramatic weather, as snow often lingers on its slopes well into summer. The southern approach from Ponte di Legno is the classic climb: 17 kilometers of a narrow road that winds past waterfalls, alpine meadows, and eventually into stark, high mountain landscapes. The final kilometers feel almost lunar, with jagged peaks surrounding the road.

The Gavia became legendary in the 1988 Giro d'Italia, when riders braved a blizzard to complete the stage, an episode etched in cycling lore as a triumph of grit over nature.

Mortirolo Pass

Though lower in altitude at 1,852 meters (6,076 feet), the Mortirolo is considered one of the hardest climbs in Europe because of its brutal gradients. From Mazzo di Valtellina, the climb stretches 12.4 kilometers with an average gradient of 10.5 percent and ramps that spike to 18 percent.

The road is narrow, twisting through dense forests with few chances to recover. At the top stands a monument to Marco Pantani, the Italian cycling champion who made his name here with an electrifying attack in the 1994 Giro d'Italia. For many riders, conquering the Mortirolo is less about scenery than about proving themselves against one of cycling's fiercest tests.

Top Scenic Routes for Cycling in Lombardy

Lake Varese Loop: A 28-kilometer (17-mile) paved circuit around Lake Varese, perfect for families and casual cyclists, with birdwatching stops, lakeside cafés, and panoramic mountain views.

Mincio Cycle Path: A 45-kilometer (28-mile) trail linking Lake Garda to Mantua, following the Mincio River through vineyards, medieval villages, and Renaissance cityscapes.

Valtellina Trail: More than 110 kilometers (68 miles) of cycle path through the Alpine valley of the Adda River, passing orchards, castles, and vineyard-covered slopes.

Lake Garda: Garda to Peschiera Path: A flat, lakeside route of about 50 kilometers (31 miles) along the southern and eastern shores, with sweeping lake views, olive groves, and charming villages.

Lake Como Greenway: A 10-kilometer (6-mile) scenic trail on the western shore between Colonno and Griante, combining lakeside stretches with hillside lanes through historic hamlets and gardens.

Lake Maggiore: Sesto Calende to Laveno: A picturesque ride of about 60 kilometers (37 miles) along the Lombard shore, passing fishing villages, sandy beaches, and views of the Borromean Gulf.

Practical Notes

Bike Rentals: Many cities, including Varese, Milan, Bergamo, and Como, have bike rental shops and e-bike options. Lakeside towns often provide short-term rentals for visitors.

Trail Sharing for Walkers and Hikers: Most lakeside and countryside routes are shared with walkers and hikers, so cyclists should ride at a moderate pace and yield when necessary.

When to Go: Spring and fall are the most pleasant seasons, with cooler temperatures and fewer crowds. Summer is lively but can be hot in the lowlands, while mountain routes open fully from June to September.

Cycling Lombardy immerses you in the region's natural beauty and living culture. Whether you glide around Lake Varese, follow the vineyards of Franciacorta, or test your endurance on the Stelvio, you will see Lombardy from a perspective few travelers ever experience.

CHAPTER TWENTY-SEVEN

Cremona's Nougat Notes

Celebrating the Torrone

Festa del Torrone Experience

Where: Cremona

When: Second and Third weekends of November.

Average Festival Temperatures: High 12°C (54°F). Low 2°C (36°F).

Event Website: https://www.festadeltorronecremona.it

Cremona

You first met Cremona in the chapter Strings of History and Harmony, where we explored the city's unmatched legacy of violin making and its Renaissance treasures. But as autumn turns to winter, Cremona adds another note to its cultural symphony: sweetness. Each November, the city fills with the aroma of honey, sugar, and roasted almonds during the Festa del Torrone, a festival that celebrates its most famous confection.

Torrone, History Wrapped in Honey and Almonds

Torrone, a nougat made of honey, sugar, egg whites, and nuts, is said to have been born in Cremona in 1441. According to tradition, the recipe was created for the wedding banquet of Francesco Sforza, Duke of Milan, and Bianca Maria Visconti. The confection was shaped to resemble the city's soaring bell tower, the Torrazzo, from which it takes its name.

From this auspicious beginning, torrone became Cremona's most celebrated sweet, prepared for centuries by local artisans and passed from family kitchens to renowned confectioners. While nougat appears in culinary traditions across the Mediterranean, Cremona's version is distinct: it is firm yet airy, richly nutty, and forever tied to the city's identity.

The Festa del Torrone was officially established in the late 20th century to honor this heritage and quickly grew into one of Lombardy's most beloved food festivals. Today, it draws thousands who come not only to sample the many variations of this special treat but also to experience reenactments of the famous 1441 wedding, historical parades, and a joyous celebration of craftsmanship, taste, and tradition.

Torrone

Festival Traditions

The Festa del Torrone is a nine-day celebration stretching across two weekends in November. Cremona's piazzas, palaces, and streets become a living stage, filled with pageantry, music, and of course, endless nougat.

Day 1: Opening Saturday

The air in Cremona crackles with anticipation as the Festa del Torrone begins. By morning, the city's elegant piazzas transform into a vibrant stage for the grand opening parade. Costumed musicians strike up Renaissance melodies, flag-throwers send bursts of color spinning through the sky, and performers in brocade and velvet evoke the grandeur of fifteenth-century Lombardy. Visitors fall easily into the rhythm of celebration, swept along by drums and trumpets echoing against the medieval facades.

As the parade winds its way through town, the first torrone tastings and artisan stalls burst into life. Wooden counters groan under the weight of endless nougat creations, classic almond and honey slabs, delicate pistachio bites, nougat dipped in chocolate, and soft varieties flavored with citrus or spices. The scent of roasted nuts and warm sugar drifts through the streets, mingling with the sound of laughter and chatter.

By evening, the heart of Cremona, Piazza del Comune, is illuminated with lights and filled with crowds. A lively open-air concert sets the celebratory tone for the days ahead, blending folk music, Renaissance fanfares, and modern performances.

Day 2: Sunday of the First Weekend

Sunday belongs to history and legend. Spectacularly, the festival's most iconic tradition is the reenactment of the 1441 wedding of Francesco Sforza and Bianca Maria Visconti. The story goes that torrone was created for this very occasion, its shape inspired by the towering Torrazzo that dominates Cremona's skyline.

The day begins with processions in full Renaissance regalia: noble couples, knights, musicians, and pageboys parade through the streets, accompanied by the steady roll of drums and the shimmering notes of trumpets. The spectacle culminates in the symbolic presentation of torrone, a theatrical moment that ties the sweet firmly to Cremona's identity.

As the historical pageant concludes, the piazzas spill over with street performers, jugglers, and fire shows, enchanting children and adults alike. Workshops invite families to try their hand at candy-making, kneading and shaping sweets under the guidance of local artisans. Meanwhile, stages across the city host live music performances ranging from traditional folk to contemporary bands.

By nightfall, Cremona glows with festivity. The combination of pageantry, laughter, music, and the irresistible crunch of the special festival treat leaves visitors immersed in a celebration that is at once deeply historical and joyfully modern.

Days 3–7: Midweek Festivities

The tempo slows but never stops. Artisan markets and tastings continue daily, alongside guided tours of Cremona's landmarks, such as the Torrazzo and Teatro Ponchielli. Visitors can attend candy-making demonstrations by local confectioners, where the craft is explained step by step. Midweek also features smaller concerts, lectures on Cremona's culinary and musical heritage, and special museum openings.

Day 8: Saturday of the Second Weekend

By the second weekend, the festival is in full swing, and the energy in Cremona rises to a crescendo. The streets burst alive once more with dazzling parades of costumed performers, jugglers balancing flaming torches, and fireworks that light the crisp November evening. Crowds throng the artisan stalls for another chance to taste their favorite torrone creations, while confectioners unveil fresh varieties and inventive new twists for eager samplers.

The popular highlights of the opening weekend return, giving latecomers a chance to experience the magic: candy workshops where visitors can stir honey and nuts into molten sweetness, historical pageants recalling the union of Sforza and Visconti, and endless tastings that showcase Cremona's mastery of its signature sweet.

The day's centerpiece is the prestigious Torrone d'Oro Award, presented in Piazza del Comune. Each year, this honor is bestowed on a cultural figure, an artist, musician, or ambassador of tradition, who has contributed to Cremona's heritage and carried its name proudly into the world.

Day 9: Closing Sunday

The final day of the Festa del Torrone is nothing short of spectacular, a grand finale that draws the entire city together. The morning begins with the last reenactment of the 1441 wedding, a reminder of the legend that gave birth to Cremona's sweetest tradition. Costumed nobles, musicians, and townsfolk fill the streets one last time, creating an atmosphere that feels both timeless and festive.

As the day unfolds, stages across the city host marching bands, choirs, and concerts, their music echoing through the piazzas and alleyways. Families linger at the markets for last-minute purchases of treats and other Lombard specialties, while street performers entertain with comedy, dance, and puppetry.

The highlight arrives with the Guinness World Record attempt, an eagerly awaited spectacle. In past editions, Cremona has unveiled the world's longest nougat, stretching across entire piazzas, or massive sculptures carved from nougat into towers, arches, and figures.

As darkness falls, the crowd gathers in Piazza del Comune for the closing ceremony. The Torrazzo, Cremona's iconic bell tower, glows in the night sky as fireworks erupt overhead, showering sparks of gold and silver over the city.

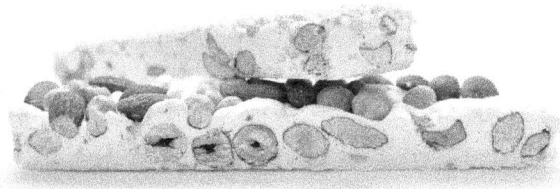

Torrone

See Chapter 21: Cremona: Strings of History and Harmony for a more detailed history of Cremona, along with information on logistics, day trips, restaurant recommendations, and accommodations.

For the Festa del Torrone, I recommend two to three nights in town to fully enjoy both the markets and the weekend spectacles.

CHAPTER TWENTY-EIGHT

Immersion Experience: Franciacorta Wine

Sparkling Wine Journey

Franciacorta Vineyard and Sparkling Wine Journey

Just outside Brescia, in the gently rolling hills between Lake Iseo and the Oglio River, lies Franciacorta, Italy's answer to Champagne. This prestigious wine region produces world-class sparkling wines using the same *méthode traditionnelle* as the famed French bubbles, yet it retains an intimate, distinctly Italian character. Visiting Franciacorta is an immersion in elegance and terroir, from walking through sun-drenched vineyards to descending into cool, stone cellars where bottles slowly mature to perfection.

A Brief History of Franciacorta

The name *Franciacorta* dates back to medieval times, believed to derive from *francae curtes*, or "free courts," referencing monastic settlements exempt from certain taxes. Yet the area's viticultural roots stretch much further, to Roman times, when vines were first planted in the fertile moraine soils left by ancient glaciers.

The modern story of Franciacorta began in 1961 when a pioneering winemaker, Guido Berlucchi, produced the first bottle of sparkling wine using the traditional method. The region's quality and reputation grew rapidly, and in 1995 Franciacorta earned Italy's first DOCG[1] status for sparkling wine, cementing its place among the world's great wine regions.

Today, over 100 producers craft Franciacorta in small quantities, focusing on artisanal quality over mass production. Every bottle is made entirely within the boundaries of the region, from grape to cork, and the result is an elegant, complex sparkling wine that rivals the best in the world.

Why Make the Trip?

A day in Franciacorta is not just a tasting, but a deep dive into history, craftsmanship, and the landscape. Italians have long cherished this area as a weekend escape, yet it remains under the radar for many international visitors. Touring here feels like stepping into an exclusive club that locals are happy to welcome you into if you take the time to visit.

Walking through the vineyards, you can smell the earth and feel the sun that nourishes the Chardonnay, Pinot Noir, and Pinot Blanc grapes. In the cellars, the quiet rows of bottles resting on wooden racks tell a story of patience and skill. And at the tasting table, each glass reveals the balance of tradition and innovation that defines Franciacorta. Pair your wine with local cheeses like Bagòss, creamy Taleggio, or Grana Padano, alongside cured meats such as bresaola or salame di Monte Isola, and you will understand why this is an experience to savor slowly.

For a first-time visit, fall during the vendemmia, the grape harvest, is especially captivating. The air is filled with the scent of ripe grapes, the hills glow in gold and crimson, and the chance to see winemakers at work offers an intimate glimpse into the heart of the region's winemaking tradition.

---

1. DOCG stands for Denominazione di Origine Controllata e Garantita (Controlled and Guaranteed Designation of Origin). It is Italy's highest quality classification for wine, ensuring that the wine is produced in a specific region, follows strict production rules, meets quality standards, and passes a government tasting panel before it can carry the DOCG label.

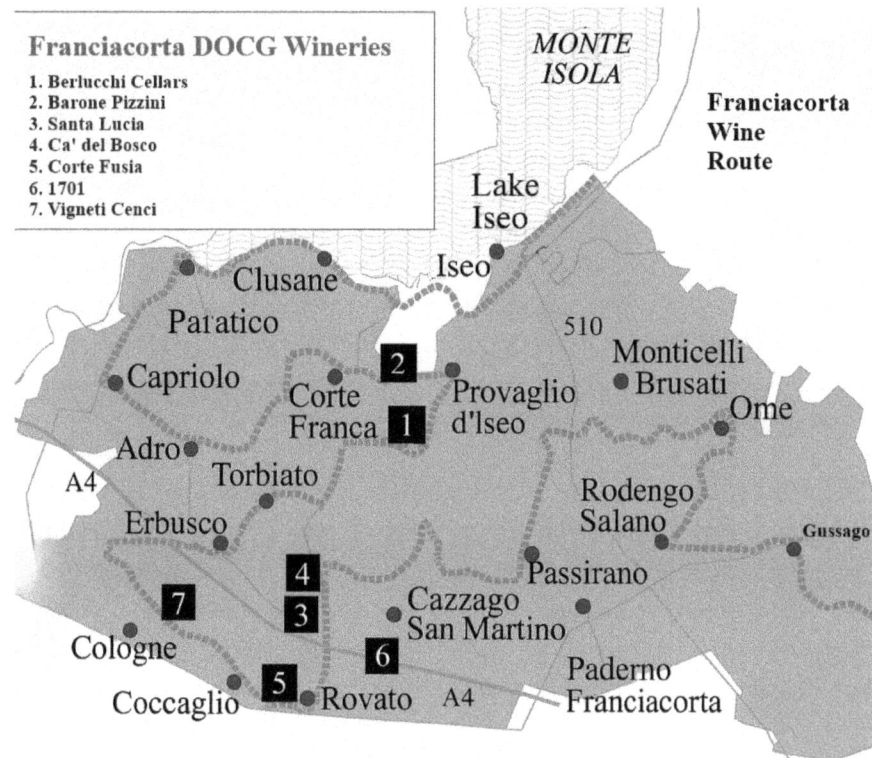

Map of Franciacorta Region

What to Expect

Vineyard Tours: Stroll through orderly rows of vines, learning about the region's unique ecosystem and grape varieties.

Cellar Visits: Descend into underground aging rooms where bottles rest for a minimum of 18 months. Guides explain the *méthode traditionnelle*, from the first fermentation to riddling and disgorgement.

Tastings: Sample a range of Franciacorta styles, from crisp Satèn to complex vintage *millesimato*. Tastings often include local food pairings.

Scenery: The landscape of vine-covered hills, medieval villages, and distant lake views is picturesque year-round.

Shopping: Many wineries sell bottles at the cellar door, often including limited editions unavailable elsewhere.

Practical Information

Location: Franciacorta wine region is about 80 kilometers (50 miles) east of Milan and 20 kilometers (12 miles) from Brescia.

Best Time to Visit: Spring and fall for mild weather and vineyard colors. September and early October coincide with the harvest and are especially atmospheric. While Franciacorta is beautiful year-round, fall is especially magical thanks to the harvest. From September to early October, the vineyards are alive with activity as workers handpick grapes and tractors carry overflowing crates to the presses.

The rolling hills glow with warm gold, red, and amber tones, creating stunning backdrops for photography. Visitors may glimpse winemakers at work, taste base wines from the new vintage, and enjoy seasonal dishes like rich risottos, wild mushroom pastas, and roasted meats, all perfect companions to Franciacorta's sparkling wines. The crisp, cool weather makes strolling through vineyards and villages comfortable and refreshing.

Duration: Half-day to full-day experience.

Booking Tips: Reserve tours and tastings in advance, especially for smaller family-run wineries.

Transportation: Best reached by car; some organized tours depart from Milan, Brescia, or Lake Iseo.

Website for Information: https://www.franciacorta.wine

Direct Winery Tours

Many Franciacorta producers offer their own guided visits and tastings.

Berlucchi. Historic winery where Franciacorta was first made in 1961. Offers cellar tours, tastings of multiple vintages, and pairing experiences. https://www.berlucchi.it

Ca' del Bosco. Known for art-filled cellars and premium wines. Tours include vineyard walks and detailed explanations of their production process. https://www.cadelbosco.com

Bellavista. Offers elegant guided tours of vineyards and underground cellars, followed by tastings. https://www.bellavistawine.it

Barone Pizzini. One of the oldest organic producers in Franciacorta, with tours focusing on sustainability. https://www.baronepizzini.it

Tour Operators

If you prefer someone to organize the entire day, these operators are well-reviewed:

Franciacorta Tour. Offers small-group and private tours including winery visits, lunch, and transport from Milan or Brescia. https://www.franciacortatour.com

Italy Luxury Tours. Customizable private tours with chauffeured transport, multiple tastings, and gourmet meals. https://www.italyluxurytours.com

Gambero Rosso Travel. Sometimes features Franciacorta wine itineraries paired with cooking classes. https://www.gamberorossointernational.com

GetYourGuide & Viator. Platforms with various Franciacorta day trips, often including vineyard visits, tastings, and time in Lake Iseo villages.

Winter Celebrations

December through February

CHAPTER TWENTY-NINE

Lecco: Celebrating San Nicolò

Lake Como Feast of St. Nicholas

Festa di San Nicolò

Where: Lecco

When: December 6

Average Festival Temperatures: High 8°C (46°F). Low 0°C (32°F).

Lecco: **Mountains, Lake, and Literature**

At the southeastern tip of Lake Como, where the waters narrow into the Adda River and the Alps rise like a natural amphitheater, lies Lecco, a city of striking contrasts and enduring charm. Its skyline is framed by jagged peaks such as Monte Resegone, whose saw-like ridge is a symbol of the town, and softened by the glittering expanse of lakefront promenades.

Lecco's story stretches back to Roman times, when its strategic position on the waterway made it a vital trading post. In the Middle Ages it grew as a fortified town under the Visconti and Sforza families of Milan, who recognized its importance as a gateway to the Alpine valleys. In later centuries, Lecco transformed into an industrial hub, especially for ironworking, yet retained its elegance with neoclassical villas, baroque churches, and airy piazzas.

Today, Lecco is known not only for its dramatic landscape but also for its literary fame. It is forever linked to Alessandro Manzoni, whose nineteenth-century novel I Promessi Sposi (The Betrothed) set many of its opening scenes along Lecco's shores. Visitors still trace his presence through monuments, museums, and the evocative views that inspired Italy's most celebrated work of fiction.

Town of Lecco and Lake Como

Celebrating St. Nicholas, Lake Como Style

What began as fervent prayers from worried families in the Middle Ages has blossomed over the centuries into a week-long celebration that transforms the entire city. The festival now weaves together solemn liturgies with joyous processions, sacred concerts with community feasts. The basilica fills with voices raised in centuries-old hymns, while the lakeside piazzas buzz with the warmth of neighbors gathering against the December chill.

Who is Saint Nicholas?

This fourth-century bishop of Myra possessed something extraordinary: a heart so generous that legends of his miracles spread like wildfire across medieval Europe. Known today as Saint Nicholas, he became the patron of sailors, children, and anyone who needed protection on treacherous waters.

Festival Traditions

Novena to San Nicolò

In the days leading up to December 6, parish groups and families gather for evening prayers and special liturgies inside the Basilica di San Nicolò. Candles, flowers, and votive offerings surround the saint's statue.

December 6: Feast Day

Morning

The Bishop of Lecco presides over the liturgy, attended by clergy, civic leaders, and delegations from across the province. Sacred music fills the basilica as hymns honor the saint.

Children's Procession

Children carry banners and lanterns through the old town, a symbolic gesture passing faith to the next generation. Small gifts and sweets are distributed in memory of the saint's generosity.

Evening

Procession and Fireworks

The statue of San Nicolò is carried from the basilica through the lakeside streets. Choirs sing, incense fills the air, and balconies are decorated with lanterns. The night concludes with fireworks over Lake Como, mirrored in the dark waters with Monte Resegone as a backdrop.

Walking Tour of Lecco

#1. Basilica di San Nicolò

In the historic center of Lecco, this nineteenth-century basilica is dedicated to the city's patron saint, protector of sailors and boatmen. Its soaring neo-Gothic bell tower, affectionately called "Il Matitone" (the Big Pencil) by locals, pierces the sky and is visible from almost every corner of town.

#2. Piazza XX Settembre

The main square of Lecco, framed by elegant arcades, cafés, and boutiques. During the festival it hosts markets, music, and holiday lights, making it a lively gathering spot for residents and visitors.

#3. Lakefront Promenade

The long walkway beside the lake offers some of the city's most iconic views. In December it glitters with lights and becomes a prime spot for watching the fireworks on the feast day.

#4. Villa Manzoni

This elegant eighteenth-century villa was the childhood home of Alessandro Manzoni, one of Italy's greatest writers and the author of I Promessi Sposi (The Betrothed). Walking through its salons and library, you can almost imagine Manzoni at his desk, drawing inspiration from the surrounding mountains and lake. The museum displays manuscripts, portraits, and period furniture, immersing visitors in the world of nineteenth-century Lombardy.

#5. Ponte Azzone Visconti

A medieval stone bridge spanning the Adda River, built in the fourteenth century by Azzone Visconti. It remains one of the most historic sites in Lecco and a scenic link between the town and its surrounding valleys.

Logistics

Train: Lecco is easily reached by frequent regional trains from Milan Centrale and Monza in about 40 minutes. The station is within walking distance of the basilica and the lakefront.

Bus: Local buses connect the train station to outlying neighborhoods and nearby towns. During the festival week, additional evening services often run to accommodate visitors attending concerts and fireworks.

Car: From Milan, take the SS36 Superstrada north toward Lecco. The drive takes about one hour, with scenic views of mountains and lakes along the route.

Parking: The historic center of Lecco has restricted traffic zones. Visitors should use designated parking lots near the station and lakefront, such as Piazza Bione, and continue on foot to festival events.

Restaurant Recommendations

Trattoria Corte Fiorina. Piazza XX Settembre, 24

A welcoming trattoria on the main square, offering traditional Lombard cuisine. Specialties include pizzoccheri, a comforting buckwheat pasta tossed with potatoes, cabbage, and melted cheese, along with polenta topped with local cheeses and hearty meat dishes. The setting, with vaulted ceilings and rustic décor, makes it a cozy place for a winter meal during the feast.

Ristorante Soqquadro. Via Belfiore, 25

A modern restaurant blending Italian classics with contemporary flair. Seasonal menus highlight lake fish, risottos, and creative desserts. Its location near the lakefront makes it a perfect choice before an evening fireworks display.

Osteria Filet. Via Ghislanzoni, 12

A small osteria known for warm service and authentic flavors of the Valtellina. Menu highlights include sciatt (fried cheese fritters), cured meats, and robust red wines from nearby vineyards. Ideal for visitors who want a genuine taste of the mountain traditions that shape Lecco's cuisine.

Day Trips from Lecco

Varenna. About 25 kilometers (15 miles) north of Lecco along the eastern shore of Lake Como. Varenna enchants with its pastel-colored houses, narrow cobblestone lanes, and the serene lakeside Villa Monastero, whose botanical gardens seem to spill right into the water. Take a stroll along the "Passeggiata degli Innamorati" (Lovers' Walk) for some of the most romantic lake views. The train from Lecco takes only about 20 minutes, making it one of the easiest and most rewarding excursions from the city.

Bellagio. Reached by ferry from Varenna, Bellagio is about 35 kilometers (22 miles) from Lecco and lives up to its title as the "Pearl of the Lake." Its elegant villas and terraced gardens, such as Villa Melzi, invite leisurely exploration, while boutique shops and cafés line the charming stepped streets. Enjoy a gelato or aperitivo with panoramic views where the three branches of Lake Como meet.

Abbey of Piona. About 30 kilometers (19 miles) north near Colico, this Cistercian abbey sits quietly on a peninsula that seems to float on Lake Como. Its Romanesque cloister and tranquil gardens offer a sense of peace that contrasts beautifully with the lively towns along the lake. After your visit, stop by the monastery shop to sample and purchase the monks' herbal liqueurs, jams, and other artisanal products, a memorable way to bring home a taste of Lake Como's contemplative side.

Lecco Festivals and Sagre Throughout the Year

Carnevale Lecchese

February or March

Lecco's Carnival fills the city with parades of children in costumes, decorated floats, and marching bands. Piazza XX Settembre becomes the center of festivities, where confetti showers and pastry stalls offer lattughe and tortelli di Carnevale.

Sagra di San Giovanni in Pescarenico

June

Held in the historic fishing district of Pescarenico, this sagra honors San Giovanni, but more broadly celebrates Lecco's connection to the lake. Expect stalls offering fresh lake fish, catch of the day style, prepared in traditional ways, alongside local wine, music, and dancing under lanterns.

Boat parades glide on the water, reflecting lights at dusk, and neighborhood bands play in the squares. This is the kind of event where you mingle with locals, stroll along waterfront alleys, taste simple but deeply satisfying food, and feel the pulse of community.

ResegUp Mountain Bike Race

Early June

For sports lovers and hiking enthusiasts alike, ResegUp is an exhilarating mountain race that starts in the center of Lecco, climbs through woods and mountain trails to the summit of Monte Resegone, then returns. Along the way, you're treated to spectacular views from the Azzoni Hut, dramatic overlooks above Lecco, and that spine-tingling sensation of being between lake and sky. Many contestants view it as a pilgrimage that bridges nature and the city.

https://www.resegup.it/

Lecco Summer Festival

July and August

Concerts, theater performances, and open-air cinema animate Lecco's piazzas and lakefront during the warm months. Both locals and tourists gather for cultural events framed by mountain sunsets and lake breezes.

Camminata Manzoniana (Manzoni Walk)

Early October

This beloved annual event invites participants to retrace the landscapes and settings featured in the novel through scenic routes that wind across Lecco and its surroundings. Choose from three routes: a 5.5 kilometers (3.4 miles) family-friendly walk ideal for casual strollers, an 11 kilometers (7 miles) intermediate route, or a 20 kilometers (12.4 miles) course for more experienced walkers.

https://www.camminatamanzoniana.it/

Natale a Lecco

December

The Advent season brings Christmas markets, ice skating rinks, light displays, and concerts to the city center. The Basilica di San Nicolò hosts nativity scenes, and Piazza Garibaldi sparkles with festive decorations.

CHAPTER THIRTY

Milan's Patron Saint Celebration

A Day of Devotion and Joy

Festa di Sant'Ambrogio

Where: Milan, Basilica di Sant'Ambrogio

When: December 7

Average Festival Temperatures: High 9°C (48°F). Low 2°C (39°F).

Feast of Saint Ambrose, Patron of Milan

December 7 marks the moment Milan becomes a stage for one of its most cherished traditions. For over fifteen centuries, longer than most nations have existed, the city has gathered to honor Saint Ambrose, their beloved patron saint, in what may be Italy's most enduring celebration.

Picture this: the ancient Basilica di Sant'Ambrogio, built directly over the saint's tomb, becomes the heart of a city in celebration. Since the early Middle Ages, pilgrims and locals alike have flocked to this sacred space, and today, tens of thousands continue the tradition. They pour in from every corner of Lombardy and beyond.

This is Milan's official start of the Christmas season. The area comes alive: haunting Ambrosian chants drift from the basilica's ancient walls, while the irresistible aroma of roasted chestnuts and warming mulled wine draws crowds through the surrounding neighborhoods. Vendors call out from the colorful stalls of the famous "Oh Bej! Oh Bej!" (Milanese dialect for Oh Beautiful, Oh Beautiful) market, a name that captures the wonder and delight that has echoed through these streets for generations.

As a public holiday, December 7th belongs entirely to this celebration. It's a day when solemn religious devotion meets infectious civic pride, when Milan's past and present converge in a spectacular display of a community spirit that has survived wars, plagues, and the passage of centuries, yet continues to captivate both faithful locals and curious visitors year after year.

Atrium of the Basilica di Sant'Ambrosio

Who was Saint Ambrose?

Born in Trier, Germany, in the mid-fourth century, Ambrose was a Roman governor in Milan when the people unexpectedly chose him as bishop in 374. This happened even before he had been baptized. His leadership was marked by pastoral care, political mediation between Church and Empire, and the introduction of the Ambrosian Rite, a unique liturgical tradition still practiced in Milan.

Ambrose was a prolific hymn writer and played a crucial role in the conversion of Saint Augustine. His defense of orthodoxy during the Arian controversy solidified his place as one of the most important bishops in Western Christianity. He died in 397 and was buried in the basilica that now bears his name. His relics remain there to this day, alongside those of Saints Gervasius and Protasius.

Festival Traditions

Morning

Opening of the Basilica and Mass

The basilica doors open early to allow pilgrims and visitors to find seating for the morning Mass. Many faithful light candles and visit the crypt for private prayer before the liturgy begins. The central liturgy of the day, presided over by the Archbishop of Milan at the high altar, in the presence of civic leaders, religious orders, and representatives of the Ambrosian Rite. The Mass features the Ambrosian chant and is often broadcast live on local television.

Following the Pontifical Mass, the relics of Saint Ambrose are displayed in the crypt. Visitors queue to kneel briefly before the saint's silver reliquary, accompanied by organ music and quiet prayer.

3:00 p.m.

Procession of the Relics

The service transitions into a formal procession. Clergy in ceremonial vestments (including the Archbishop of Milan, local priests, and members of Ambrosian confraternities) move the silver reliquary containing the relics of the saint (and often those of Saints Gervasius and Protasius) from the crypt or high altar. The procession slowly advances through the central nave, accompanied by Ambrosian hymns and the gentle glow of candlelight.

All Day

Oh Bej! Oh Bej! Market

Running from morning until evening, the market fills the piazza and the surrounding streets with over three hundred stalls. Visitors browse artisan crafts,

Christmas ornaments, antiques, toys, and regional delicacies such as roasted chestnuts, honey cakes, nougat, and mulled wine.

Evening

La Scala Opera Season Opening

Though not part of the religious feast, the gala at Teatro alla Scala on December 7 has become inseparable from Milan's celebration of Saint Ambrose. The date unites the city's spiritual devotion by day with its cultural splendor by night.

The season opening is one of the world's most prestigious opera events, attracting dignitaries, artists, and Milan's elite in dazzling evening dress. Red-carpet arrivals, televised nationwide, fill Piazza della Scala with excitement. Inside, the Italian anthem signals the start of a new season, often with a Verdi or Puccini masterpiece performed at the highest level.

Even without a ticket, the surrounding streets and cafés buzz with energy, as locals view the La Scala premiere as the elegant evening chapter of Sant'Ambrogio Day.

La Scala Operahouse

https://www.teatroallascala.org/en/index.html

Basilica di Sant'Ambrogio

Stepping into the Basilica di Sant'Ambrogio feels like entering the very heart of Milan's Christian heritage. Founded by the saint himself in the 4th century and rebuilt in Romanesque style between the 11th and 12th centuries, the basilica preserves its historic character with warm brick walls, arcaded courtyards, and a sense of solemn grandeur.

Nave and Romanesque Columns

Inside, solid Romanesque columns and alternating brick and stone draw the eye to the golden high altar, crowned by a 9th-century baldachin on porphyry columns. Beneath it, the relics of St. Ambrose and Saints Gervasius and Protasius rest in a crystal and silver reliquary, a powerful site of devotion during feast days.

The marble pulpit, supported by an ancient Roman sarcophagus, still hosts readings and sermons, while off the right aisle, the Chapel of San Vittore in Ciel d'Oro glows with 5th-century mosaics of Saint Victor the Moor, among the finest in Milan. In the apse, a 13th-century mosaic of Christ Pantocrator shimmers in gold light, completing this masterpiece of faith, art, and history.

Museum of the Basilica

Next to the church, the small museum preserves liturgical vestments, manuscripts, and ancient relics, as well as fragments from the original 4th-century structure. It offers valuable historical context for what you see inside the basilica.

Restaurant Recommendations Near the Basilica di Sant'Ambrogio

Osteria Carbonaia Mare. Via Cardinale Federico Borromeo, 12, about a 3-minute walk.

A cozy osteria offering Milanese and Northern Italian classics, including risotto alla Milanese and cotoletta (breaded veal cutlets), along with fresh pasta and seasonal specialties. Warm rustic décor and a welcoming atmosphere make it a splendid choice after the morning liturgy.

La Magolfa. Via Magolfa, 15 is about an 8-minute walk.

A relaxed trattoria popular with locals, serving hearty traditional dishes and pizzas. The outdoor seating is especially pleasant in early December when the market is in full swing nearby.

CHAPTER THIRTY-ONE

Sirmione Christmas Markets

Shopping at an Illuminated Castle

Natale a Sirmione

Where: Sirmione

When: December 8 to January 6.

Average Festival Temperatures: High 8°C (46°F). Low 2°C (36°F).

Sirmione: A Jewel on Lake Garda

On a slender peninsula that reaches into the shimmering waters of Lake Garda stands a fairytale castle, watching over the town of Sirmione. Today it is home to just 8,367 residents, who live in what is truly one of Italy's most enchanting places and one of my personal favorites. Long before Instagram, Roman poet Catullus was already bragging about his villa here, calling Sirmione the "jewel of peninsulas." Smart man, for those famous thermal springs have been drawing everyone from battle-weary legions to modern spa-goers seeking the waters' healing touch.

During the Middle Ages, Sirmione fell under the protection of the powerful Scaliger family, who ruled Verona and much of the surrounding territory between the 13th and 14th centuries. Known for their military prowess and political ambition, the Scaligers fortified Sirmione with thick walls and the imposing Rocca Scaligera, transforming it into a key defensive outpost on Lake Garda. The castle's towers and battlements still bear their emblem, the ladder ("scala"), a lasting reminder of the dynasty that once controlled the region.

The medieval Scaliger castle still commands the town entrance like something from a storybook, complete with drawbridges and crenellated towers. There's something thrilling about approaching those ancient gates.

I'll never forget racing across the moat with our luggage as thunder rumbled overhead, feeling like we were fleeing from medieval knights on horseback! The relief of crossing into the castle's protective walls was pure magic, and somehow we made it to Hotel Sirmione without getting drenched by the storm. We stayed for five nights, and I did not want to leave.

Creative souls have always found refuge here. Opera legend Maria Callas made Sirmione her sanctuary, joining centuries of artists drawn to this place where ancient stones seem to hum with stories and lake light dances like music made visible.

Scaliger Castle from inside the Medieval Gate

The Christmas Festival of Sirmione

What began centuries ago as quiet parish celebrations has blossomed into Natale a Sirmione, a winter wonderland that transforms this lakeside jewel from Advent through Epiphany.

Picture the mighty Scaliger Castle bathed in golden light, its medieval towers reflected in the moat like floating stars. The fortress that once defended against invaders now welcomes families with open drawbridges, its ancient walls becoming the perfect backdrop for twinkling illuminations that would make any Disney movie jealous.

In Piazza Carducci, local artisans peddle everything from hand-blown ornaments to steaming cups of vin brulé that warm both hands and hearts. The air fills with the mingled scents of roasted chestnuts, spiced wine, and fresh panettone;a sensory symphony that draws visitors from across Lombardy and beyond.

Festival Traditions

Advent Markets

Wooden chalets line Piazza Carducci and the narrow lanes of the old town. Stalls brim with Christmas ornaments, nativity figures, and handmade crafts.

Castle Illuminations

Each evening, the Scaliger Castle is bathed in colorful lights, its moat shimmering with reflections. The illuminated towers and battlements become the centerpiece of Sirmione's Christmas celebrations and a favorite spot for evening strolls.

Concerts and Cultural Performances

Churches and piazzas host sacred music concerts, choirs, and occasional theatrical performances inspired by the season. Local schools also take part, adding a family-friendly touch to the schedule.

Christmas Eve and Christmas Day

Parish liturgies bring the community together, with midnight Mass at Santa Maria Maggiore and festive bells ringing across the peninsula. Restaurants and homes serve traditional holiday dishes, many with flavors of the Garda region such as freshwater fish, polenta, and regional wines.

Epiphany Celebrations

On January 6, the festival concludes with the arrival of the Befana, Italy's beloved gift-bringing figure. Children gather in the piazzas for treats, while markets and concerts provide a final flourish before the season closes.

Walking Tour of Sirmione

#1. Scaliger Castle

The visit begins as you cross the narrow drawbridge over the moat and pass through the castle gate, the Porta di Sirmione, the historic entrance to the old town fortress. This dramatic gateway immediately transports you back to the thirteenth century, when the Scaliger Castle was built by the powerful della Scala family of Verona to guard the southern shores of Lake Garda and control access to the peninsula. This perfectly preserved fortress, with its crenellated walls, slender towers, and enclosed harbor, once protected both the town and the Scaliger fleet.

Inside, you can explore the courtyards, climb the narrow staircases, and walk along the ramparts, imagining the sentinels who once kept watch over the lake. From the highest tower, the view stretches across the water and down the narrow spine of Sirmione. During Natale a Sirmione, the castle glows with festive lights reflected in the moat, turning this medieval stronghold into one of the most enchanting holiday scenes in Lombardy.

#2. Piazza Carducci

Just beyond the castle lies Piazza Carducci, the lively heart of Sirmione. Cafés and shops frame the square, which hosts the Christmas markets each December. Wooden stalls, carolers, and families with mulled wine fill the piazza, while holiday lights add sparkle to the evening atmosphere.

#3. Santa Maria Maggiore

This fifteenth-century parish church stands on the site of an earlier Lombard church, and its foundations may even date back to early Christian times.

Dedicated to the Virgin Mary, Santa Maria Maggiore served as the principal place of worship for the fishermen, artisans, and families of Sirmione for centuries.

Its simple stone façade opens into a single-nave interior with Gothic arches, fragments of late-medieval frescoes, and a carved wooden choir that speaks to the devotion of the community that built it. The church's nativity scene, carefully arranged each Advent, is a highlight for visitors of all ages. On Christmas Eve, Midnight Mass fills the nave with candlelight, music, and the scent of incense, creating one of the most atmospheric moments of the holiday season in Sirmione.

#4. Grotte di Catullo

At the far tip of the peninsula, the Grotte di Catullo are the remains of an enormous Roman villa built between the late first century BC and the first century AD. Despite the name, the poet Catullus never lived here, but the ruins bear witness to the luxurious lakeside retreats of wealthy Roman families. You can still trace the outlines of reception halls, porticoes, and baths, imagining the grandeur of the villa in its prime.

The site's elevated position offers sweeping views of Lake Garda, and in December, the combination of pale winter light and mist rising from the water gives the ruins an almost dreamlike quality. While the villa hosts cultural events tied to the Callas Festival in summer, at Christmastime it becomes a tranquil escape, inviting visitors to wander slowly among its columns and arches, far from the festive bustle of the town below.

Casa della Bougainvillea

#5. The Bougainvillea House of Sirmione

A postcard-perfect corner where brilliant purple blossoms spill across medieval stone walls, creating one of the town's most iconic and beloved sights. The vivid bougainvillea frames shuttered windows and stone archways, making it a favorite photo stop for visitors. This charming house captures the timeless beauty of Sirmione's historic center and is best enjoyed in the soft evening light when the colors glow even more vibrantly. I have never been to Sirmione at Christmas, so when you go, let me know if this is still blooming in December! The vivid purple blooms typically peak in late spring to early autumn.

#6. Lakefront Promenade

End the tour with a leisurely stroll along Sirmione's lakefront promenade, which curves gently along the eastern shore of the peninsula. The paved walkway begins near the castle and stretches for about one kilometer (just over half a mile), following the water's edge past cafés, small docks, and park benches perfect for pausing to take in the view. In winter, strings of holiday lights reflect on the calm surface of Lake Garda, and vendors sell roasted chestnuts, mulled wine, and sweet treats that add to the festive atmosphere.

If you continue all the way to the northern tip, you will eventually reach the park near the Grotte di Catullo, where the panorama opens wide toward the mountains and the lake's northern branch. As you look back, the sight of the illuminated castle towers in the distance reminds you that Sirmione is both a fortress of history and a place of celebration.

Biking Lake Garda

If you have extra time and want to see more of the lake at a leisurely pace, consider renting a bike before leaving Sirmione. Several shops in the historic center and near the ferry dock offer bike rentals, including city bikes, mountain bikes, and electric bikes, making it easy for every traveler to join in. The lakeshore road heading north toward Lugana and Peschiera del Garda offers a mostly flat ride with spectacular views of the water, vineyards, and snow-tipped peaks in winter.

For more adventurous cyclists, ferries make it possible to plan a loop that includes stops in Garda, Bardolino, or even Malcesine before returning. In the warmer months, the Ciclovia del Garda, a breathtaking cliffside cycling path near Limone sul Garda, allows riders to pedal above the lake with uninterrupted views of the deep blue water, an unforgettable experience for active travelers.

Logistics

Train: Sirmione does not have a train station. The nearest stations are Desenzano del Garda and Peschiera del Garda, both about 10 kilometers (6 miles) away. From there, buses and taxis connect directly to Sirmione.

Bus: Regular bus services run from Desenzano and Peschiera to Sirmione's historic center. During the Christmas season, additional buses are often scheduled to accommodate visitors heading to markets and concerts.

Car: From Milan or Verona, take the A4 Autostrada and exit at Sirmione. The drive from Milan takes about one and a half hours and from Verona about forty minutes. The road to the peninsula narrows near the old town, so patience is needed during busy holiday weekends.

Parking: The historic center of Sirmione is a restricted traffic zone. Visitors should park outside the old town in designated lots such as Piazzale Monte Baldo or Piazzale Europa. From these lots, shuttle buses or a short walk lead to the castle and Christmas events.

Restaurant Recommendations

Ristorante Piccolo Castello. Via Dante, 7

A hidden gem tucked at the foot of the Scaliger fortress, with sweeping views of the castle, moat, and lake. We ate here on a beautiful summer evening, and the soft glow of candles flickering across the terrace created the perfect sense of refuge. The staff greeted us with genuine warmth, guiding us to a balcony table right above the moat, where the castle's silhouette shimmered in the lamplight.

The food was memorable in flavor and presentation, with fresh lake fish, hand-rolled pasta, and a delightful swordfish entrée that they filleted right at our table. Every dish felt thoughtful; the service was attentive without being overbearing.

Trattoria La Fiasca. Via Santa Maria Maggiore, 11

A cozy trattoria in the heart of the old town. Offers traditional Lombard and Garda specialties such as risotto with lake fish, homemade pastas, and hearty meat dishes. The intimate setting makes it a favorite for families and couples seeking authentic flavors during the festival season.

Day Trips: Nearby Sites, Cities, and Towns

Verona. 40 kilometers (25 miles) east of Sirmione, Verona is one of northern Italy's most beautiful cities. Famous for its Roman Arena, Juliet's balcony, and elegant piazzas, Verona is also home to excellent museums and Renaissance churches. Trains from nearby Peschiera del Garda reach Verona in about 20 minutes, or you can drive directly in under an hour. During December, Verona glows with Christmas markets in Piazza dei Signori and festive lights strung along its medieval streets.

Padua. 120 kilometers (75 miles) east of Sirmione, Padua is a city of faith and learning. The Basilica of Saint Anthony attracts pilgrims year-round, while the Scrovegni Chapel with Giotto's frescoes is one of the greatest treasures of Italian art. Padua is also lively with arcaded streets, vibrant markets, and elegant cafés. The train from Desenzano to Padua takes about an hour and a half with a change in Verona, making it a peaceful day trip from Lake Garda.

Garda (by ferry). The town of Garda lies 30 kilometers (19 miles) north along the lake's eastern shore. From Sirmione you can reach Garda by ferry during much of the year, though schedules are reduced in winter. The ferry ride, when available, takes about one hour and offers splendid views of castles, lakeside villas, and snow-dusted peaks in December. Garda itself charms with a colorful waterfront promenade, narrow lanes, and small historic center that hosts holiday events and markets. If ferries are not running, Garda can be reached by car in about 45 minutes.

Limone sul Garda (by ferry). On the western shore, Limone sul Garda is a picturesque village set against steep cliffs and known for its lemon groves, narrow lanes, and inviting waterfront. Ferries connect Sirmione and Limone in most seasons, making it a beautiful way to cross the lake. Stroll the peaceful harbor, visit the historic lemon houses, and enjoy a coffee with stunning views of the surrounding mountains. In the cooler months, the quiet atmosphere and misty lake views add to its charm.

Malcesine (by ferry). Malcesine, with its medieval core, is a treasure further north on the eastern shore. The town is dominated by the striking Scaligero Castle, whose tower offers breathtaking views of the lake and Monte Baldo. Its cobbled streets are filled with artisan shops and trattorias, perfect for a leisurely lunch. The lakefront promenade is ideal for a sunset stroll before taking the ferry back to Sirmione.

Sirmione Festivals and Sagre Throughout the Year

Carnevale di Sirmione

February

The historic center is filled with parades, costumed children, and confetti. Local associations decorate floats that wind through Piazza Carducci, while pastry stalls sell lattughe and tortelli di Carnevale. The laughter and music bring a playful warmth to the quiet winter streets.

Festival della Lugana

Late September

Held in the nearby hamlet of Lugana di Sirmione, this wine festival celebrates the crisp white Lugana DOC. Tastings, food pairings, concerts, and markets highlight the wine culture of the southern shores of Lake Garda. Visitors can stroll through vineyard stands, meet producers, and enjoy lake views framed by grapevines.

Sirmione in Festa

Early September

A lively civic festival featuring outdoor concerts, art exhibitions, food stalls, and a fireworks show over the lake. The event unites locals and visitors in a joyful celebration of Sirmione's community spirit at the end of summer. As fireworks reflect on the water, the castle and peninsula glow in a magical evening atmosphere.

CHAPTER THIRTY-TWO

Milan and the Three Kings

A Procession of Knights and Light

Festa dell'Epifania

Where: Milan

When: January 6

Average Festival Temperatures: High 6°C (43°F). Low 0°C (32°F).

When Medieval Splendor Takes Over Milan's Streets

On January 6th, Milan transforms into something extraordinary. The crisp January air fills with the thunder of drums and the flutter of ancient banners as the city becomes a living medieval tapestry where kings walk among mortals and miracles feel within reach.

The magic begins at the foot of the magnificent Duomo, where the grand Three Kings Parade assembles in all its glory. Costumed figures in rich medieval robes gather, their crowns catching the winter light as they prepare to recreate one of history's most sacred journeys. The Magi themselves, resplendent in royal attire, stand ready to follow the same star that guided wise men over two millennia ago.

Duomo di Milano

As the procession unfolds, Milan's historic streets transform into an ancient pilgrimage route. Tens of thousands of spectators bundle against the January chill, their breath forming clouds of anticipation as they line the cobblestones. The air pulses with the rhythm of medieval drums, while skilled flag-throwers send colorful banners dancing against the gray winter sky. Parish groups proudly carry their centuries-old standards, each one telling its own story of faith and community.

A Journey to Sacred Ground

But this celebration goes far beyond pageantry. This is a pilgrimage with profound meaning. The procession's destination, the ancient Basilica of Sant'Eustorgio, holds one of Christianity's most tantalizing mysteries. For centuries, this sacred church safeguarded what many believed to be the actual relics of the Three Kings themselves. Though these precious remains were spirited away to Cologne in the 12th century (a tale worthy of its own medieval drama), Sant'Eustorgio remains forever linked to the Magi's story.

Today, as the costumed kings approach the basilica's weathered facade, they complete a circle that began nearly a thousand years ago. The church bells ring out across the city, welcoming home the kings in a moment that bridges the earthly and the divine.

Surviving Through Storm and Story

For over a millennium, through plagues and wars, foreign occupations and political upheavals, Milan has refused to let this celebration die. Wars may have silenced the drums temporarily, but they always returned, sometimes stronger than before.

In the depths of Lombardy's coldest month, when the city could easily retreat indoors, Milan instead chooses spectacle. The Corteo dei Magi brings more than light to the dark January days. It proves that even in our modern world, we still hunger for wonder, for stories that connect us to something larger than ourselves.

Who Were the Magi?

The story of the Magi comes from the Gospel of Matthew, which tells how wise men from the East followed a star to Bethlehem to honor the birth of Christ. Tradition gives them the names Caspar, Melchior, and Balthazar, and describes them as kings who brought gifts of gold, frankincense, and myrrh. Each gift carried symbolic meaning: gold for kingship, frankincense for divinity, and myrrh for Christ's future suffering and death.

The relics of the Magi were long venerated at the Basilica of Sant'Eustorgio in Milan, brought here in late antiquity. In 1164, they were taken to Cologne by the Holy Roman Emperor Frederick Barbarossa, where they remain today. Despite their transfer, Milan has never forgotten its ancient guardianship of the relics, and the Epiphany procession continues to affirm this bond.

Why January 6?

The date of January 6 has been observed since the early centuries of Christianity as the feast of the Epiphany, meaning "manifestation." In the Western Church, it marks the day when Christ was revealed to the nations through the visit of the Magi, while in the Eastern Church, it also celebrates Christ's baptism in the Jordan.

In Milan, the Epiphany procession has been held for nearly a thousand years, making it one of the city's oldest public celebrations. The day also marks the traditional close of the Christmas season in Italy. Families take down nativity scenes, children receive sweets and small gifts from the folkloric Befana, and the city gathers to walk the ancient route from the Duomo to Sant'Eustorgio with the Three Kings.

Festival Traditions

Morning

The day begins with Mass in the Duomo, where the Archbishop of Milan recalls the journey of the Magi and the meaning of the Epiphany. Families gather early, many with children dressed as shepherds or angels, adding to the atmosphere of devotion and celebration.

2:00 p.m.

Corteo dei Magi

The grand parade sets off from Piazza Duomo, framed by the soaring spires of Milan's cathedral. Three men representing the Magi, in richly embroidered robes and jeweled crowns, ride on horseback through the streets of central Milan.

They are followed by a procession of hundreds: civic groups in medieval costume, bands of drummers and trumpeters, flag-throwers tossing bright banners into the air, and children carrying symbolic gifts of gold, frankincense, and myrrh. The air fills with music, the clatter of hooves on stone, and the laughter of families who line the route, creating a spectacle that blends faith, folklore, and pageantry.

3:30 p.m.

Arrival at Sant'Eustorgio

The parade makes its way through the heart of the city before reaching the Basilica of Sant'Eustorgio, long associated with the relics of the Magi. The atmosphere shifts from festive to reverent as the procession enters the basilica.

The faithful follow the Magi inside to honor the memory of the relics that once rested here, pausing before the ancient sarcophagus of the Three Kings. Hymns echo through the nave, accompanied by the glow of candles, as prayers close the formal religious celebration. Outside, the crowd lingers in the piazza, savoring the feeling of having taken part in a tradition that has animated Milan for nearly a thousand years.

Basilica of Sant'Eustorgio

All Day

Markets and Festivities

Around the city, especially near the Duomo and Sant'Eustorgio, stalls sell sweets, toys, and winter treats. Among the most popular is la Befana, the good witch of Italian folklore who brings gifts to children on Epiphany night. Vendors sell Befana dolls, candies, and stockings filled with chocolates, keeping alive the blend of Christian and folk traditions that make the day so beloved.

Restaurant Recommendations near Sant'Eustorgio

Ristorante Sant'Eustorgio. Piazza Sant'Eustorgio 6

A classic restaurant right beside the basilica, serving Milanese specialties such as ossobuco (slow cooked beef) with saffron risotto and cotoletta alla milanese (veal cutlets). The outdoor terrace is especially pleasant when the piazza fills with festival crowds.

Al Pont de Ferr. Ripa di Porta Ticinese 55

Located along the Navigli canals, a short walk from Sant'Eustorgio, this Michelin-recognized restaurant blends tradition with innovation. Known for creative takes on Lombard classics and a superb wine list.

CHAPTER THIRTY-THREE

Brescia, the Lioness of Lombardy

Roman Ruins and Festival Joy

Festa di San Faustino e Giovita

Where: Brescia

When: February 15

Average Festival Temperatures: High: 10°C (50°F). Low: 2°C (36°F).

Feast of Saints Faustinus and Jovita

Before exploring Brescia's most beloved festival, it is worth remembering that this proud Lombard city, known as La Leonessa d'Italia for its heroic role in Italy's unification, has a history stretching back to Roman times. Its layers of ancient ruins, medieval fortifications, and Renaissance architecture create a setting that feels both monumental and intimate. For more about Brescia's history and key sites, see Chapter 12, Brescia: Classic Cars & Timeless Elegance.

Brescia's most beloved civic and religious celebration is the Festa di San Faustino, a vibrant day honoring the city's patron saint. Taking place every February 15, the festival spiritedly combines faith, tradition, and commerce. Streets in the historic center overflow with stalls selling everything from handmade crafts and local delicacies to clothing, home goods, and toys. The scent of roasted chestnuts and freshly fried frittelle fills the air, and the cheerful hum of shoppers and families creates an atmosphere that feels both timeless and joyfully modern.

Local cafés and trattorie join in the spirit by offering seasonal specialties, while musicians and street performers keep the mood lively.

Who are the brothers Giovita and Faustino?

San Faustino, together with his brother San Giovita, is deeply tied to Brescia's spiritual history. According to tradition, the two were noblemen from Brescia who converted to Christianity in the early 2nd century AD during a time of Roman persecution. Both dedicated their lives to preaching the Christian faith, aiding the poor, and strengthening the community's resolve in the face of oppression.

Their steadfast devotion eventually led to their arrest and martyrdom under Emperor Hadrian. It is said that their example of courage inspired many in Brescia to embrace Christianity despite the dangers. Over the centuries, San Faustino became especially venerated as a protector of the city. He was formally declared co-patron of Brescia, and his feast day has been celebrated with processions and gatherings for generations.

Festival Traditions

Morning

From early morning, Brescia's historic center comes alive with the sound of vendors setting up their stalls along the main streets and piazzas. Aromas of coffee, pastries, and street food quickly permeate the air. The Church of Santi Faustino e Giovita opens its doors to welcome pilgrims and locals who come to pay their respects. At dawn, the first Mass is said, and then worshipers arrive steadily during the morning.

By 9:00 a.m., the fair is in full swing. Over 600 stalls line the streets radiating from Piazza Loggia, Via San Faustino, and Corso Mameli. Shoppers browse everything from artisan crafts and handmade jewelry to colorful scarves, ceramics, and toys. The food stands offer a tempting variety, from roasted chestnuts and grilled sausages to creamy polenta and regional sweets.

Church of Saints Faustino And Giovita

Midday

At midday, the most solemn religious moment takes place. A special Mass in honor of San Faustino is celebrated at the Chiesa dei San Faustino e Giovita. The liturgy includes prayers for the city and blessings for its residents, invoking the saint's protection and guidance. Many Brescian families attend together before continuing their day at the festival.

Restaurants and cafés offer festive menus for lunch, often featuring traditional Lombard dishes such as casoncelli, a half moon shaped stuffed pasta filled with meat, cheese, and herbs, braised meats, and rich polenta, paired with local wines from the Franciacorta region. Street performers and musicians appear in the main squares, entertaining the crowds with live music, folk songs, and theatrical acts.

Afternoon

The afternoon sees the fair at its busiest. Families stroll between the stalls, children clutching candy and balloons, while shoppers haggle for bargains or hunt for unique finds. Cultural associations sometimes host small exhibitions or guided walks to highlight Brescia's history and its connection to San Faustino.

The lively mood is accompanied by the constant hum of conversation and the occasional church bells echoing over the rooftops. In some years, small parades or costumed figures representing the saints make appearances, greeting the crowd and adding a touch of pageantry.

Evening

As evening falls, the lights of the stalls cast a warm glow over the cobbled streets. Many visitors linger for a final round of shopping or a last taste of festival food. The day concludes with the final evening Mass at Santi Faustino e Giovita, where candles flicker and hymns fill the church. When night is over, the stalls disappear, and the city quiets.

For the Walking Tour, Restaurant Recommendations, Day Trips and Festivals throughout the Year please **see Chapter 12, Brescia**.

Special Festival Food

Torte di San Faustino

No celebration in Brescia is complete without a taste of something sweet, and the Festa di San Faustino is no exception. The name "torte di San Faustino" actually refers to several kinds of cakes and pastries made just for the patron saint's day. You'll find soft sponge cakes filled with custard or cream, flaky puff-pastry treats glazed with sugar, and fruit tarts dusted with powdered sugar.

Bakers sometimes include almonds, citrus, or chocolate to give added richness and contrast. These sweets are often small enough to share, perfect for pairing with a café-nero or a glass of sweet wine. The timing of the festival, falling just one day after Valentine's Day, adds a playful culinary overlap.

Local chocolatiers seize the moment to showcase their finest creations, offering pralines and hand-crafted chocolates that celebrate both love and devotion. Sampling these treats in the heart of Brescia allows visitors to connect directly with the spirit of the festival.

Chapter Thirty-Four

Immersion Experience: Thermal Bliss

Lombardy's Spa Experiences

From Turn-of-the-Century Grandeur to Alpine Wellness

Imagine stepping into warm, mineral rich water that has bubbled up from deep underground for centuries, surrounded either by snow-capped peaks or by French inspired Belle Époque architecture with elegant colonnades, wrought-iron balconies, and pastel facades that recall the glamour of early twentieth century spa culture.

This is the essence of Italy's terme, thermal spa complexes where natural spring water is used for bathing, relaxation, and wellness. Long treasured for their healing properties, these waters are rich in minerals like calcium, magnesium, and sulfur, which many believe soothe muscles, ease joint pain, and improve circulation. Visiting the thermal spas is a cherished cultural ritual, a chance to slow down, soak, and rest after days of touring or hiking while savoring the moment.

San Pellegrino Terme: Elegance, History, and a Personal Favorite

I have personally experienced the beauty of QC Terme San Pellegrino, and I can say it is truly magnificent. The building itself is a work of art, and the approach through winding mountain roads sets the stage for an unforgettable visit. While I have also been to the terme at Sirmione, this one stands above the rest. Whether you spend a full day or even just a half-day with lunch in your robe, you will find countless wellness and relaxation areas, San Pellegrino water flowing on tap, and an atmosphere that makes it feel like a complete immersion into Italy's spa culture.

Situated in the Brembana Valley along the banks of the Brembo River, San Pellegrino Terme is a place where elegance, history, and wellness meet. The mineral springs here have been known since medieval times, when local shepherds and travelers noticed the naturally carbonated water bubbling up from the ground. By the fourteenth century, documents record the use of these waters for their curative effects, with visitors coming from nearby Bergamo and Milan to drink from the springs.

The fame of San Pellegrino grew steadily, especially in the nineteenth century when the spa culture swept across Europe. In 1901, the elaborate Grand Hotel and the ornate Casinò Municipale opened, attracting royalty, aristocrats, and the wealthy elite from across the continent. These magnificent structures, with their flowing organic lines and decorative flourishes typical of early 1900s design, created a setting where guests came not only to bathe in the thermal waters but also to enjoy concerts, dances, and fine dining amid lavish architectural beauty. The mineral water, bottled and sold under the now world-famous San Pellegrino brand, became a symbol of refined Italian taste and an ambassador for the town's reputation.

Today, the jewel of the spa experience is the QC Terme San Pellegrino, housed in a restored early twentieth-century building. Inside, marble floors, frescoed ceilings, and grand windows frame pools fed by warm mineral waters. Visitors can wander between indoor baths and open-air pools overlooking the river, step into saunas infused with mountain herbs, or relax in quiet rooms that once hosted high-society gatherings.

A visit often includes a stroll through the town to admire its Belle Époque villas, riverside promenade, and historic porticoes. Many visitors pause for a meal featuring local Bergamasco specialties such as casoncelli pasta and creamy polenta taragna, continuing a tradition of hospitality that has defined this spa town for centuries.

San Pellegrino Terme

https://www.qcterme.com/destinations/san-pellegrino/qc-spa-spl

Sirmione Terme: Healing Waters of Lake Garda

On a slender peninsula that juts into the southern waters of Lake Garda, Sirmione has long been known as a place of healing and beauty. Ancient Roman poets, including Catullus, praised its charms, and archaeological remains at the Grotte di Catullo suggest that wealthy Romans came here to relax amid views of the lake. At the heart of Sirmione's wellness tradition are its thermal springs, rich in sulfur, bromine, and iodine, which bubble up from deep underground at a steamy 69°C (156°F).

The modern spa experience centers on Terme di Sirmione, one of Italy's most celebrated wellness complexes. The Aquaria Thermal Spa, set right on the lakefront, offers indoor and outdoor thermal pools with panoramic views, hydromassage stations, saunas, steam baths, and relaxation rooms. Visitors can also indulge in therapeutic mud treatments, massages, and skin therapies that draw on the mineral-rich properties of the waters. At night, the outdoor pools glow against the castle-lit skyline, creating a magical lakeside atmosphere.

I have also been to the terme at Sirmione and found it to be a wonderfully relaxing visit. The combination of soothing waters, breathtaking lake views, and the charm of the historic town makes the experience truly special. While I recommend San Pellegrino above all others for its grandeur and immersive atmosphere, Sirmione offers something different, the romance of Lake Garda paired with the serenity of spa culture.

A visit to Sirmione combines wellness with history. Before or after a spa session, wander the cobblestone streets of the old town, explore the medieval Scaliger Castle guarding the harbor, or stroll out to the Roman villa ruins at the tip of the peninsula. Many visitors end the day with a lakeside dinner, pairing local Lugana wine with fresh pasta or lake fish.

Official Website: https://www.termedisirmione.com/

Bormio Terme and QC Terme Bagni Nuovi: Alpine Wellness with Ancient Roots

High in Valtellina, surrounded by snow-capped peaks, Bormio's thermal waters have been treasured since ancient times. The earliest written record comes from the Roman historian Pliny the Elder in the first century AD, who praised their therapeutic qualities. Archaeological remains reveal that the Romans built public baths here, using ingenious stone channels to divert naturally hot water into pools for relaxation and healing.

Today, visitors can choose between two main spa experiences. Bormio Terme, the municipal facility, offers a welcoming and authentic atmosphere with both indoor and outdoor pools, Roman-style baths under stone vaults, and sweeping views of the Alps. The waters emerge from underground springs at a steady 37 to 40 degrees Celsius, rich in minerals believed to promote wellness.

For those seeking a more luxurious retreat, QC Terme Bagni Nuovi is the largest alpine spa in Europe. Set in a grand historic hotel, it features over 30 different wellness stations, from panoramic outdoor pools and scenic whirlpools to saunas, steam rooms, and relaxation gardens. The design blends Alpine elegance with modern spa innovation, creating an indulgent sanctuary for both body and mind.

In winter, both places provide an unforgettable experience of warm water, falling snow, and crisp mountain air. Many visitors pair their spa day with skiing or snowboarding in the surrounding slopes, or hiking in nearby Stelvio National Park in the warmer months.

Bormio Terme https://www.bormioterme.it/en
https://www.qcterme.com/destinations/bormio/qc-spa-bagni-nuovi

Why You Should Go

A day at the thermal baths is a chance to rest your body, clear your mind, and connect with Italy's centuries-old tradition of wellness. This is not just a spa day; it is a ritual that Italians and Europeans have quietly cherished for generations, often passing along favorite terme destinations by word of mouth rather than glossy advertisements. Many visitors from abroad are unaware of how deeply embedded these places are in local culture, where a trip to the thermal baths is as natural as a weekend lunch with family.

The joy of visiting these terme lies in how they blend history, nature, and a slower pace of life. Italians know that these waters do more than relax muscles; they nourish the soul, invite unhurried conversation, and offer a moment to simply be present. Discovering them for yourself means stepping into a world that most travelers overlook, yet one that locals have treasured for centuries.

Include experiences like this in your itinerary to make your journey through Italy more memorable. Soak in the waters, breathe in the mountain air, and let yourself slow down. This is an experience you will remember long after you leave.

Practical Information

Duration: Half day to full day

Best Time to Visit:

San Pellegrino year-round.

Sirmione Terme is wonderful in every season; spring and autumn offer mild weather and fewer crowds, while summer brings lively lakefront energy.

Bormio Terme and QC Terme Bagni Nuovi are especially magical in winter, and also excellent in summer after hiking or cycling.

Age Requirement:

Guests must be at least 14 years old to enter the spa. Minors between 14 and 18 years of age must be accompanied by an adult and provide written parental authorization. Children under 14 are not permitted in the wellness areas, pools, or saunas.

CHAPTER THIRTY-FIVE

Milan Fashion Week: The Style Capital

Fashion, Film, and Lifestyle

Milan Fashion Week

Where: Milan

When: Twice annually. February/March for Autumn and Winter collections, and late September for Spring and Summer collections.

Average Festival Temperatures: High 14 °C (57 °F). Low 5 °C (41 °F).

Official website and schedule: https://www.cameramoda.it/en/

A Global Stage for Style

Milan Fashion Week is one of the "Big Four" fashion weeks in the world, together with Paris, London, and New York. Organized by the Camera Nazionale della Moda Italiana, it has been a centerpiece of Milanese culture since 1958. For decades, Milan's runways have defined global style, elevating iconic Italian brands such as Prada, Armani, Versace, and Dolce & Gabbana. The event also introduces new and emerging designers who carry Italian creativity forward.

For one week in February or March and again in September, the city transforms. Sleek black cars with tinted windows glide through cobblestone streets as designers, buyers, journalists, and celebrities converge on the fashion capital. The Palazzo delle Stelline echoes with the rapid-fire clicking of cameras, while converted warehouses in Porta Nuova buzz with anticipation before each show. Even outdoor squares become impromptu runways where the scent of Italian leather mingles with espresso from nearby cafés.

Fashion Week in the City

During Fashion Week, Milan fills with more than one hundred and fifty official events: runway shows, presentations, cocktail parties, and exhibitions. While many shows are invitation-only, the festive spirit spills into the streets. In the golden light filtering through the Galleria Vittorio Emanuele II's glass dome, models in oversized coats pause for street style photographers. Via Montenapoleone hums with energy as buyers negotiate in rapid Italian-English, while the Brera district showcases pop-up installations and limited edition collections.

Digital access also makes Fashion Week widely available. Many of the shows are streamed online, giving visitors the chance to watch a Milanese sunrise backdrop a 9:00 a.m. presentation or catch the drama of an evening show from a café in Navigli. Museums such as the Armani Silos or Fondazione Prada often schedule exhibitions to coincide with Fashion Week, creating moments where centuries-old art meets cutting-edge design under the same roof.

Festival Traditions

Runway Shows: Top designers present new collections in venues ranging from Renaissance palaces to sleek modern studios.

Pop Up Shops and Installations: Temporary boutiques and creative displays appear throughout the Quadrilatero della Moda and Corso Como.

Exhibitions and Open Houses: Several fashion houses and museums create special exhibitions tied to fashion and design.

Fashion Film Festival Milano: A global celebration of the intersection of fashion and cinema, held during Fashion Week. Hundreds of films compete, from short experimental pieces to feature-length productions, alongside panels, talks, and public screenings. The festival highlights emerging voices in both film and fashion and adds a cultural dimension to the week's events.

Nightlife and Celebrations: Exclusive parties welcome the global fashion elite, but citywide bars, restaurants, and clubs share in the atmosphere.

Main Fashion Week Venues in Milan

Palazzo Reale: Historic palace near the Duomo often used for high-profile shows and exhibitions.

Teatro alla Scala: The city's famed opera house occasionally transforms into a glamorous fashion venue.

Fondazione Prada: A contemporary art and cultural space hosting groundbreaking presentations.

Fashion Houses' Showrooms: Many top brands stage shows in their own headquarters and ateliers, spread across Milan's central districts.

Via Tortona: A creative hub known for design studios and loft-style spaces, buzzing with fashion events and street style photographers.

Porta Nuova: A modern district of glass towers and sleek plazas where major labels sometimes host shows and pop-up experiences.

Visiting Tips

Plan Early: Hotels in Milan fill quickly for Fashion Week, especially in September, so make reservations far in advance.

Seek Public Events: While the main runway shows are private, many installations, exhibitions, and pop-ups are open to the public and free.

Dress Stylishly: Even if you are not attending a show, Milan reaches peak style during Fashion Week, and locals as well as visitors often take part in the spectacle.

Combine Fashion with Culture: Enhance your Fashion Week experience by visiting Milan's cultural treasures such as the Duomo, the Last Supper, and aperitivo in Navigli.

Milan's March and April Celebrations

Stramilano

March

This beloved running event attracts tens of thousands of participants, from casual runners to elite athletes. The route winds through Milan's historic streets, and the city buzzes with energy during race weekend.

Milan–San Remo

March

Known as "La Classicissima," this is one of cycling's most prestigious one-day races. Starting in Milan and finishing on the Ligurian coast in San Remo, it attracts the world's top cyclists and immense crowds of fans.

https://www.milanosanremo.it/en/

Milan Marathon

April

A major international marathon drawing athletes from around the world. The course highlights Milan's landmarks, from the Duomo to Sforza Castle, while relay options and charity runs make it accessible to many.

Salone del Mobile & Milan Design Week (Fuorisalone)

April

The world's premier furniture and design fair, transforming Milan into an open-air museum of creativity. Beyond the exhibition halls, neighborhoods host installations, pop-up galleries, and events that attract visitors from across the globe.

Milano Art Week

April

A week of contemporary art exhibitions, gallery openings, and museum initiatives across the city. Special programs at institutions like the Fondazione Prada and PAC showcase Milan's creative edge.

Fiori e Sapori sul Naviglio Grande

April

This spring festival fills the Naviglio canal with flowers, plants, and food stalls. The colorful displays are paired with tastings of Lombard specialties, offering a scenic way to welcome the season.

Milano Cortili Aperti

Late April (date varies)

On one special weekend, Milanese families open the doors of their historic private courtyards, allowing visitors to step inside normally hidden gardens and palazzi. A unique chance to see the city's architectural gems up close.

Pittori sul Naviglio

April–May (several weekends)

Artists set up easels along the Naviglio Grande, turning the canal district into an open-air gallery. Paintings inspired by Milan and Lombardy can be admired and purchased directly from the artists.

Estate all'Idroscalo

Begins in late spring

Known as "Milan's sea," the Idroscalo lake comes alive with outdoor concerts, theater, water sports, and family activities.

Orticola

Late Spring

A prestigious flower and plant exhibition held in the Indro Montanelli Gardens.

Spring Celebrations

March and April

Chapter Thirty-Six

FestaFusion in Bergamo

Jazz Festival & Bergamo Film

FestaFusion Bergamo

#1. Bergamo Film Meeting. An internationally respected celebration of cinema, presenting over a hundred films from across the globe, including retrospectives, avant-garde screenings, competitions, and director talks in the city's historic venues.

#2. Bergamo Jazz Festival. A world-class jazz gathering that fills Bergamo with the sounds of internationally acclaimed musicians, intimate performances, and experimental collaborations in stunning theaters and open-air spaces.

#FestaFusion: When two festivals converge in the same town around the same time, your journey becomes twice as magical.

Where: Bergamo

When: March. Film Festival second week. Jazz Fest, third week.

Average Temperatures: High 14°C (57°F). Low 3°C (37°F).

Event Websites: https://www.bergamofilmmeeting.it/

https://www.teatrodonizetti.it/en/seasons-and-festivals/bergamo-jazz-festival/

Bergamo: The City of Two Souls

Bergamo is a city unlike any other in Lombardy, divided into two distinct yet harmonious halves: the medieval Città Alta, perched on its hilltop with stone walls, and the more modern Città Bassa spreading elegantly across the plain below. Together, they form a tapestry of history, culture, and daily life that enchants visitors from their first glimpse.

First settled by Celtic tribes and later conquered by the Romans, Bergamo's position at the foot of the Alps made it both a trading hub and a fortress. Centuries of Venetian rule left their mark in the form of magnificent defensive walls, now recognized as a UNESCO World Heritage Site. The city's blend of architectural styles, from Romanesque churches to Renaissance palaces, speaks to its layered past.

We fell in love with Bergamo the moment we took the cable car up to the Città Alta. As the carriage rose, the streets of the lower city gave way to sweeping views of tiled rooftops, church towers, and the soft curve of surrounding hills. Stepping out onto the cobblestone lanes felt like walking into a dream, with narrow streets opening into lively piazzas, elegant arcades sheltering cafés, and the scent of fresh pastries drifting from historic bakeries.

#1. Bergamo Film Meeting

The Bergamo Film Meeting has been a cornerstone of the city's cultural calendar since its founding in 1983. Created by a group of passionate cinema enthusiasts, the festival was designed to bring independent and international cinema to a wider audience, offering an alternative to the mainstream releases that dominated Italian theaters. Over the decades, it has grown into one of Italy's most respected film festivals, drawing directors, actors, critics, and film lovers from around the world.

The event takes place at multiple venues across the city, from the elegant Teatro Sociale in the Città Alta to modern cinemas in the Città Bassa. Screenings often spill into smaller, atmospheric spaces, where the intimacy between audience and filmmaker makes for unforgettable exchanges. The program typically includes retrospectives dedicated to filmmakers, competitive sections for emerging talent, thematic strands exploring pressing social issues, and tributes to underappreciated cinematic gems.

For me, the charm of the Bergamo Film Meeting lies in how it blends high-level artistry with the warmth of community. You might find yourself discussing a thought-provoking documentary with its director over coffee in Piazza Vecchia, or attending a Q&A in a centuries-old theater that seems tailor-made for storytelling. Even casual visitors are quickly drawn into the rhythm of screenings, conversations, and impromptu gatherings in the city's cafés and wine bars.

While the line-up changes each year, the essence of the festival remains constant: a commitment to cinema as a living art form that challenges, entertains, and connects people. While the line-up changes each year, the essence of the festival remains constant: a commitment to cinema as a living art form that challenges, entertains, and connects people. Most films are screened in their original language with Italian subtitles, and some include English subtitles, making it a truly international experience that welcomes film lovers from around the world.

Special Festival Foods
Polenta e Osei

No festival in Bergamo feels complete without a taste of the city's most iconic sweet, Polenta e Osei. Despite its rustic name, this is not the traditional polenta dish with game birds, but a delicate cake that has become a symbol of Bergamo's celebrations. Layers of sponge cake are filled with chocolate and hazelnut cream, then covered in golden marzipan to mimic the look of a mound of polenta.

Tiny marzipan birds perch on top, giving the dessert its playful name. You will find this cake in pastry shops throughout the year, but it takes on special meaning during feast days such as the Festa di Sant'Alessandro, when locals gather in Bergamo Alta to honor their patron saint. Enjoying a slice of Polenta e Osei during the festivities is more than just indulging in something sweet.

#2. Bergamo Jazz Festival

The Bergamo Jazz Festival is one of Italy's most prestigious jazz events, with roots reaching back to the late 1960s. Originally launched as a small gathering of enthusiasts in the Teatro Donizetti, it quickly gained a reputation for adventurous programming and for attracting some of the greatest names in jazz. Over the decades, legends such as Miles Davis, Ornette Coleman, and Chick Corea have graced its stages, alongside a new generation of innovative performers pushing the boundaries of the genre.

The festival takes place each March, often overlapping with the Bergamo Film Meeting, creating a rare opportunity for visitors to experience two world-class cultural events in a single trip.

The main concerts are held at the grand Teatro Donizetti and the more intimate Teatro Sociale, but the festival's spirit spills into the city's streets, piazzas, and bars. Late-night jam sessions, masterclasses, and informal performances create a sense of spontaneity that mirrors the improvisational heart of jazz itself.

One of the festival's hallmarks is its willingness to explore jazz in all its forms, from classic big band arrangements and soulful ballads to avant-garde experimentation and cross-genre collaborations. The program often pairs internationally renowned artists with rising talents, ensuring that audiences discover fresh voices while enjoying established masters.

For me, what makes the Bergamo Jazz Festival truly special is how it transforms the city into a living soundtrack. Strolling through the Città Alta at night, you might hear a trumpet solo drifting from an open window, or pass a bar where a trio is swinging in full stride. It's a celebration of music not as a distant performance, but as something woven into the very fabric of Bergamo's life.

Walking Tour of Bergamo

#1. Piazza Vecchia

After you take the funicular up to the high city you will begin the tour in the heart of the Città Alta at Piazza Vecchia, a Renaissance masterpiece framed by elegant arcades and historic buildings. The square's centerpiece is the Contarini

Fountain, surrounded by the Palazzo della Ragione and the Palazzo Nuovo, which now houses the Angelo Mai Library. The Torre Civica (Campanone) rises above the square, and its massive bell still chimes 100 times every evening at 10:00 p.m., a tradition dating back centuries.

#2. Cappella Colleoni

Next to the basilica stands the Cappella Colleoni, an exquisite 15th-century Renaissance chapel built as the mausoleum for condottiere Bartolomeo Colleoni. Its polychrome marble façade, detailed sculptures, and harmonious proportions make it one of Italy's finest examples of Lombard Renaissance architecture. Inside, the gilded ceiling and richly frescoed walls reflect the power and ambition of its patron. The chapel was designed by Giovanni Antonio Amadeo, whose mastery is evident in the intricate decorative program, from biblical reliefs to allegorical figures. Every detail glorifies Colleoni's legacy, blending religious devotion with a statement of civic pride. Even today, the building's striking colors and sculptural richness make it an unmissable highlight of Bergamo's Città Alta.

Cappella Colleoni Facade

#3. Basilica di Santa Maria Maggiore

A short walk from Piazza Vecchia brings you to the 12th-century Basilica di Santa Maria Maggiore, a masterpiece of Lombard Romanesque architecture.

Commissioned in 1137, it was originally intended as a civic vow to the Virgin Mary in gratitude for protection from the plague. The church is adorned with ornate portals by Giovanni da Campione, whose sculptural details display a mix of Gothic elegance and symbolic imagery.

Inside, the contrast with the austere exterior is breathtaking; rich Baroque decoration fills every surface with golden stucco, frescoed ceilings, and elaborate side chapels. The intricately carved wooden choir stalls, designed by Lorenzo Lotto, depict biblical scenes with astonishing detail and craftsmanship. The basilica's sumptuous interior speaks to Bergamo's historical wealth and devotion, making it one of the city's most cherished and celebrated places of worship.

#4. Duomo di Bergamo (Cattedrale di Sant'Alessandro)

Directly opposite the Cappella Colleoni stands the Duomo di Bergamo, dedicated to Sant'Alessandro, the city's patron saint and martyr. Built on the site of an earlier church and completed in its current form in the 19th century, the cathedral's neoclassical façade contrasts with the ornate Renaissance and Baroque interiors. Its bright, harmonious interior is crowned by an elegant cupola that bathes the space in natural light.

Beautiful Ceilings of the Duomo

Among its most notable artworks is the serene Madonna and Child by Giovan Battista Moroni, alongside canvases by other Lombard masters. The Duomo also houses important relics of Sant'Alessandro, which are venerated during the saint's feast day in August. Serving as the spiritual core of Bergamo, the cathedral offers a peaceful and contemplative counterpoint to the lavish splendor of the neighboring basilica and chapel.

#5. Rocca di Bergamo

Stroll uphill to the Rocca, a medieval fortress surrounded by gardens and offering sweeping views of the Città Bassa and the surrounding plains. Today it houses the Museo dell'Ottocento, which recounts Bergamo's history during the 19th century, particularly the Risorgimento era.

#6. Venetian Walls (Mura Venete)

From the Rocca, walk along the UNESCO-listed Venetian Walls, built in the 16th century when Bergamo was under the rule of the Republic of Venice. The pathway provides panoramic views, passing through gates such as Porta San Giacomo, whose white marble façade gleams in the sun.

#7. Teatro Sociale

Make your way to the Teatro Sociale, an intimate 19th-century theater in the Città Alta that hosts concerts during both the Bergamo Film Meeting and the Bergamo Jazz Festival. Restored to its original charm, it's a beautiful venue that blends history with world-class acoustics.

#8. Funicolare to Città Bassa

Descend to the Città Bassa via the historic funicular railway. The ride offers spectacular views as you glide between the medieval hilltop and the elegant lower town.

#9. Sentierone and Teatro Donizetti

In the Città Bassa, stroll along the Sentierone, Bergamo's grand promenade lined with trees, cafés, and shops. At its heart stands Teatro Donizetti, named for the city's famous composer, Gaetano Donizetti. This neoclassical theater is the principal venue for the Bergamo Jazz Festival and a hub for the city's cultural life.

#10. Accademia Carrara

End the walking tour at the Accademia Carrara, one of Italy's top art galleries. Its collection includes masterpieces by Botticelli, Bellini, Raphael, and Titian, offering a final cultural flourish to your exploration of Bergamo.

Logistics

Train: Bergamo is well-connected by Trenord and Trenitalia regional services, making it a simple trip from Milan, Brescia, and other Lombard cities. From Milan Centrale, direct trains take around 50 minutes, while from Brescia the journey is just over an hour. The train station is located in the Città Bassa, about a 25-minute walk or a short bus ride to the Città Alta.

Bus: Local buses operated by ATB (Azienda Trasporti Bergamo) connect the train station, Città Bassa, and Città Alta. During major events such as the Bergamo Film Meeting and Bergamo Jazz Festival, extra evening services are often scheduled to accommodate concertgoers and festival audiences. Regional buses link Bergamo to nearby towns such as Clusone, Sarnico, and Lovere on Lake Iseo.

Car: Bergamo is easily reached by car via the A4 Autostrada (Milan–Venice). From Milan, the journey takes roughly 45 minutes depending on traffic. The historic Città Alta is mostly within a ZTL (Zona a Traffico Limitato), meaning vehicle access is restricted to residents and authorized vehicles. Visitors arriving by car should plan to park in the Città Bassa or in designated lots outside the walls and use the funicular or bus to reach the upper city.

Parking: Popular parking options include Parcheggio Piazza Libertà and Parcheggio Piazza della Repubblica in the Città Bassa, both within walking distance of the funicular. Near the Città Alta, Parcheggio Stadio and Parcheggio San Giovanni offer convenient access to the city gates. Spaces can fill quickly during festivals, so arriving early is advisable.

Restaurant Recommendations

Mimì – La Casa dei Sapori. Via Bartolomeo Colleoni, 26 (Città Alta)

Nestled in the heart of the old town under stone vaults and gingham tablecloths, this charming trattoria is your go-to for regional Bergamasque cooking.

This is our go-to spot!

We enjoy the local dishes including casoncelli□alla□bergamasca, traditional ravioli filled with sausage, butter, and sage, tagliatelle with porcini mushrooms, coniglio con polenta, rabbit with creamy polenta, as well as a selection of cured meats, cheeses from the Orobie valleys, and local honey and wine. We usually eat in their courtyard, which offers lovely outdoor dining, particularly in summer.

Da Mimmo. Via Bartolomeo Colleoni, 17 (Città Alta)

A Bergamo institution, Da Mimmo is known for its classic Lombard and Italian dishes served in an elegant yet welcoming setting. Handmade pasta, wood-fired pizza, and hearty meat dishes share the menu with seasonal specials. The location along the main street of the Città Alta makes it perfect for a pre- or post-festival dinner.

Ristorante Lalimentari. Via Tassis, 3 (Città Alta)

Nestled just steps from Piazza Vecchia, this cozy spot combines deli, wine bar, and restaurant. Plates highlight regional cheeses, cured meats, and inventive pasta dishes, all paired with a well-curated wine list. The intimate dining room makes it ideal for a relaxed evening after a concert or film screening.

Trattoria Camozzi da Claudio. Via Camozzi, 73 (Città Bassa)

A favorite of seafood lovers, offering fresh daily catches prepared with Mediterranean flavors. Even though Bergamo is inland, this trattoria is celebrated for its impeccable quality and refined yet unpretentious service.

Vesuvio. Largo Porta Nuova, 12 (Città Bassa)

A lively pizzeria and restaurant known for its wood-fired pizzas and generous pasta portions. The location near Teatro Donizetti makes it a convenient choice before or after a jazz performance.

Day Trip Options: Nearby Sites, Towns, and Scenic Spots

Clusone. 35 kilometers (22 miles) from Bergamo. This charming medieval town in the Seriana Valley is famous for the Oratorio dei Disciplini, whose exterior frescoes "Triumph of Death" and "Dance of Death" are among Italy's most striking examples of late medieval art. The town's cobbled streets, small piazzas, and artisan shops make it ideal for a leisurely wander.

Lovere (Lake Iseo). 42 kilometers (26 miles) from Bergamo. Perched at the northern tip of Lake Iseo, Lovere is one of Italy's most beautiful villages. Its lakeside promenade offers stunning views, while the historic center features narrow lanes, towers, and the Accademia Tadini art museum. Perfect for a relaxed afternoon by the water.

Cornello dei Tasso. 26 kilometers (16 miles) from Bergamo. A remarkably preserved medieval hamlet accessible only on foot, Cornello dei Tasso was once a key stop on the Via Mercatorum trade route. It's also the ancestral home of the Tasso family, pioneers of the European postal system. Stone arcades, quiet courtyards, and mountain views make it feel untouched by time.

Schilpario. 55 kilometers (34 miles) from Bergamo. A peaceful Alpine village in the upper Scalve Valley, known for scenic hikes, cross-country skiing in winter, and artisan cheese production. In the warmer months, the surrounding mountains and waterfalls are perfect for nature walks.

Bergamo Festivals and Sagre Throughout the Year

Festa di Sant'Alessandro

August 26

Bergamo's patron saint is honored with a full day of celebrations that blend devotion and festivity. The day begins with solemn religious processions and special Masses in the Duomo dedicated to Sant'Alessandro, the Roman soldier martyred for his Christian faith. As evening falls, the city transforms into a lively open-air stage: piazzas fill with music, food stalls serve Bergamasque specialties, and children's activities bring families together. Historic buildings often open their doors for rare guided tours, while streets and monuments are illuminated to create a festive atmosphere. It is the perfect moment to experience Bergamo's faith, culture, and community spirit all at once.

Palio di Città Alta

September

A lively neighborhood competition in the upper town, featuring costumed participants, traditional games, and parades through the medieval streets. Local food stalls serve regional dishes, and musicians add to the celebratory atmosphere. Each district competes for pride and honor in playful challenges that recall Bergamo's medieval traditions, from flag throwing to relay races. The cobbled lanes of Città Alta come alive with color, laughter, and the sound of drums, making it a wonderful way to experience the spirit of the city's historic heart.

Donizetti Opera Festival

November

Celebrating Bergamo's most famous composer, Gaetano Donizetti, this festival stages opera productions, concerts, and recitals in theaters across the city. Events often include lectures, exhibitions, and special tours focused on the composer's life and works. The main performances take place at the beautifully restored Teatro Donizetti, where international artists and young talents reinterpret Donizetti's masterpieces with fresh energy. For visitors, it's a rare chance to see Bergamo through the lens of its musical heritage and to feel the city's deep pride in its native son.

Mercatini di Natale di Bergamo (Christmas Markets)

December

The historic center transforms into a festive wonderland with market stalls selling artisan crafts, holiday decorations, roasted chestnuts, and mulled wine. Piazza Dante in the Città Bassa and Piazza Vecchia in the Città Alta are especially atmospheric with lights and music.

CHAPTER THIRTY-SEVEN

Mantua: Faith & Gonzaga Splendor

Island City Between Two Lakes

Festa di Sant'Anselmo

Where: Mantua

When: March 18

Average Festival Temperatures: High: 15°C (59°F). Low: 3°C (37°F).

Mantua: City of Dukes and Devotion

Mantua, surrounded on three sides by artificial lakes created in the Middle Ages, rises like a dream from the water. Driving across the long bridge, the walled city appears almost like an island, its skyline marked by domes, towers, and the silhouette of the Gonzaga palaces. Today, Mantua is home to around 49,000 residents, a number that matches its character as both vibrant and welcoming, while still preserving the intimacy of its historic core.

When I visited Mantua, this view took my breath away. We drove over the bridge, parked outside the city walls and entered through the main gate, stepping directly into a town that feels like a stage set from history. Compact and easily walkable, Mantua reveals itself square by square: Renaissance piazzas framed by arcades, cobblestone streets opening to palaces, and churches filled with masterpieces.

At lunchtime we enjoyed an incredible local meal, savoring the flavors of Mantua's cuisine. The city is known for its bold specialties, including dishes made with cavallo (horsemeat), a culinary tradition that may surprise visitors. We did not try that specialty that day, but the other regional dishes more than satisfied, reinforcing Mantua's reputation as a place where art, history, and food are deeply intertwined.

With its layers of Etruscan origins, Roman foundation, and flowering under the Gonzaga dynasty, Mantua is truly a city of dukes and devotion. The Gonzaga family, who ruled from 1328 to 1707, transformed Mantua into one of the great courts of Renaissance Europe. They commissioned masterworks of art and architecture, inviting geniuses such as Andrea Mantegna, Leon Battista Alberti, and Giulio Romano to shape the city's palaces, churches, and piazzas.

Their legacy remains visible at every turn. The Palazzo Ducale, a sprawling complex of over 500 rooms, served not only as the family's residence but as the stage for courtly life, diplomacy, and power. Inside, Mantegna's Camera degli Sposi (wedding chamber) dazzles with illusionistic frescoes that celebrate the Gonzaga lineage, while ornate chapels and galleries reflect their role as both secular rulers and patrons of faith.

About 2 kilometers (1.2 miles) south of the city center, the Palazzo Te, designed by Giulio Romano, was created as a pleasure palace where dukes entertained guests with lavish banquets, theater, and music. Its frescoes, including the famous Sala dei Giganti, illustrate the grandeur and playful extravagance of Gonzaga taste. These buildings, along with Mantua's churches and piazzas, turned the city into a living theater of Renaissance power.

Beyond architecture, the Gonzaga elevated Mantua as a cultural beacon. Their patronage extended to music and literature, making Mantua a hub for innovation in the arts. They supported sacred relics and religious institutions as well, ensuring their rule was tied both to the civic pride of the city and to its enduring devotion.

Today, Mantua is celebrated not only as a UNESCO World Heritage Site but also as one of Italy's most atmospheric historic centers. Walking its compact streets, visitors encounter the enduring imprint of the Gonzaga dynasty, where secular glory and sacred devotion coexist.

Feast of Saint Anselm

Mantua's most heartfelt civic and religious celebration is this event, honoring the city's patron saint. While smaller in scale compared to the grand feasts of Milan or Brescia, this day carries deep meaning for Mantovani, linking faith with local identity.

The festival begins with solemn Masses celebrated in Mantua's churches, especially in the Basilica of Sant'Andrea and other historic sanctuaries connected to the city's spiritual life.

Basilica di Sant'Andrea

In the historic center, small markets and food stalls recall older traditions, adding a festive atmosphere to the day. Though more intimate than the massive fairs of other Lombard cities, the Festa di Sant'Anselmo reflects Mantua's powerful sense of community, where devotion and heritage are shared quietly but with profound pride.

Who was Saint Anselm?

Saint Anselmo, born in Mantua in the 11th century, rose to prominence as Bishop of Lucca and was later canonized for his piety, learning, and reforming spirit. A contemporary of the Gregorian Reform movement, he worked to strengthen clerical discipline and to defend the independence of the Church during a turbulent period. Despite his role as bishop in Lucca, his Mantuan birth cemented his identity as a native son, and the city has long honored him as patron.

According to tradition, Anselmo was deeply committed to justice and compassion, qualities that made him beloved among the faithful. His feast day, March 18, has been marked in Mantua for centuries, blending the city's religious devotion with civic recognition of one of its most illustrious figures.

Festival Traditions

March 16

Opening of the Urn

Opening of the urn containing Saint Anselm's relics in the Cathedral at 5:30.

Feast Day: March 18

Morning

The day of the festival begins quietly as church bells ring across Mantua's compact center. Early morning Mass is celebrated in several churches, most notably the Basilica di Sant'Andrea, where worshippers gather to pray for the city and its people. Local families arrive together, and the liturgy sets a reverent tone for the day. In Piazza Sordello and the surrounding streets, vendors set up stalls offering seasonal produce, local cheeses, and baked goods. The smell of fresh pastries and coffee drifts through the arcades, inviting visitors to linger.

Afternoon

The afternoon takes on a lighter, more communal feel. Children wander the piazzas with sweets in hand, while locals browse the small market stalls for artisanal goods and regional products. Cultural associations sometimes organize exhibitions or talks recalling the life of Saint Anselm and the city's medieval past under the Gonzaga. The compact size of Mantua makes it easy to stroll from one piazza to another, with each square offering a glimpse of the city's layered history.

Evening

As evening falls, the day concludes with a final Mass dedicated to the saint. Hymns echo within the softly lit churches, candles flicker, and the faithful give thanks for their patron's enduring presence. Outside, the city slowly quiets as vendors close their stalls and families return home. Unlike the large, bustling fairs of Brescia or Bergamo, Mantua's celebration is more reflective, its strength lying in the intimacy of devotion shared among its people.

Walking Tour of Mantua

#1. Piazza Sordello

Exploration begins in Piazza Sordello, the city center of Mantua. Surrounded by the imposing Ducal Palace (Palazzo Ducale) and the Cathedral of San Pietro, this square has been the political and spiritual center of Mantua since medieval times. The cobblestones echo with centuries of history, from Gonzaga court ceremonies to modern civic events.

#2. Mantua Cathedral (Duomo di San Pietro)

On the edge of Piazza Sordello stands the cathedral, dedicated to Saint Peter. Originally built in the early Christian era, it was later transformed by Giulio Romano in the Renaissance. Its neoclassical façade conceals a richly decorated interior filled with paintings, altars, and chapels. The cathedral is an essential stop for understanding Mantua's religious devotion and its role in honoring Saint Anselm.

#3. Palazzo Ducale

Stretching across more than 34,000 square meters, the Palazzo Ducale is less a single palace than an entire city within the city. For nearly four centuries it was the residence of the Gonzaga family, who filled it with art, architecture, and symbols of their authority. The complex is a labyrinth of courtyards, gardens, frescoed halls, and ornate apartments that together form one of the largest palace structures in Europe.

The highlight for most visitors is the Camera degli Sposi (Bridal Chamber), painted by Andrea Mantegna between 1465 and 1474. This room is one of the masterpieces of Renaissance art, famous for its pioneering illusionistic frescoes. The ceiling's painted oculus, with cherubs peering playfully over a balustrade, creates the illusion of open sky and was revolutionary in its use of perspective. Wall frescoes depict Ludovico II and his court, celebrating the Gonzaga family with scenes of dominance, compromise, and home life. The Bridal Chamber art immortalizes the Gonzaga as both worldly rulers and refined patrons, cementing Mantua's status as a Renaissance cultural capital.

Exploring the Palazzo Ducale's corridors and chambers offers a vivid glimpse into the wealth, taste, and political influence of one of Italy's greatest dynasties. Beyond Mantegna's chamber, visitors can discover chapels, galleries, and apartments richly adorned with frescoes and stuccoes that reflect centuries of Gonzaga patronage.

Tickets and Information: Entry to the Palazzo Ducale requires a ticket, which includes access to the Camera degli Sposi. Reservations are strongly recommended, especially during weekends and festival periods. Tickets and updated visitor information are available on the official website: www.mantovaducale.beniculturali.it.

#4. Piazza delle Erbe and Palazzo della Ragione

A short walk brings you to Piazza delle Erbe, Mantua's bustling medieval market square. Arcaded buildings frame the piazza, and the lively atmosphere recalls the city's mercantile traditions. On one side stands the Palazzo della Ragione, a 13th-century civic hall once used for public assemblies. Its austere brick walls and crenellations contrast with the energy of the piazza below, where cafés and shops invite you to linger.

#5. Rotonda di San Lorenzo

Next to Piazza delle Erbe is the Rotonda di San Lorenzo, Mantua's oldest church, dating back to the 11th century. Built in a circular plan inspired by the Holy Sepulchre in Jerusalem, it exudes an intimate, mystical atmosphere. Step inside to admire fragments of frescoes that transport you back to the city's early medieval faith.

Rotonda di San Lorenzo

#6. Basilica di Sant'Andrea

Walk toward Piazza Mantegna to discover the Basilica di Sant'Andrea, designed by Leon Battista Alberti in the 15th century. This monumental church is one of Mantua's greatest treasures, built to house a sacred relic said to contain drops of Christ's blood. Its soaring nave, harmonious proportions, and chapels adorned with Renaissance frescoes create a breathtaking sense of grandeur.

#7. Teatro Bibiena

Continue to the Teatro Bibiena, an 18th-century gem with an intimate horseshoe-shaped interior decorated in Baroque style. Even Mozart performed here as a young prodigy in 1770. Today the theater remains a jewel of Mantua, where music and culture continue to flourish. A guided visit reveals the exquisite details of its stucco work and gilded décor.

#8. Lungolago Walk

Conclude the walking tour with a gentle stroll along the shores of the Lago di Mezzo, one of Mantua's encircling lakes. From here, the city's skyline of domes, bell towers, and walls is perfectly framed by the water. At sunset, the view recalls the same magical impression you experience when first driving across the bridge into Mantua, a city suspended between land and water, history and devotion.

Logistics

Train: Mantua is well connected by regional trains, though it is not on Italy's high-speed network. From Milan, the journey takes about 1 hour and 45 minutes with a direct Trenitalia service. Verona, a major hub, is just 45 minutes away, while Modena and Parma are also reachable in under an hour. The train station lies just outside the historic center, a pleasant 15-minute walk to Piazza Sordello, or a short bus ride if carrying luggage.

Bus: Local buses, operated by APAM, provide frequent service within the city and to nearby towns in Lombardy and Emilia-Romagna. The main bus terminal is near the train station. During major events, additional services are often scheduled to accommodate visitors.

Car: Mantua is located along the A22 Autostrada, with convenient exits connecting it to Verona in the north and Modena in the south. Driving from Milan takes about two hours. Roads are well maintained, and the signage is clear. However, entry into the centro storico is restricted because of the ZTL (Zona a Traffico Limitato). It is best to leave your car in one of the parking areas outside the walls and continue on foot.

Parking: Several parking options are available near the city walls, including Piazza Anconetta, Campo Canoa, and the Mazzini parking areas. Rates are reasonable, and from each lot, it is a short walk to the main gates and historic center. On festival days, parking fills quickly, so early arrival is recommended.

Restaurant Recommendations

Osteria dell'Oca. Via Trieste, 10

This cozy osteria offers a menu steeped in Mantua's culinary heritage. Specialties include stracotto d'asino (slow-cooked donkey stew, another local tradition) and fresh handmade pasta. The intimate dining room makes it ideal for a long, relaxed meal.

Antica Osteria ai Ranari. Via Pescheria, 13

Situated in the heart of the historic center, this osteria takes its name from the frog catchers who once worked along Mantua's lakes. Today it serves refined interpretations of local classics, paired with an excellent wine list featuring Lombard and Veneto labels.

Ristorante Il Cigno dei Martini. Piazza Carlo d'Arco, 1

A refined restaurant housed in a historic palazzo, offering elegant dining with a focus on seasonal ingredients. Dishes highlight the sophistication of Mantuan cuisine, from pumpkin-based specialties to inventive takes on traditional recipes. The setting, with vaulted ceilings and tasteful décor, makes it perfect for a memorable evening.

Day Trip Options: Nearby Sites, Cities, and Towns

Peschiera del Garda. 40 kilometers (25 miles) from Mantua, is a fortified lakeside town where the Mincio River flows out of Lake Garda. Its star-shaped fortress, part of the UNESCO Venetian Works of Defense, offers a fascinating glimpse into the military history of the region. The charming historic center is encircled by canals and lined with shops, cafés, and gelaterie, perfect for a leisurely stroll.

We always enjoy visiting Peschiera del Garda. Crossing the moat to enter the old castle walls feels like stepping back in time, and the sunset views over the medieval bridge are unforgettable. The town's compact, walkable size makes it easy to explore on foot, whether wandering along the waterfront or stopping for a coffee in one of its inviting piazzas.

Peschiera is also an excellent base for exploring Lake Garda by ferry. From its port you can reach towns such as Sirmione with its castle and Roman ruins, Bardolino with its lakeside promenade and wine culture, Lazise with its medieval walls, and Garda with its colorful harbor, making it easy to craft your own lake itinerary.

Verona. 45 kilometers (28 miles) from Mantua. Verona enchants visitors with its Roman amphitheater, the Arena, which still hosts grand operas and concerts. The historic center, a UNESCO World Heritage Site, brims with medieval towers, Renaissance palaces, and lively piazzas. A day trip offers the chance to wander the streets of Shakespearean legend, visit Juliet's balcony, and savor the elegance of Veneto cuisine.

My family visited Verona during the summer to have dinner and attend a performance inside the Arena, and it was one of the most memorable evenings of our travels. As the sun set over the ancient stone arches, we joined the crowd of beautifully dressed Italians making their way to the theater. The atmosphere was pure magic, with music drifting through the warm air, candles flickering along the steps, and a sense of timeless elegance that made the entire night feel like stepping into a living opera.

Parma. 60 kilometers (37 miles) from Mantua. Renowned for its rich culinary tradition, Parma is home to Parmesan cheese and Parma ham, as well as elegant architecture. The pink-marble Baptistery and frescoed Cathedral are highlights of Italian Romanesque art. I visited Parma with two friends for the Palio di Parma, and the city was alive with color and pride. Everywhere we went, locals spoke passionately about their contrade, eager to share the traditions that have defined their community for centuries. It was a beautiful event filled with pageantry, music, and heartfelt devotion.

Festivals and Sagre in Mantua and Nearby Towns Throughout the Year

Carnevale di Mantova

February or March (dates vary)

While not as large as Venice's, Mantua's Carnival has deep roots. Colorful parades, costumes, and masked balls take place in the city center. Piazza Sordello becomes the lively heart of the festivities, filled with music, confetti, and families in costume. Traditional sweets such as chiacchiere and tortelli di Carnevale are sold at stalls, and performances bring the Renaissance spirit of the city to life.

Palio di Goito

May

In the nearby town of Goito, this historic palio commemorates medieval traditions with colorful parades, flag-throwing, and competitions between districts. The event includes costumed processions, reenactments, and stalls featuring local specialties such as salumi and cheeses.

Sagra del Risotto alla Pilota in Villimpenta

Late June

Just outside Mantua in the town of Villimpenta, this sagra is dedicated to the region's signature dish: risotto alla pilota, prepared with local rice and sausage. The event fills the town with food stalls, music, and dancing, drawing thousands of visitors each year.

Sagra del Tortello di Zucca in Various Towns around Mantua (Pumpkin Festival)

September and October

Several towns near Mantua host festivals celebrating the area's beloved pumpkin-filled pasta, tortelli di zucca. Each community adds its own twist, with tents serving hundreds of plates, paired with local wines.

Festivaletteratura (Literary Festival)

Early September

Mantua's most celebrated cultural event, this international literary festival transforms the city into an open-air stage for authors, poets, and thinkers from around the globe. Readings, lectures, and workshops take place in historic palaces, theaters, and piazzas. The atmosphere is lively yet intimate, attracting both local audiences and international visitors.

https://www.festivaletteratura.it/it/home

Festa dell'Uva di Quistello (Wine Festival)

September

Quistello, southeast of Mantua, celebrates the grape harvest with a vibrant sagra. Visitors enjoy tastings of local wines, grape-themed sweets, and festive parades. The event highlights the agricultural richness of the Mantovano countryside.

CHAPTER THIRTY-EIGHT

Seven Spectacular Lombardy Carnivals

Masks, Music & Alpine Traditions

While Venice often steals the spotlight during Carnival, Lombardy hosts its own dazzling array of celebrations, blending history, folklore, and Alpine charm. From Milan's unique Ambrosian calendar to the wooden masks of Schignano, each Carnival here offers a fresh perspective on this beloved Italian tradition.

Whether you prefer grand parades through bustling cities, rustic Alpine dances, or medieval settings, Lombardy's Carnivals immerse you in a world of costumes, satire, music, and community spirit. Adding a Carnival stop to your Lombardy itinerary expands your journey far beyond Milan's Duomo into small towns where centuries-old traditions still thrive.

What is Carnival?

Lent is the forty-day period before Easter, dedicated to prayer, fasting, and reflection in preparation for the holiest day of the Christian year. Carnival is the season that comes just before Lent, a time of joy and celebration marked by parades, costumes, music, and feasting. Carnival generally takes place in February. It culminates on Fat Tuesday, known in Italian as Martedì Grasso and in the

UK as Shrove Tuesday, the day before Ash Wednesday. On Ash Wednesday, Christians receive ashes on their foreheads or over their scalps as a sign of repentance, and the solemn season of Lent begins.

Carnival Events Across Lombardy: Folklore & Festivity

1. Milan: Carnevale Ambrosiano

Carnival Highlight: Celebrations extend until Saturday after Ash Wednesday, following the Ambrosian Rite.

Milan's Carnival is unlike any other in Italy. Because the city follows the Ambrosian Rite, festivities last four days longer than elsewhere. The main event is the grand parade on Saturday, when floats, musicians, stilt-walkers, and masked groups converge on Piazza Duomo. Children in costumes fill the streets, showered with confetti, while pastry shops serve chiacchiere and tortelli. Leading up to Saturday, schools, parishes, and cultural associations hold smaller parades and theatrical performances.

It's an unmissable twist for those wanting something special. The combination of sacred tradition and Milanese flair makes this an essential stop.

2. Crema: Carnevale di Crema

Carnival Highlight: Huge allegorical floats parading through Piazza del Duomo on February Sundays.

Crema's Carnival is one of Lombardy's most spectacular, drawing visitors from across northern Italy. Each Sunday in February, giant allegorical floats parade through the historic Piazza del Duomo, accompanied by satirical skits, brass bands, dancers, and confetti storms. The final Sunday parade is the peak, with the largest floats, costumed competitions, and awards for creativity. Food stands serve tortelli cremaschi and other local specialties, while side events include concerts and children's games.

It's a family-friendly spectacle with the scale of Venice but a warmer, more local feel. Perfect for travelers wanting both grandeur and community spirit.

3. Bagolino (Brescia): Carnevale di Bagolino

Carnival Highlight: The Balarì, masked dancers performing in traditional black and red costumes to violin music.

This centuries-old Alpine Carnival is steeped in Renaissance traditions. Over three days, masked Balarì dancers in black jackets, red sashes, and elaborate hats perform choreographed dances through Bagolino's cobbled streets, accompanied by haunting violin music unique to the region.

On Fat Tuesday, the celebration reaches its peak, with musicians, dancers, and villagers filling every corner of the old town. Carnival food is central here: steaming bowls of gnocchi and sweet frittelle are shared in taverns and family homes.

Authentic, folkloric, and deeply tied to Alpine culture. Bagolino's Carnival feels like stepping into another century.

4. Schignano (Como): Carnevale di Schignano

Carnival Highlight: Grotesque wooden masks representing the Bei (wealthy) and Brut (poor).

Perched in the mountains above Lake Como, Schignano's Carnival is renowned for its dramatic wooden masks. Characters are divided into the Bei (wealthy, elegant, and proud) and the Brut (poor, ragged, and comical).

On Fat Tuesday, the full cast of characters parades through the village, accompanied by raucous music, cowbells, and theatrical antics. The satire is biting but humorous, mocking social inequalities with grotesque exaggeration. Bonfires and village feasts close the night, extending well past midnight.

For a Carnival unlike any other, full of satire, laughter, and incredible mask craftsmanship. A photographer's dream.

5. Soncino (Cremona): Carnevale di Soncino

Carnival Highlight: Medieval reenactments and masked parades through the walled town.

Within the medieval walls of Soncino, Carnival becomes a historical pageant. The town center is filled with masked nobles, knights, jesters, and allegorical figures parading against the backdrop of the Rocca Sforzesca fortress. Events include jousting reenactments, fire performances, artisan markets, and food stalls with chiacchiere and roasted chestnuts.

The final Sunday parade features costumed groups from neighboring towns, creating a festive but intimate atmosphere within the walled streets.

A Carnival for history lovers, combining Renaissance architecture with festive pageantry.

6. Castiglione delle Stiviere (Mantua Province): Carnevale di Castiglione

Carnival Highlight: Colorful floats and masked parades fill the historic streets.

In the Renaissance town of Castiglione delle Stiviere, Carnival takes on a joyous, community-driven atmosphere. For several Sundays leading up to Lent, the streets become a stage for giant allegorical floats, costumed groups, brass bands, and children in vibrant masks. The procession winds through the heart of town, with satirical skits poking fun at politics and everyday life, echoing the playful spirit of Venetian and Viareggian traditions but in a more intimate, local setting.

Alongside the parades, the squares host live music, children's activities, and food stalls offering traditional carnival treats such as chiacchiere and tortelli di carnevale. Families gather on balconies and along the piazzas, cheering as confetti rains down in a kaleidoscope of color.

Castiglione's carnival is one of southern Lombardy's liveliest, balancing spectacular floats with small-town warmth. It's ideal for travelers wanting to experience a festive celebration without the overwhelming crowds of bigger cities, a chance to enjoy authentic Lombard hospitality and Renaissance scenery alongside the joy of Carnival.

7. Carnevale di Cantù (Como Province)

Carnival Highlight: Huge allegorical floats and Lombardy's largest parade.

Cantù, near Lake Como, hosts one of the region's most spectacular Carnival parades, with massive papier-mâché floats that rival those of Viareggio. The event typically takes place on consecutive Sundays in February, drawing thousands of spectators. Alongside the floats, marching bands, dancers, and masked groups fill the streets with color and energy.

This is the Carnival for those who love spectacle. With its scale, artistry, and festive energy, Cantù's parade is often called "the Venice of Lombardy."

Festival Foods
Carnival Specialities in Lombardy

Lattughe: Thin, fried pastries dusted with powdered sugar. In Lombardy they are often called lattughe ("lettuce leaves") for their crinkled shape. Universally found at Milan's Ambrosiano Carnival and throughout the region.

Tortelli di Carnevale: Small fried dough balls, sometimes plain and sometimes filled with cream, custard, or jam. A staple across Lombardy during Carnival, especially in Milan and Crema.

Tortelli Cremaschi (Crema): A unique, sweet-savory stuffed pasta from Crema, usually served at festive occasions. While more of a year-round specialty than a carnival street food, some stalls highlight them during the Carnevale di Crema to emphasize local identity.

Polenta e frittelle (Bagolino). Hearty Alpine dishes often accompany the music and dancing, with sweet frittelle (fried doughnuts) offered as snacks during the processions.

Local sweets in Soncino and Schignano: Stalls sell roasted chestnuts, nougat (torrone, also a Cremona specialty), and simple rustic pastries made with honey and nuts, foods tied to medieval and Alpine traditions.

CHAPTER THIRTY-NINE

Bormio: Easter in the Alps

I Pasquali Pageant of Faith

Easter and I Pasquali

Where: Bormio

When: Easter Sunday

Average Festival Temperatures: High 12°C (54°F). Low 2°C (36°F).

Discover Bormio: Alpine Heritage and Thermal Springs

Steam rises from ancient stone pools as snow-capped peaks tower overhead. Welcome to Bormio, where Romans once soaked their weary bones in the same thermal waters that beckon travelers today. The mineral-rich springs bubble up at a soothing 37°C (99°F), carrying with them the faint scent of sulfur and centuries of history.

Framed by the mountains in the Valtellina Valley at 1,225 meters (4,019 feet), this mountain town of 4,000 residents commands a spectacular position at the foot of the Stelvio Pass. Here, the crisp mountain air carries the sound of church bells echoing off medieval stone walls, while the aroma of wood smoke mingles with the earthy fragrance of pine forests.

Bormio's history stretches back to Roman times, when soldiers and traders first discovered these natural hot springs bubbling from the earth. In the Middle Ages, the town prospered under the Visconti and later the Sforza of Milan, who prized both its strategic location and the rich bounty of its alpine valleys, wheels of aged cheese, air-dried bresaola, and robust red wines that still grace local tables today.

Walking through the town's narrow cobbled streets, your footsteps echo against weathered stone houses whose thick walls have withstood centuries of alpine winters. Frescoed churches reveal glimpses of vibrant colors with deep blues and golden yellows that seem to glow even in the mountain's filtered light, while ancient towers stand sentinel over squares where the clatter of morning markets has echoed for generations.

Though internationally known as a ski resort and challenging stage of the Giro d'Italia cycling race, Bormio's most heartfelt celebration comes not in winter or summer, but at Easter. Each year, the townspeople revive the tradition of I Pasquali, a pageant of faith, craftsmanship, and community spirit that fills the streets with the rustle of period costumes and the warm glow of hundreds of candles on Easter Sunday.

I Pasquali Easter Tradition

The tradition of I Pasquali is one of the most distinctive Easter celebrations I have ever seen. It blends religious devotion with Alpine craftsmanship with community pride. As dawn breaks on Easter Sunday, the scent of fresh pine boughs and wildflowers fills the air while the steady rhythm of hammers and whispered prayers echo from workshops across Bormio's ancient neighborhoods.

The custom dates back to the Middle Ages, when Bormio's contrade (neighborhood guilds) expressed their faith at Easter by preparing offerings for the parish church. The creak of wooden wheels on cobblestones announced the arrival of these humble gifts, carried by hands calloused from mountain work. Over time, these simple offerings blossomed into elaborate wooden floats decorated with cascades of spring flowers, fragrant evergreen boughs, and intricately hand-carved figures depicting biblical scenes of the Passion and Resurrection.

By the sixteenth century, I Pasquali had become an established part of Bormio's Easter observances, organized with great care by the contrade. The sweet fragrance of wood shavings mingles with incense as master craftsmen work by candlelight, their weathered fingers coaxing life from alpine timber. Each group competed not for prizes but for honor and recognition, presenting the most beautiful and meaningful creation as a testimony of faith.

When the procession begins, the ancient stone streets come alive with the soft shuffle of hundreds of feet and the gentle rustle of hand-sewn medieval costumes. Children clutch bouquets of mountain violets while residents lean from flower-draped balconies, their voices joining in centuries-old hymns that seem to rise with the morning mist. The floats themselves are marvels to behold: life-sized figures with expressions so tender they seem to breathe, surrounded by garlands of early spring blooms whose petals catch the filtered Alpine sunlight.

What Are Pasquali?

The word pasquali comes from Pasqua, the Italian word for Easter, and in Bormio it refers to the elaborate wooden floats that form the heart of the town's Easter celebration. Each pasquale is created by one of Bormio's historic neighborhoods, or contrade, and represents a union of faith, craftsmanship, and community tradition.

The floats are built on sturdy wooden frames and decorated with greenery, flowers, fabrics, and hand-carved figures that portray scenes from the Passion and Resurrection of Christ or symbolic images of renewal and hope. Some are intimate in scale, while others are large, intricate tableaux that fill entire piazzas with color and meaning.

Months of preparation are required for each creation. Families contribute in every way, with men working the wood, women preparing costumes and floral arrangements, and children gathering branches and blossoms. On Easter Sunday, the floats are lifted onto the shoulders of young men dressed in traditional Alpine costume, accompanied by women and children in festive attire who process alongside them through the streets.

Men from a contrada in the procession with a pasquale.

The Role of the Contrade

Bormio is divided into historic districts known as contrade, traditional neighborhoods that serve as the backbone of the town's civic and cultural life. These contrade: Dossiglio, Dossorovina, Combo, Maggiore, and others are both community hubs and guardians of local identity.

Each contrada prepares its own pasquale, and months of preparation go into constructing the floats. Men and women carve wood, weave branches, and design figures, while children and elders gather greenery and flowers to decorate the final creation. On Easter morning, the completed floats are carried on the shoulders of men and boys dressed in traditional Alpine costume, accompanied by women in regional dress and children in festive attire.

The pride of the contrade is evident in every detail. Their collective effort ensures that I Pasquali is not only a religious procession but also a living expression of Bormio's communal spirit, transforming the town into a moving tableau of faith and artistry.

Faith and Community

Each float tells a story: Christ carrying the Cross, the Last Supper, the Resurrection, or symbolic images of hope and renewal. When they arrive at the

Church of San Vitale in the town center, the creations are blessed by the parish priest before being displayed in the piazza for all to admire.

When I first saw the procession, I was surprised and delighted to notice that the local children also marched proudly alongside the adults. They carry small versions of the pasquali, some of which I even saw made from Legos. Though the floats are heavy, even for the children, they beam with pride as they show off their creations. Dressed in medieval costumes, they walk with the same dignity as their relatives, eager to be part of the town's cherished tradition.

Festival Foods

Easter Breads and Alpine Specialties

Colomba Pasquale: The classic dove-shaped Easter bread, soft and fragrant, symbolizing peace and resurrection. Topped with almonds and pearl sugar, it graces nearly every holiday table across Italy. This is my favorite Easter Treat.

Uova di Pasqua: Large chocolate eggs, often wrapped in colorful foil and filled with small surprises for children. A joyful Easter tradition enjoyed by families throughout the country.

Pizzoccheri: The signature dish of the Valtellina valley, made from hearty buckwheat pasta cooked with potatoes, greens, butter, and layers of local cheese. Comforting and rich, it represents the Alpine spirit of Bormio.

Sciatt: Small, golden fritters with a crisp exterior and melted cheese center, served hot from the pan. These irresistible bites are a beloved local treat during festivals and family celebrations alike.

Local Meats and Wines: Easter feasts in Bormio often feature cured mountain meats and regional wines from nearby vineyards, bringing a savory balance to the table and completing the celebration of spring.

Walking Tour of Bormio

#1. Piazza Cavour and the Kuerc

Begin the exploration in Piazza Cavour, the main square of Bormio. At its center stands the Kuerc, a medieval structure with an open loggia that once served as the town hall and a gathering place for citizens. During I Pasquali, the square fills with people as the floats pass by on their way to the blessing, making it one of the best vantage points for the celebration.

#2. Collegiate Church of San Gervasio and Protasio

From the piazza, visit the parish church dedicated to Saints Gervasius and Protasius. With origins in the ninth century and later Gothic and Baroque additions, the church preserves frescoes, carved wooden altars, and sacred treasures. It remains a spiritual center of Bormio and an important stop during Easter observances.

#3. Piazza San Vitale

Walk through the narrow lanes to reach Piazza San Vitale, where the blessing of the pasquali takes place on Easter Sunday. The small Church of San Vitale provides the backdrop for this moving ceremony. Outside of festival days, the piazza retains its charm with traditional stone houses and mountain views.

#4. The Civic Museum at Palazzo De Simoni

A quick stroll residence that now houses Bormio's Civic Museum. Exhibits include local art, historical documents, and displays on Alpine life, giving insight into the cultural background that nourishes traditions such as I Pasquali.

#5. Via Roma

Walk along Via Roma, the town's main street lined with noble palazzi, frescoed façades, and shops selling local products. During the procession, this street becomes one of the most atmospheric routes as the floats advance between the medieval stone walls and the lively crowd.

#6. Thermal Baths of Bormio

Conclude the tour with a visit to one of Bormio's famed thermal baths, celebrated since Roman times. The natural hot springs have made the town a place of relaxation for centuries. Today, visitors can choose between historic baths such as Bagni Vecchi or modern spa facilities at Bagni Nuovi. After the intensity of the festival, soaking in the warm mineral waters provides a perfect balance of rest and reflection. See Chapter 38, Immersion Experience: Thermal Bliss.

Logistics

Train: Bormio does not have its own railway station. The nearest station is Tirano, about 30 kilometers (19 miles) away, which is served by Trenord regional trains from Milan. The journey from Milan to Tirano takes around 2.5 hours. From Tirano, regular buses connect to Bormio in about 45 minutes.

Car: For those driving, Bormio can be reached from Milan in approximately 3.5 hours. Take the SS36 north toward Lecco, continue through Valtellina following signs for Sondrio and Tirano, then proceed along the SS38 to Bormio. From Switzerland, scenic routes across the Stelvio Pass and Bernina Pass connect to the valley, though some passes are closed in winter and early spring. Roads during Easter are busy, so allow extra travel time.

Parking: During I Pasquali, traffic in Bormio's historic center is restricted. Designated parking areas are available on the outskirts, with shuttle services and walking routes into the town. Arriving early on Easter Sunday is strongly advised to secure a parking spot, as thousands of visitors come for the parade and blessing.

Restaurant Recommendations

Ristorante Al Filò. Via Dante 6

Set inside a former hayloft with vaulted stone ceilings and candlelit charm, Al Filò is one of Bormio's most atmospheric restaurants. The menu highlights Valtellina specialties such as pizzoccheri, sciatt (fried cheese fritters), and braised meats, paired with Nebbiolo wines from the valley.

Ristorante Vecchia Combo. Via Roma 77

Named after one of Bormio's historic contrade (neighborhoods), this restaurant specializes in homemade pasta and seasonal mountain fare. Dishes like deer stew, risotto with local mushrooms, and buckwheat desserts make it a favorite during festival days.

Day Trip Options: Nearby Sites, Cities, and Towns

Tirano and the Bernina Express. 30 kilometers (19 miles) from Bormio. Tirano, the southern terminus of the famous Bernina Express, is a must for visitors who wish to combine Alpine tradition with one of Europe's most spectacular train journeys. The Bernina line, a UNESCO World Heritage Site, winds through dramatic mountain landscapes, glaciers, and viaducts before descending into Switzerland. See Chapter 24, Immersion Experience: Bernina Express.

Stelvio Pass. 20 kilometers (12 miles) from Bormio. One of the highest paved mountain passes in Europe at 2,757 meters (9,045 feet), the Stelvio Pass is legendary among cyclists and motorists for its twisting hairpin bends and panoramic views. The road usually opens in late May or early June, depending on snow conditions, so visitors arriving around Easter may only be able to ascend part of the route. For cycling information, see Chapter 26, Giro di Lombardia and Cycling in Lombardy.

Livigno. 35 kilometers (22 miles) from Bormio. This duty-free Alpine town near the Swiss border is a lively shopping and sports destination. Known for its ski slopes in winter and hiking trails in summer, Livigno also has a growing reputation for gastronomy, with mountain restaurants serving both Valtellina and Engadine specialties. Its high-altitude location and modern amenities provide a striking contrast to Bormio's medieval charm.

Festivals and Sagre in Bormio and Nearby Towns Throughout the Year

Fiera di San Gervasio e Protasio, Bormio

June 19

This annual fair honors the patron saints of Bormio, Gervasius and Protasius, with religious ceremonies, a festive market in Piazza Cavour, and music in the streets. It is both a devotional occasion and a lively community celebration.

Bormio Stelvio Festival

July and August

A summer cultural festival that brings classical music, chamber concerts, and art events to Bormio and neighboring villages in the Stelvio National Park. Concerts are often held in churches, piazzas, and scenic mountain settings, blending natural beauty with artistic excellence.

Festa della Madonna della Neve, Santa Caterina Valfurva

August 5

In the mountain village of Santa Caterina Valfurva, locals honor the Madonna of the Snow with an outdoor Mass, processions, and traditional food stalls. The setting at high altitude makes this festival especially atmospheric.

Sagra dei Pizzoccheri, Teglio

September

Visitors can sample pizzoccheri prepared in the traditional style with buckwheat pasta, greens, potatoes, and local cheese, all served in the rustic dining halls of the historic town.

Fiera di Ognissanti, Bormio

November 1

Held on All Saints' Day, this historic fair fills Bormio's streets with stalls selling produce, livestock, crafts, and seasonal foods. It is one of the town's oldest traditions, linking back to its medieval role as a trading center for Alpine communities. The atmosphere is lively and authentic, with locals dressed in traditional attire and musicians performing folk tunes. Visitors can sample mountain cheeses, honey, and cured meats while browsing handmade goods that reflect the craftsmanship of the region.

Essentials: Milan and Lombardy

Eat Well, Stay Well, Travel Smart

CHAPTER FORTY

Regional Dishes and Local Specialities

A Culinary Journey

The Flavors of Milan and Lombardy

Lombardy's cuisine reflects the region's geographic diversity, ancient traditions, and refined tastes. From Alpine pastures to elegant urban cafés, each dish tells a story. In Milan, you'll find creamy risottos, delicate braised meats, and beautifully plated dishes served in stylish surroundings. In the countryside and lake towns, food is heartier and often rooted in centuries-old rural customs.

This is a region that prizes high-quality ingredients, slow cooking, and seasonal variety. Olive oil and tomato sauces take a backseat here. Instead, butter, cream, cheese, and polenta are the stars of many dishes, with rice and meat playing important roles as well.

Whether you're enjoying an elegant meal in a Milanese trattoria or savoring fresh lake fish in a quiet village along Lake Como, the food of Lombardy invites you to sit down, take your time, and enjoy every bite.

Lombard Specialties: What to Eat in Milan and Lombardy

Many of Lombardy's dishes are seasonal and tied to tradition. For example, pumpkin-filled pasta often appears in autumn, while hearty stews or game-based dishes are more common in the colder months. Travelers may not find every specialty on menus year-round, but this seasonality is part of the region's authentic rhythm of eating.

Starters and Small Plates

Bresaola della Valtellina: Air-dried salted beef aged until tender and served in thin slices. Typically dressed with lemon juice, arugula, and shaved Grana Padano. A specialty of the Valtellina valley.

Sciat:. Crispy fried cheese fritters made with buckwheat flour, served hot and melty. Beloved street food from the Alpine region.

Lardo di Colonnata: Cured pork fat aged in marble basins with herbs and spices. Served thin on warm bread or polenta.

Insalata di Nervetti: A traditional salad made with veal cartilage, onions, and vinegar. A humble but deeply traditional Milanese dish often found in local osterias.

Pasta, Rice, and First Courses

Risotto alla Milanese: A creamy rice dish made with saffron, beef marrow, white wine, and butter. This luxurious golden risotto is often served alongside ossobuco and is a symbol of Milan's culinary elegance.

Pizzoccheri della Valtellina: Buckwheat pasta tossed with cabbage, potatoes, butter, and melting alpine cheese like Bitto or Casera. Perfect after a day in the mountains.

Tortelli di Zucca: Pumpkin-filled pasta from Mantua seasoned with nutmeg and crumbled amaretti biscuits. Served with melted butter and sage.

Casoncelli alla Bergamasca: Stuffed pasta from Bergamo filled with meat, breadcrumbs, and cheese. Traditionally topped with browned butter, pancetta, and sage.

Minestrone alla Milanese: A vegetable soup with rice enriched with lard or butter. Warm, hearty, and full of seasonal flavor.

Main Courses and Meats

Ossobuco alla Milanese: Braised veal shanks cooked with white wine and vegetables until tender. Served with gremolata, a topping of parsley, garlic, and lemon zest. Often paired with risotto alla Milanese.

Cotoletta alla Milanese: A breaded veal cutlet fried in butter until crisp and golden. Traditionally made with bone-in veal and served simply with lemon.

Cassoeula: A rustic winter stew of pork ribs, sausage, and Savoy cabbage. Rich, warming, and best enjoyed on a wintry day.

Pesce in Carpione: Lake fish such as perch or trout, lightly fried and marinated in vinegar with onions and herbs. Common in lake towns like Como and Iseo.

Bollito Misto: A celebratory dish of boiled meats served with condiments like salsa verde and mostarda di Cremona, a sweet and spicy fruit preserve.

Polenta, Vegetables, and Side Dishes

Polenta Taragna: A creamy polenta made with cornmeal and buckwheat flour, stirred with cheese and butter until rich and smooth. A mountain specialty.

Funghi Porcini: Porcini mushrooms from Lombardy's forests are prized for their earthy flavor. Grilled, sautéed, or added to risotto and polenta.

Mostarda di Cremona: Candied fruits preserved in mustard syrup. A bold companion to meats, cheeses, and holiday feasts.

Asparagi alla Milanese: White or green asparagus topped with a fried egg and shaved cheese. Elegant and seasonal.

Cheeses and Dairy

Taleggio: A soft, washed-rind cheese from Val Taleggio with a pungent aroma and creamy texture. Served on cheese boards or melted into risotto and polenta.

Grana Padano: Hard, aged cheese similar to Parmigiano Reggiano but native to Lombardy. Used for grating over pasta, risotto, and soups.

Bitto: An alpine cheese from Valtellina made with cow's milk and a touch of goat's milk. Aged for months or even years, it develops a complex, nutty flavor.

Breads and Baked Goods

Michetta (Rosetta): A hollow, crusty bread roll typical of Milan. Light and airy inside, perfect for sandwiches or aperitivo spreads.

Desserts and Sweets

Panettone: A tall sweet bread filled with raisins and candied fruit. Originally from Milan, it is now an international symbol of Italian Christmas.

Torrone di Cremona: A traditional nougat made with honey, egg whites, and nuts. Sweet, chewy, and deeply tied to Lombard celebrations.

Torta Sbrisolona: A crumbly almond cake from Mantua, often broken by hand and served with coffee or dessert wine.

Amaretti di Saronno: Crunchy almond cookies often served after meals or paired with sweet wine.

Gelato alla Crema Milanese: A rich custard-style gelato flavored with lemon zest and vanilla. Found in historic gelaterie across Milan.

Digestivi and After-Dinner Drinks

Amaro Ramazzotti: A herbal liqueur born in Milan, often served as a digestivo after meals. Balanced bitterness with notes of citrus and spice.

Fernet-Branca: A bold, bitter digestivo created in Milan in 1845. Known for its intense herbal profile and often enjoyed neat or with soda.

Wines and Drinks

Franciacorta: Lombardy's finest sparkling wine, produced near Brescia using the same method as Champagne. Dry, crisp, and elegant.

Valtellina Superiore: A red wine made from Nebbiolo grapes grown on terraced mountain vineyards. Pairs beautifully with game and stews.

Bonarda: A fruity red wine from the Oltrepò Pavese area, served slightly chilled and ideal with cold cuts and rustic dishes.

Milanese Aperitivo: Enjoy a Campari, Negroni Sbagliato, or Aperol Spritz during aperitivo hour, along with olives, focaccia, and cured meats.

Insider Tips for Dining in Milan and Lombardy

Join the aperitivo tradition. Milan is famous for its pre-dinner drinks and snacks, often enjoyed in beautiful courtyards or stylish lounges.

Lingering Over Meals: The Italian Way. In Lombardy, as in much of Italy, eating is never rushed. Mealtimes are not simply a way to refuel but a social ritual and a chance to savor life. It is perfectly normal (and encouraged) to order antipasto, primo, secondo, contorno, and dolce, enjoying each course at a leisurely pace. A traditional lunch or dinner may last two or even three hours, especially on weekends.

Why It's Important. Many of Lombardy's most beloved dishes, like ossobuco alla milanese, brasato al Barolo, or slow-cooked risotti require time to prepare and are meant to be enjoyed slowly. Dining here is part of the "slow food" movement, a concept that was born in Italy as a reaction to fast food culture.

Reserve ahead. Milan's restaurants, especially those near the Duomo and the lakes, are popular. It's best to plan your meals in advance.

Buon appetito!

CHAPTER FORTY-ONE

Best Dining, Gelato & Drinks in Milan

Beautiful Spots in the Center

Where to Eat and Drink in Milan and Lombardy

Lombardy offers a wide range of dining experiences, from traditional trattorias in quiet villages to elegant restaurants with skyline views in Milan. Knowing what to look for can help you enjoy the region's rich culinary culture more fully:

Trattoria or Osteria: Casual, family-run spots serving local specialties like risotto, braised meats, and house-made pasta.

Ristorante: More formal restaurants, often with a focus on modern presentation and elegant service. Expect wine lists, reservations, and multi-course menus.

Caffè or Bar: Perfect for an early espresso, late-night grappa, or the beloved Milanese aperitivo.

Pasticceria: Bakeries that serve traditional sweets, fresh pastries, and rich coffee.

Gelateria Artigianale: These are often labeled artigianale, meaning the gelato is crafted by hand in small batches using fresh, natural ingredients.

Chocolate Shops: For chocolate lovers, Milan offers refined chocolate shops that combine craftsmanship, innovation, and irresistible flavor

Milan's Best Aperitivo Culture

Aperitivo in Milan is a cherished ritual. Starting around 6:00 p.m., locals gather at cafés and bars to unwind before dinner. A typical aperitivo includes a drink, such as a Negroni Sbagliato, Aperol Spritz, or Campari soda, paired with light snacks like olives, focaccia, and slices of prosciutto. These small bites are known as stuzzichini, a word that loosely translates to "little teasers" or "nibbles."

Stuzzichini can range from simple offerings like nuts and crisps to more refined bites such as crostini with ricotta and honey, tramezzini, miniature quiches, or even arancini. Some bars and lounges, especially in Milan, elevate the aperitivo into a full experience with buffet-style spreads that include pasta salads, risottos, grilled vegetables, and warm dishes, all included in the price of your drink.

Try enjoying aperitivo at a rooftop bar with skyline views or a quiet courtyard café near the Brera district. Look for places buzzing with locals. That is where you will find the most authentic experience, where conversation flows as freely as the prosecco and the stuzzichini keep arriving as you linger a little longer.

Apericena: A Milanese variation of the traditional aperitivo, where the drinks are accompanied by an abundant buffet of food, often enough to serve as dinner.

Where to Enjoy a Memorable Aperitivo in Milan

Bar Basso. Via Plinio 39

Inventor of the Negroni Sbagliato, Bar Basso is a Milanese icon. Order the classic and enjoy it served in an oversized glass with a side of potato chips.

Ceresio 7. Via Ceresio 7

A stylish rooftop with pools, skyline views, and an elegant aperitivo menu. Come for sunset and stay for the scene.

Camparino in Galleria. Piazza del Duomo 21

Located inside the Galleria Vittorio Emanuele II, this historic bar once served Campari to Verdi and Toscanini. The marble counters and polished brass speak of old-world elegance.

Nottingham Forest. Viale Piave 1

Consistently ranked among the world's top bars, this tiny spot serves molecular cocktails and exotic infusions. A unique experience for those craving something unusual.

Dining Recommendations

Centro Storico (Duomo, Galleria, and Surroundings)

Luini. Via Santa Radegonda 16

Famous for its panzerotti, crispy fried dough pockets stuffed with mozzarella and tomato. A local tradition and an ideal quick lunch near the Duomo.

Giacomo Arengario. Via Guglielmo Marconi 1 (inside Museo del Novecento)

An upscale dining experience with a view of the Piazza del Duomo. Elegant Milanese dishes served in a space that balances history and modern design.

Camparino in Galleria. Piazza del Duomo 21

A historic aperitivo bar inside the Galleria Vittorio Emanuele II. Order a Campari-based cocktail and enjoy the timeless ambiance.

Gelateria Artico. Via Dogana 1

Ideal for a post-museum treat or evening stroll through the center.

Brera Neighborhood

Trattoria Torre di Pisa. Via Fiori Chiari 21

A classic Tuscan trattoria with Milanese charm. A neighborhood favorite for its warm atmosphere, house-made pastas, and fine Chianti.

N'Ombra de Vin. Via San Marco 2

Set in a historic cellar, this wine bar offers a romantic setting with a vast wine selection. Perfect for aperitivo with aged cheeses and meats.

Gelateria Marghera Brera. Via Cusani 10

Smooth textures and bold flavors define this stylish gelato shop just steps from Sforza Castle.

Navigli Neighborhood

Osteria del Gnocco Fritto. Via Pasquale Paoli 2

Known for its namesake fried dough served with prosciutto, mortadella, and cheese. The atmosphere is casual and joyful, with generous portions.

El Brellin. Alzaia Naviglio Grande 14

Located in a historic building along the canal, this elegant restaurant specializes in Milanese classics like ossobuco (slow-cooked beef) and risotto alla Milanese.

Mag Café. Ripa di Porta Ticinese 43

One of the city's most iconic cocktail bars. Creative mixology, vintage decor, and a prime canal-side location make this a favorite for aperitivo.

Gelateria Latteneve. Via Vigevano 27

All-natural, seasonal ingredients and innovative flavor combinations. Try the Sicilian almond or fig and ricotta.

Porta Romana Neighborhood

Trippa. Via Giorgio Vasari 1

This trattoria has gained cult status for its modern take on traditional Milanese dishes. Expect bold flavors and a lively local crowd.

Osteria della Via Appia. Via Orti 10

Small and rustic, this osteria serves comforting dishes like cassoeula (winter stew) and brasato (beef cooked in wine) with polenta. Warm service and an old-world feel.

Lacerba. Via Orti 4

Known for its inventive cocktails and steampunk design, this stylish bar is a go-to spot for aperitivo lovers in Porta Romana.

Ciacco Lab Gelato. Via Spadari 13

A short walk away and worth the detour. This gelateria offers gourmet gelato with pure, traceable ingredients. Their pistachio and hazelnut are exceptional.

Isola Neighborhood

Ratanà. Via Gaetano de Castillia 28

Housed in a former industrial building, Ratanà serves sophisticated Lombard cuisine with an emphasis on sustainability and regional sourcing.

Il Liberty. Viale Monte Grappa 6

Elegant and creative cuisine in a refined Art Nouveau setting. The tasting menu is a true journey through contemporary Italian flavors.

Bob Milano. Via Borsieri 30

A fun and modern cocktail bar known for its signature drinks and energetic vibe. Aperitivo includes gourmet finger foods.

Artico Gelateria. Via Luigi Porro Lambertenghi 15

One of the best-rated gelaterias in Milan. Artisanal gelato made in-house with an excellent selection of classic and seasonal flavors.

Porta Venezia Neighborhood

Osteria del Binari. Via Tortona 1

Lush garden seating and classic Milanese fare. A great spot for traditional risotto, roast meats, and rich desserts.

Pavé. Via Felice Casati 27

One of Milan's best pastry shops. Known for buttery croissants, filled brioche, and smooth coffee. Perfect for breakfast or a mid-afternoon break.

Nottingham Forest. Viale Piave 1

A tiny, world-renowned cocktail bar offering molecular cocktails and experimental drinks. Reservations are a must.

Gelato Giusto. Via San Gregorio 17

A charming shop with creative and beautifully balanced flavors. Known for pistachio, lemon with basil, and gianduja.

Milan's Finest Chocolate

For chocolate lovers, Milan offers refined chocolate shops that combine craftsmanship, innovation, and irresistible flavor. Whether you prefer classic pralines, velvety ganache, or artistic creations, these shops provide a luxurious taste of Milan's sweet side.

Zaini Milano. Via de Cristoforis 5 (Porta Garibaldi / Corso Como area)

A stylish chocolate boutique and café from one of Italy's historic chocolate producers, dating back to 1913. Inside, you'll find vintage packaging, thick hot chocolate, and a beautiful selection of handcrafted pralines, bars, and truffles. Ideal for gifts or an indulgent treat.

Chocolat Milano. Via Giovanni Boccaccio 9 (near Cadorna / Sempione)

A modern favorite known for rich hot chocolate in the winter and chocolate gelato in the summer. Their truffles and chocolate-dipped fruits are beautifully crafted, and the stylish atmosphere attracts both locals and visitors.

Odilla Chocolat. Via Andrea Maffei 10 (Porta Romana)

A boutique from Piedmont with a loyal Milan following. Known for its silky gianduja (chocolate of Turin) and hazelnut-rich creations, Odilla offers traditional flavors with an artisanal touch. Try their soft chocolate spreads or handmade chocolate-covered cherries.

Insider Tips for Dining in Milan

Try the aperitivo culture. Milan is where the tradition began. A single drink often includes complimentary snacks, or in some places, access to a full buffet.

Order like a local. Cotoletta alla Milanese is typically veal, bone-in, and fried in butter. Risotto alla Milanese is often served as a first course, not a side dish.

Make reservations. Popular spots fill quickly, especially on weekends and during Fashion Week or Design Week.

Explore by neighborhood. Each area has its own style, flavor, and personality. Let the local atmosphere guide your palate.

From stylish rooftop drinks to canal-side meals, and from hidden osterias to bustling aperitivo bars, Milan's food scene invites you to savor every moment of your stay.

Buon appetito!

CHAPTER FORTY-TWO

Best Coffee and Pastries in Milan

A Taste of Tradition

Coffee Culture in Milan

Coffee in Milan is more than a drink. It is part of the city's rhythm, a moment of pause, a spark of conversation. Whether you are sipping a quick espresso at the bar before a meeting or lingering over a cappuccino and pastry in a quiet courtyard, Milan offers countless ways to enjoy this daily ritual.

In Milan, as in much of Italy, the most authentic coffee experience is often enjoyed al banco, standing at the bar. Locals step inside, greet the barista, and order their coffee in a simple, direct manner. At busy times, you might first pay at the register and take the receipt to the bar, where the barista will prepare your drink. More often, you simply catch the barista's eye, and when they are ready, they will ask "Prego?" or "Cosa le porto?" which means "Please?" or "What can I get you?" This is your cue to order.

Standing at the bar is quick and sociable, and prices are often lower than sitting at a table. Many Milanese treat it as a brief but essential pause in their day, a chance to exchange a few words with the barista or other patrons before returning to work or errands. If you prefer a slower pace, cafés and pasticcerie also offer seated service, often with an array of beautiful pastries, but be prepared to pay a higher coperto or service charge for the privilege.

To order like a local, simply say:
"Vorrei un caffè, per favore"

I would like a coffee, please.

Keep in mind that "caffè" in Italy refers to espresso. There is no need to specify unless you want something different:

- *Caffè lungo* is a milder espresso with more water

- *Caffè macchiato* is espresso with a splash of milk

- *Cappuccino* is milk and foam, typically enjoyed only in the morning

- *Caffè americano* is espresso with added hot water

- *Caffè corretto* is espresso with a shot of liquor

- *Latte macchiato* is hot milk "stained" with a small amount of espresso, usually served in a tall glass

Locals often drink their coffee standing at the bar, where it costs less, and the service is fast. Sitting at a table usually includes a small service charge, but offers the chance to relax, read, or people-watch.

Centro Storico and Duomo

Pasticceria Marchesi 1824. Galleria Vittorio Emanuele II

A Milan institution. Elegant interiors, impeccable service, and finely crafted sweets make this a memorable stop. Sip espresso surrounded by gilded walls and velvet armchairs. I placed this in centro storico but there are actually three locations around town.

Taveggia. Via Uberto Visconti di Modrone 2

Established in 1909, Taveggia is a landmark for coffee and cake lovers. Try the Sacher-style chocolate cake or their signature cannoncini filled with cream.

Pasticceria Cucchi. orso Genova, 1

Near the Basilica of San Lorenzo. Take a step back in time at this historic café that has been serving up coffee in true Milan tradition since 1936. Indulge in a perfectly brewed cappuccino and a delicately baked brioche to start your morning off right.

Brera Neighborhood

Pasticceria Cova. Via Cusani 10

Elegant and historic, Cova serves traditional Milanese pastries with refined coffee in a quiet corner just steps from the Brera Art Gallery. Try the panettone in winter or a fruit tart with your macchiato year-round. I find that if there is a wait to get in the line moves quickly; it is worth it.

Bar Jamaica. Via Brera 32

A longtime artist hangout with a literary past. Known for its strong espresso and old-world atmosphere, it is perfect for a mid-morning coffee after exploring the nearby art district.

Navigli Neighborhood

Panificio Pattini. Via Solari 3

Technically a bakery, but their coffee and morning pastry offerings draw locals daily. Grab a cappuccino and fresh brioche before a walk along the canal.

Taglio. Via Vigevano 10

Modern and relaxed, Taglio serves high-quality coffee and pastries with a small gourmet shop in the back. It is a favorite brunch and breakfast stop in the Navigli area.

Porta Venezia Neighborhood

Pavé. Via Felice Casati 27

Our favorite coffee in Milan. Known for buttery croissants, warm brioche, and excellent cappuccinos, all served in a retro, welcoming space. Great any time of day.

Gelsomina. Via Galvano Fiamma 2

Renowned for maritozzi, pistachio brioche, and a charming terrace setting.

Cafezal Specialty Coffee. Via S. Gregorio 29A

A top-rated specialty coffee spot brought to life by Milan's pioneering Cafezal roastery. Here you'll find expertly crafted espresso, filter coffee, cold brew, and even decaf options, alongside breakfast and lunch offerings in a stylish setting. The café is laptop-friendly, dog-friendly, and offers vegan options, outdoor seating, and a take-away window for quick stops.

Isola Neighborhood

Caffè Pascucci. Piazza Gae Aulenti

Overlooking one of Milan's most modern piazzas, this sleek café is ideal for a break between shops or museums. Espresso, fresh juice, and pastries are served all day.

L'Ile Douce. Via Luigi Porro Lambertenghi 15.

A stylish Italian-French-inspired patisserie offering artisanal desserts and a cozy, homey vibe.

Lambrate area

Panetteria Amordi. Via Porpora 150

A local favorite known for authentic Italian baked goods, pizzas, and hearty offerings at accessible prices.

Porta Romana Neighborhood

Loste Café. Via Francesco Guicciardini 3

Minimalist and modern, this café is known for its expertly brewed coffee, fresh croissants, and sourdough-based pastries. A hidden gem for breakfast or a mid-morning break.

Bar Luce. Largo Isarco 2 (inside Fondazione Prada)

Designed by filmmaker Wes Anderson, Bar Luce offers retro vibes, artistic flair, and excellent coffee and sweets. A cultural stop that blends espresso with style.

Pasticceria Sissi. Piazza Risorgimento 6

A charming, bohemian pâtisserie famed for its fresh brioches filled at the counter and inviting courtyard patio.

Milano Centrale Station

If you find yourself arriving or departing through Milano Centrale, you can still enjoy a good coffee experience. Inside the station, you'll find several bars where you can stand at the counter for a quick espresso before catching your train. Look for Motta Milano 1928, Caffè Napoli, WASCOFFEE Lab, or Storie di Caffè e Pastaria right in the main concourse, all offer reliable coffee and pastries without leaving the station.

For something more atmospheric, step outside the main entrance and look for **Pave – Break** (Via della Moscova, 25), a short walk or one metro stop away, where you can sit down and enjoy artisan pastries with your cappuccino. If you want a classic Milanese experience near the station, try **Caffè Pascucci** or **Panificio Pattini** for an espresso and brioche. This is a perfect way to slow down, even for a few minutes, before continuing your journey.

Buona pausa caffè!

CHAPTER FORTY-THREE

Shopping Experiences Milan

Haute Couture to Local Markets

M ilan is not only Italy's financial powerhouse; it is also its undisputed capital of fashion, design, and style. To shop here is to step onto a living catwalk where couture, craftsmanship, and creativity spill from storefronts into the very streets themselves. From the glamour of the Quadrilatero della Moda to bustling antique markets along the canals, from gourmet food emporiums to art supply shops that keep the city's creative spirit alive, Milan's shopping scene is an experience that engages all the senses.

The Quadrilatero della Moda

Milan's fashion heart beats in the Quadrilatero della Moda, a chic rectangle of streets, Via Montenapoleone, Via della Spiga, Via Sant'Andrea, and Via Manzoni lined with the world's most prestigious boutiques. Strolling here is a must, even without stepping inside.

On Via Montenapoleone, Prada, Gucci, Valentino, and Dolce & Gabbana sparkle in museum-worthy window displays. Via della Spiga, pedestrian-only and intimate, hosts Moschino, Tod's, and Roberto Cavalli, while Via Sant'Andrea features Chanel and Hermès. Via Manzoni links fashion to culture, leading toward Teatro alla Scala.

Milan's jewelry and watchmaking tradition also shines here, from Buccellati's Renaissance-inspired goldwork to Pisa Orologeria's luxury timepieces. Even empty-handed, you'll leave dazzled, the air scented with designer perfume and espresso, the sidewalks alive with stylish locals. During Milan Fashion Week, the district becomes a runway, with photographers, models, and editors filling the streets. It's Milan at its most glamorous, where fashion, culture, and lifestyle converge.

Department Stores and Concept Spaces

Milan balances luxury and exclusivity with grand public shopping experiences. La Rinascente, steps from the Duomo, is the city's legendary department store. Across ten floors you'll find fashion, beauty, home design, and a gourmet food hall. Its rooftop terrace, with sweeping cathedral views, is ideal for an espresso or a sunset aperitivo.

Excelsior Milano offers a sleek, modern take on shopping, combining designer fashion, lifestyle products, and fine food under one striking roof. For something truly distinctive, visit 10 Corso Como. Created by Carla Sozzani in a converted industrial space, it blends fashion, art, books, and a serene garden café. Browsing its concept store and gallery feels like stepping into Milan's creative soul.

Markets and Vintage Finds

Milan's lively markets offer a welcome contrast to its luxury boutiques. Mercato di Viale Papiniano is one of the city's largest open-air markets, packed with stalls selling discounted clothing, shoes, and accessories. Mercato di Via Fauche mixes fashion with food vendors, attracting stylish locals searching for bargains while doing their weekly shopping.

Vintage lovers flock to East Market Milano, a cult favorite in a former aircraft factory, where retro clothing, records, and quirky collectibles draw a young, creative crowd. The most famous market is the Mercatone dell'Antiquariato along the Naviglio Grande. On the last Sunday of each month, over 300 stalls line the canal with antiques, furniture, art, and books. The atmosphere is magical, with sunlight g on the water, the buzz of visitors exploring, and cafés waiting nearby for a leisurely lunch.

Food Shopping: Gourmet Treasures

No Milan shopping guide is complete without its culinary icons. Peck, founded in 1883, is a temple of Italian gastronomy, offering artisanal cheeses, charcuterie, chocolates, and pastries. Its vast wine cellar is a destination in itself, and its upstairs restaurant lets visitors savor Peck's delicacies in style. Eataly Milano Smeraldo celebrates Italian food culture with restaurants, teaching kitchens, and a market perfect for taking home olive oil, wine, or sweets. For a taste of Milanese tradition, historic pastry shops like Pasticceria Marchesi and Cova serve elegant desserts and the city's iconic panettone.

Books, Art, and Design

As Italy's publishing capital, Milan boasts bookstores that mirror its intellectual spirit. Libreria Hoepli, founded in 1870, is one of Europe's largest, while Libreria Bocca in the Galleria Vittorio Emanuele II has been a hub for art and philosophy lovers since 1775. Modern shops like Feltrinelli Duomo offer a sleek space to browse Italian and international titles.

Art enthusiasts can explore Ferrario Belle Arti, serving painters and designers since 1919, and Zecchi Milano, known for its traditional pigments and tools that connect today's artists with Milan's creative past. For design lovers, the Kartell flagship store and the Brera district's mix of artisan shops and galleries are perfect places to find stylish gifts and inspiration.

Antiques and Artisan Discoveries

Brera is Milan's bohemian heart, known for its art academy, museum, and boutiques selling antiques, jewelry, and artisan crafts. Its cobbled streets and hidden courtyards invite slow wandering, with galleries and shops offering rare prints and unique decorative pieces. The Navigli district, once a working canal network designed in part by Leonardo da Vinci, is now a hub for vintage shops and artisan studios by day and a lively dining and nightlife scene after dark.

CHAPTER FORTY-FOUR

Milan Walking Tours and Must-See Sights

Explore Milan at Your Own Pace

M ilan rewards travelers who slow down, looking beyond fashion boutiques
to discover a city of ancient basilicas, Renaissance masterpieces, and
dynamic piazzas. These itineraries are designed to let you walk between sites
logically, weaving together art, faith, and history while giving you the flexibility
to linger where inspiration strikes.

One Day: Historic Core

If you only have a single day in Milan, the best approach is to concentrate on the
historic heart of the city. While it isn't possible to see everything, you can choose
the highlights that interest you most. Begin in the city's iconic central square,
a gathering place for centuries, framed by monumental architecture and alive
with the energy of locals and visitors alike. From here, Milan's most celebrated
landmarks and treasures are all within easy reach.

Duomo di Milano. The largest church in Italy and the symbol of Milan, the
Duomo is a masterpiece of Gothic architecture that took nearly six centuries
to complete. Inside, its soaring nave is illuminated by immense stained-glass

windows telling biblical stories in radiant color. Outside, climb to the rooftop terraces early in the day to wander among spires and statues with unmatched panoramic views of the city skyline. Tickets should be purchased in advance online, especially for rooftop access and the elevator option.

Museo del Duomo. Housed in the Palazzo Reale complex, this museum is included with cathedral admission and offers a deeper look at the Duomo's history. Visitors can admire original statues, stained-glass panels, gargoyles, and architectural models that once adorned the cathedral itself. The collection provides context for the monumental effort of constructing such a vast Gothic landmark over many generations.

https://www.duomomilano.it

Palazzo Reale. Once the royal palace of Milan's rulers, this neoclassical building now serves as the city's premier exhibition venue. Its spacious galleries host blockbuster shows ranging from Renaissance masters to contemporary art. Even if you are not attending an exhibition, the palace itself is worth a visit for its elegant halls and sweeping views of Piazza del Duomo.

https://www.palazzorealemilano.it

Galleria Vittorio Emanuele II. Step into one of the world's most beautiful shopping arcades, a 19th-century glass-and-iron masterpiece often called the "living room of Milan." Its mosaics, luxury boutiques, and cafés make it as much an architectural gem as a shopping destination. Be sure to spin on the mosaic bull set into the floor, a quirky local tradition said to bring good luck.

Palazzo Marino. Facing Piazza della Scala, this 16th-century palace is today Milan's City Hall. Its Renaissance façade and grand interiors reflect the power and prestige of the families who once lived here. Free guided tours (available by advance booking) allow visitors to admire its frescoed rooms and discover the role Palazzo Marino has played in civic life for centuries.

Piazza Mercanti. Tucked just behind the Duomo, this charming square was the center of Milan's medieval commercial life. Surrounded by Gothic and Renaissance palaces, it feels worlds away from the bustle of the cathedral square. Look for the Loggia degli Osii, decorated with statues and balconies from which official proclamations were once read to the public.

Lunch Suggestion: Camparino in Galleria. At the entrance to the Galleria Vittorio Emanuele II, this historic café opened in 1915 and quickly became a Milanese institution. Known as the birthplace of the Campari aperitivo, it is the perfect spot to enjoy a light lunch or midday drink. The art nouveau interiors and lively atmosphere make it as memorable as the aperitivo itself.

Castello Sforzesco & Musei del Castello. A short walk brings you to this massive 15th-century fortress built by the Sforza family, one of Renaissance Italy's most powerful dynasties. Today, its courtyards are open to all, while its museums hold treasures ranging from Egyptian artifacts to musical instruments. The highlight is Michelangelo's unfinished Rondanini Pietà, his final work, displayed in a simple, moving setting.

https://www.milanocastello.it/

Parco Sempione & Arco della Pace. Behind the castle stretches Milan's most beloved park, Parco Sempione, laid out in the 19th century. Shady pathways, ponds, and open lawns make it ideal for a late-afternoon stroll. Continue through to the Arco della Pace, the "Arch of Peace," whose sculpted horses and triumphant figures glow in the golden light of sunset, a perfect finale to your first day in Milan.

Day 2: Renaissance and Baroque Marvels

Santa Maria delle Grazie and The Last Supper. This UNESCO World Heritage church is home to Leonardo da Vinci's masterpiece, *The Last Supper,* one of the most celebrated works of Western art. The painting captures the dramatic moment Christ announces his betrayal, with astonishing detail and emotional intensity. Only small groups are admitted for 15 minutes at a time, so reservations are required months in advance.

https://cenacolovinciano.org

Leonardo's Vineyard (Vigna di Leonardo). Across from Santa Maria delle Grazie lies a restored vineyard once owned by Leonardo da Vinci. Given to him by Ludovico Sforza, it was Leonardo's retreat while painting The Last Supper. Today, visitors can stroll the tranquil garden, explore the historic Casa degli Atellani, and enjoy a glimpse into the master's daily life beyond his art.

https://www.vignadileonardo.com

San Maurizio al Monastero Maggiore. Known as the Sistine Chapel of Milan, this church dazzles with frescoes by Bernardino Luini and his workshop covering nearly every surface. Biblical scenes unfold across walls and ceilings, immersing visitors in Renaissance color and devotion. Once part of a Benedictine convent, its hidden nuns' choir holds some of the most exquisite frescoes in the city.

Pinacoteca Ambrosiana. Founded in 1618 by Cardinal Federico Borromeo, this gallery houses masterpieces by Caravaggio, Raphael, Botticelli, and Titian. Its collection also includes Leonardo da Vinci's Codex Atlanticus, a compilation of his scientific sketches and inventions. The Ambrosiana combines art, history, and scholarship in one unforgettable visit. This is my favorite museum in Milan.

https://www.ambrosiana.it

Casa degli Omenoni. Built in the sixteenth century for sculptor Leone Leoni, this palace is named for the eight massive stone figures on its façade. These muscular statues give the building a strikingly dramatic presence, unusual even in a city rich with Renaissance architecture. Though the interior is rarely open, the exterior is a remarkable example of Milan's architectural boldness.

Casa Manzoni. The residence of novelist Alessandro Manzoni, author of I Promessi Sposi, has been preserved as a museum. Visitors can see his library, furnishings, and personal items that reflect nineteenth-century Milanese life. Exhibitions here also highlight his enduring influence on Italian literature and culture.

https://www.casadelmanzoni.it

San Fedele. Built in the late sixteenth century for the Jesuit order, this church reflects their emphasis on clarity and devotion. Inside are elegant altars and artworks, including pieces by Simone Peterzano, the teacher of Caravaggio. The crypt has been reimagined as a contemporary art space, creating a unique dialogue between tradition and modernity.

https://www.centrosanfedele.net

San Giorgio al Palazzo. Founded in the eighth century and later rebuilt, this church holds significant frescoes by Bernardino Luini. Its intimate interior encourages quiet reflection, while its chapels display Renaissance artistry in an unassuming setting. Located close to the heart of Milan, it makes for a peaceful yet inspiring stop.

Evening in Brera. End the day wandering the artistic Brera district, with its cobbled lanes, boutiques, and inviting restaurants. Once the haunt of artists and intellectuals, Brera still exudes a bohemian atmosphere that contrasts with Milan's grander districts. Enjoy a relaxed dinner at a trattoria, accompanied by a glass of local Lombard wine.

https://pinacotecabrera.org

Day 3: Sacred Heritage and Hidden Gems

Basilica di Sant'Ambrogio. Founded in the 4th century by Milan's patron saint, this basilica is one of the most important examples of Romanesque architecture in Italy. The interior has a striking simplicity, with golden mosaics in the apse and the shrine of Saint Ambrose alongside Saints Gervasius and Protasius. The basilica's cloisters and museum provide further insight into its long spiritual and civic history.

https://www.basilicasantambrogio.it

Archaeological Excavations Beneath the Duomo. Included with certain Duomo tickets, these excavations reveal Milan's ancient foundations. Visitors descend below the cathedral to see the remains of early Christian baptisteries and Roman walls. The site evokes the many layers of Milan's history, adding a fascinating dimension to a visit already centered on the great Gothic church.

https://www.duomomilano.it

Basilica di San Lorenzo Maggiore and Colonne di San Lorenzo. This early Christian basilica is among the oldest churches in Milan, rebuilt over centuries and notable for its octagonal chapel of Saint Aquilino with stunning mosaics. In front of the church stand the ancient Roman Colonne di San Lorenzo, sixteen Corinthian columns that evoke the city's imperial past. The square here has become a lively gathering place, blending antiquity with the rhythm of modern life.

https://www.basilicasanlorenzo.com

Civico Museo Archeologico. In a former monastery near San Lorenzo, this archaeological museum showcases Milan's Roman heritage. Visitors can explore artifacts from the Roman, Etruscan, and early medieval periods, as well as the remains of Milan's Roman walls and towers. The cloisters and gardens offer a peaceful setting to reflect on the city's deep history.

https://museoarcheologicomilano.it

Santa Maria presso San Satiro. A small but remarkable church designed by Bramante, it is famous for its illusionistic apse. The brilliant use of perspective creates the impression of a deep choir space, though it is only a few feet deep. This architectural trick, combined with elegant Renaissance details, makes San Satiro one of Milan's most fascinating sacred spaces.

Basilica di Sant'Eustorgio. Traditionally associated with the relics of the Magi, Sant'Eustorgio is an essential stop for those interested in Milan's early Christian history. The highlight is the Portinari Chapel, a Renaissance jewel decorated with magnificent frescoes by Vincenzo Foppa. The basilica also houses an archaeological area and museum that trace its long evolution.

https://www.basilicasanteustorgio.it

Basilica di San Nazaro Maggiore. Founded by Saint Ambrose in the 4th century, this basilica was originally dedicated to the Apostles. Its distinctive Romanesque plan includes the circular Chapel of Saint Aquilino, rich with mosaics and relics. Although quieter than the Duomo or Sant'Ambrogio, it is a place of great historical and spiritual resonance.

Naviglio Grande and Museo Diocesano. In the afternoon, head to the Navigli district, where Milan's historic canals once linked the city to Lake Maggiore and beyond. The lively Naviglio Grande is now lined with cafés, boutiques, and art studios, making it a perfect spot for an evening stroll and aperitivo. Nearby, the Museo Diocesano offers a fine collection of sacred art housed in the former cloisters of Sant'Eustorgio.

https://museodiocesano.it

Day 4: Brera and the Northwest

Pinacoteca di Brera. Milan's premier art gallery, the Pinacoteca di Brera holds an extraordinary collection of Renaissance and Baroque masterpieces. Highlights include Raphael's *Marriage of the Virgin*, Caravaggio's *Supper at Emmaus*, and works by Mantegna, Piero della Francesca, and Bellini. The museum is located in the historic Brera Palace, which also houses an elegant botanical garden.

https://pinacotecabrera.org

Brera District. Surrounding the Pinacoteca is Milan's most artistic neighborhood, known for its bohemian charm. Narrow cobbled streets are lined with art galleries, antique shops, and inviting cafés, creating an atmosphere that has long attracted artists and intellectuals. The district is especially lively in the evenings, when locals and visitors gather for aperitivo.

Ponte delle Gabelle. A charming canal bridge near Via San Marco, the Ponte delle Gabelle is one of the few reminders of Milan's once-vast network of waterways. Its name recalls the taxes once collected on goods transported through the canals. Today, it is a quiet and photogenic corner, ideal for a short stroll or a memorable photo stop.

Chiuse di Leonardo (Locks of Leonardo). Nearby are canal locks designed with input from Leonardo da Vinci as part of the Navigli system. These ingenious works of engineering allowed boats to navigate different water levels, boosting Milan's importance as a trading city. Visitors can still see the historic lock gates, a reminder of Leonardo's enduring influence on Milan's infrastructure.

San Marco. This Gothic church is one of the largest in Milan and has played host to figures such as Leonardo da Vinci and Mozart. The façade blends Gothic and Baroque elements, while the interior preserves impressive altars and artworks. The organ is among the oldest and most important in the city, and concerts are often held here.

Orto Botanico di Brera. Tucked behind the Pinacoteca, this historic botanical garden offers a peaceful escape from the bustle of the city. Established in the 18th century by the Austrian Habsburgs, it features rare plants, medicinal herbs, and ancient trees. It remains a hidden gem, perfect for a tranquil stroll.

https://ortibotanici.unimi.it

Day 5: Civic Icons and Modern Treasures

Piazza Cordusio. Once the financial heart of Milan, this square is surrounded by elegant late 19th and early 20th century buildings. Today it is a hub for shops, cafés, and offices, but it keeps the grandeur of its Belle Époque origins. From here, it is only a short walk back to the Duomo or the Galleria Vittorio Emanuele II.

Piazza Affari and Palazzo Mezzanotte. This square is home to Milan's stock Exchange, housed in the Palazzo Mezzanotte built in the 1930s. Outside stands the famous sculpture *L.O.V.E.* by Maurizio Cattelan. The combination of classical architecture and bold modern art captures Milan's dual character.

Palazzo Litta. One of Milan's oldest Baroque palaces, Palazzo Litta has hosted emperors, nobles, and cultural events for centuries. The grand courtyard and richly decorated interiors illustrate the wealth and taste of Milan's ruling families. Today, it is used for exhibitions, concerts, and events, continuing its role as a center of Milanese culture.

https://palazzolitta.org

Museo del Novecento. Located beside the Duomo in the Palazzo dell'Arengario, this museum focuses on 20th-century Italian art. Visitors can admire works by Futurists such as Boccioni and Carrà, as well as pieces by Morandi, De Chirico, and Fontana. The top floor offers a spectacular view of the Duomo's spires, making it both an artistic and architectural highlight.

https://museodelnovecento.org

Bagatti Valsecchi Museum. Located in Milan's Fashion District, this house museum is one of Europe's best preserved examples of a Renaissance Revival residence. Its ornate rooms are filled with decorative arts, arms, and furnishings collected by the Bagatti Valsecchi brothers in the 19th century. Walking through the richly decorated interiors and intimate courtyard feels like stepping back into another era.

https://museobagattivalsecchi.org

San Bernardino alle Ossa. This unusual church is famous for its ossuary chapel, decorated with human skulls and bones arranged in intricate patterns. Established in the 13th century when the cemetery overflowed, it is both eerie and fascinating. The main church is peaceful, but the ossuary leaves a lasting impression on all who visit.

Experience-Based Enhancements

These curated experiences and tours are offered through Milan-based providers and trusted platforms such as Viator. Whether you seek culinary indulgence, design discovery, or cultural immersion, these are wonderful ways to deepen your connection with the city at the end of long sightseeing days.

Patisserie Tour or Chocolate Walk. For travelers with a sweet tooth, Milan offers historic pastry shops and chocolatiers worth discovering. A guided walk introduces visitors to delicate pralines, artisan cakes, and iconic Milanese desserts such as panettone. It is a delightful way to combine culture with indulgence while supporting local traditions.

Local Wine Tastings. Milan's enotecas (wine bars) provide intimate tastings of Lombard wines, particularly from regions such as Franciacorta and Valtellina. Many of the best venues are in the Navigli or Porta Romana districts, where sommeliers explain the history of each varietal. This experience pairs perfectly with aperitivo and offers a flavorful introduction to Lombardy's wine heritage.

Fashion and Design Tours. Milan is Italy's fashion capital, and guided tours offer access to showrooms, ateliers, and designer districts. In the Quadrilatero della Moda, visitors can explore the boutiques of Via Montenapoleone and Via della Spiga while learning about the city's sartorial (tailor-made) history. For design lovers, visits to showrooms during Milan Design Week or curated walking tours highlight the city's cutting-edge creativity.

Cooking Classes in Milan. Hands-on cooking experiences in Milan often focus on traditional Lombard dishes such as risotto alla Milanese or ossobuco. Local chefs welcome visitors into kitchens for small-group classes that end with a shared meal. It is a warm and interactive way to carry a taste of Milan home.

https://cesarine.com/en

CHAPTER FORTY-FIVE

Itineraries for Milan & Lombardy

Lake Como and Lake Garda

Milan is often a gateway city, but it deserves more than a single rushed night at the beginning or end of a journey. Its soaring Gothic Duomo, Renaissance treasures, and world-class shopping provide enough to fill several days, while its position at the heart of northern Italy makes it an ideal springboard to the lakes, the Alps, and nearby historic towns.

These itineraries are designed to help you plan time in Milan in combination with the wider region. Each balances art, culture, and leisure while leaving room for aperitivo hours and lakeside strolls. Trains connect most of these destinations efficiently, though renting a car offers flexibility if you plan to explore small towns or wineries.

Classic Northern Italy Week (9–10 Nights)

Arrive in Milan: 3 nights

Settle into the city and spend three days exploring its highlights: the Duomo rooftop, Leonardo's *Last Supper* at Santa Maria delle Grazie, and the frescoed splendor of San Maurizio al Monastero Maggiore. Stroll the Galleria Vittorio

Emanuele II, linger in the Brera district, and enjoy an evening performance at La Scala if tickets are available.

Lake Como: 3 nights

From Milano Centrale, trains to Como or Varenna take less than an hour. Base yourself in Como town or in romantic Bellagio. Spend your days gliding across the lake by ferry, visiting villas such as Villa Carlotta and Villa del Balbianello, and dining on terraces with mountain views.

Verona: 2 nights

Travel east to Verona, city of opera and romance. Visit the Roman Arena, still hosting summer performances, Juliet's House with its famous balcony, and elegant Renaissance piazzas alive with cafés. Stroll across the Ponte Pietra bridge for views of the Adige River winding through the city. A day trip into the Valpolicella wine country pairs history with tastings of Amarone in family-run vineyards, a perfect complement to Verona's timeless charm.

Return to Milan: 1 night

Spend your final night back in Milan. Shop along Via Montenapoleone, enjoy a farewell aperitivo on a rooftop bar overlooking the Duomo, and prepare for your flight home.

Milan & the Lakes (7 Nights)

Milan: 3 nights

Dedicate your first days to the city: art at the Pinacoteca di Brera, shopping in the Quadrilatero della Moda, and evenings in the Navigli canals district.

Lake Como: 2 nights

Choose **Varenna** if you prefer a quieter village atmosphere with easy train access from Milan, or **Bellagio** if you want the postcard-perfect lake setting with elegant villas, gardens, and boutique shopping. From either base, ferries run frequently, making it simple to hop between towns. Spend one day gliding across the water, stopping in **Menaggio** or **Tremezzo** to explore villas and lakeside cafés. Don't miss Villa Carlotta, with its sculpture galleries and gardens cascading down to the shore, or Villa del Balbianello, famed for its terraced gardens and film appearances in *James Bond* and *Star Wars*.

In the evenings, stroll the lakeside promenade as the mountains reflect in the water, their peaks glowing at sunset. Enjoy dinner at a trattoria overlooking the lake, where risotto al pesce persico (perch risotto) is a specialty. For walkers, Varenna offers a scenic lakeside path, the Passeggiata degli Innamorati (lovers walk), while Bellagio has narrow cobbled lanes that climb up from the waterfront, filled with artisan shops and wine bars.

Lake Garda: 2 nights

Take a train from Milan to either **Desenzano del Garda** or **Peschiera del Garda**, both lively towns with excellent connections and ferry services. Desenzano has a cosmopolitan feel, with a broad lakeside promenade, Roman villa remains, and vibrant piazzas, while Peschiera is a fortified town whose historic walls are a UNESCO World Heritage Site.

Dedicate one day to **Sirmione**, a fairytale peninsula town crowned by the Scaliger Castle. Climb the castle tower for sweeping views of the lake and Alps, then relax at the town's historic thermal baths, known since Roman times for their healing waters. The Grotte di Catullo, the ruins of a vast Roman villa at the tip of the peninsula, offer a fascinating glimpse into antiquity framed by olive groves and turquoise water.

On your second day, take a ferry eastward to **Bardolino** or **Lazise**. Bardolino is famous for its red wines, with tastings available at lakeside enotecas, while Lazise charms visitors with its medieval walls, small harbor, and café-lined streets. Both towns are best enjoyed at a leisurely pace, wander, sip a spritz by the water, and allow the rhythm of lake life to slow you down. Evenings on Lake Garda are magical, with warm breezes, lakeside dining, and the lights of hillside villages twinkling across the water.

Return to Milan for onward travel.

Milan & the Alps (7–8 Nights)

Milan: 2 nights

Focus on the city's iconic sights: the Duomo, Galleria Vittorio Emanuele II, and Castello Sforzesco.

Bernina Express via Tirano: 1 night
Take the train to Tirano (2.5 hours), where the Bernina Express begins. This UNESCO-listed railway winds through glaciers and alpine valleys to St. Moritz in Switzerland. Stay overnight in St. Moritz or return to Tirano.

Lake Como: 3 nights
Relax after your alpine adventure with a few days on the lake. Explore gardens, hike trails above Varenna, or simply linger with gelato by the water.

Milan return: 1 or 2 nights
Wrap up with a last chance for shopping or an evening at La Scala before flying home.

Art & History Focus (7 Nights)

Milan: 4 nights
Dive deep into the city's cultural treasures. Spend time at the Pinacoteca Ambrosiana to view Leonardo's *Codex Atlanticus*, visit San Maurizio al Monastero Maggiore for Luini's frescoes, and tour the Museo del Novecento for modern Italian art. Don't miss Bramante's perspective illusion at Santa Maria presso San Satiro.

Day trips from Milan:

- *Pavia:* Visit the Certosa di Pavia, one of the most ornate Renaissance monasteries in Europe.

- *Bergamo:* Wander the medieval Città Alta and admire the frescoes in Cappella Colleoni.

Bergamo: 2 nights
Stay in the hilltop town to enjoy quiet evenings after day-trippers depart. Its winding alleys, historic churches, and panoramic views over Lombardy make it one of northern Italy's most atmospheric towns.

Milan return: 1 night
Enjoy a final dinner in Brera or the Navigli district before departure.

Practical Notes

- **Trains**: Trenitalia and Italo connect Milan with Verona, Como, Bergamo, and Pavia. High-speed trains are best booked in advance (www.trenitalia.com, www.italotreno.it).

- **Local transport**: Metro and trams are efficient in Milan. Ferries on Lake Como and Lake Garda are ideal for exploring lakeside towns.

- **Timing flights**: Always return to Milan the night before departure, as early trains can be delayed.

These itineraries combine the elegance of Milan with the beauty of northern Italy's lakes and towns, allowing travelers to experience both city sophistication and timeless landscapes.

Extend Your Journey with my Immersion Travel Italy Podcast

For those who want to go even deeper into the lakes, I've created two dedicated podcast series:

- **Lake Garda Podcast Series (5 episodes)** covering the north, south, east, and west shores, plus activities from hiking and biking to wine tasting.

- **Lake Como Podcast Series (5 episodes)** exploring the western, northern, and eastern branches of the lake, with history, town guides, ferry tips, and recommendations for dining with a view.

- **Lago Maggiore Podcast Series (5 episodes)** featuring the Italian and Swiss shores, the famous Borromean Islands, plus villa gardens, lakeside towns from Stresa to Locarno, and cable car excursions to mountain viewpoints.

You can listen to both series on my **Immersion Travel Italy Podcast** here: https://katerinaferrara.com/video-podcast/

CHAPTER FORTY-SIX

Stay in Style: Accommodations

Milan First, Lombardy by City

Accommodation Recommendations

Milan then Beyond

Milan is the natural starting point for any journey through Lombardy. As the region's transportation hub, most visitors begin and end their stay here, so this chapter opens with detailed neighborhood recommendations for the city.

Here you will find the hotel recommendations for Milan followed by the rest of the Lombardy towns included in this guide. Each town has its own section, making it easy to locate where to stay whether you are attending a festival in Bergamo, exploring Mantua's Renaissance treasures, or enjoying the lakeside atmosphere of Sirmione.

This structure allows you to compare options across the region at a glance while still providing the depth and detail needed for each destination.

Milan's Best Neighborhoods and Accommodations

Choosing the right neighborhood in Milan can transform your experience. From the elegance of Brera to the creative pulse of Isola and the timeless beauty near the Duomo, each district offers a unique atmosphere and local flavor. This chapter will guide you through the most popular neighborhoods and recommend hotels that reflect the character and convenience of each.

Understanding Hotel Options

Milan offers everything from five-star luxury in historic palazzi to boutique hotels in fashionable quarters and design-forward stays in up-and-coming areas. When choosing your accommodation, consider your interest in museums, shopping, nightlife, or proximity to the train station or metro lines.

Three-star hotels
Comfortable and well-situated, these often feature modern design or classic Milanese charm. Ideal for travelers seeking value with reliable amenities.

Four-star hotels
Often found in historic buildings or modern boutique settings, four-star hotels offer higher service standards, elegant interiors, and upgraded breakfasts.

Five-star hotels
Expect luxury service, refined design, and locations near the city's cultural heart. These are often located near Via Montenapoleone, the Duomo, or Parco Sempione.

Boutique and design hotels are abundant in Milan and often highlight the city's artistic flair, with curated decor and personalized service.

Milan: Recommended Hotels by Neighborhood

Duomo and Centro Storico

I prefer to stay as close to the Duomo in any Italian town as possible. The Duomo is almost always the absolute center of the town, the hub of daily life, and the focal point of any major events or celebrations. In Milan, this area is home to the breathtaking Duomo, the Galleria Vittorio Emanuele II with its soaring glass arcades, and some of the most elegant shops, cafés, and restaurants in the city.

Staying here means you are in the very heart of the action, with the majority of the centro storico's historic streets, architectural gems, and cultural sites just a short stroll away. You can wander from morning coffee to evening aperitivo without ever needing a taxi or public transport, making it the most convenient and atmospheric base for exploring Milan.

Park Hyatt Milan. Via Tommaso Grossi 1

Five-star elegance in a neoclassical palazzo just steps from the Duomo. Sophisticated design, attentive service, and luxurious rooms make this a favorite for discerning travelers.

Room Mate Giulia. Via Silvio Pellico 4

Boutique hotel with a playful modern design just behind the Galleria. Artistic interiors inspired by Milanese culture, warm hospitality, and an unbeatable central location.

Hotel Spadari al Duomo. Via Spadari 11

Elegant and quiet, just minutes from the Duomo. Art-filled rooms, professional service, and local charm make this four-star a favorite for repeat visitors.

Brera and Montenapoleone

Historic charm, high-end fashion, and an artsy atmosphere. Ideal for elegant strolls, café culture, and boutique shopping.

Hotel Milano Scala. Via dell'Orso 7

Eco-conscious four-star hotel with vertical gardens and rooftop views. Near Teatro alla Scala and the Brera district's art galleries.

Hotel Manzoni. Via Santo Spirito 20

Tucked into the fashion district, this boutique luxury hotel is ideal for shoppers and design lovers. Interiors blend classic Italian elegance with contemporary details.

Brera Apartments. Multiple locations in Brera

Stylish serviced apartments ideal for travelers who want a longer stay or more independence. Excellent for those looking to explore Milan at a relaxed pace.

Navigli and Porta Genova

Lively and romantic, known for canals, nightlife, and a bohemian spirit. Great for evening walks and aperitivo culture.

Maison Borella. Alzaia Naviglio Grande 8

Charming four-star hotel with canal views, rustic wooden beams, and a peaceful inner courtyard. A romantic base in a lively district.

Combo Milano. Ripa di Porta Ticinese 83

Design-forward hostel meets boutique hotel. Offers private rooms and shared spaces with an artsy vibe. Ideal for younger travelers and creatives.

Art Hotel Navigli. Via Angelo Fumagalli 4

Modern hotel with contemporary decor, an excellent rooftop terrace, and spa facilities. A comfortable stay close to bars and galleries.

Isola and Porta Garibaldi

A hub for innovation, architecture, and nightlife. Easy access to transport and trendsetting cafés.

Hotel VIU Milan. Via Aristotele Fioravanti 6

Five-star modern luxury with a rooftop pool, panoramic views, and sleek interiors. Walking distance to Piazza Gae Aulenti and the Bosco Verticale.

Porta Venezia

Elegant and residential with Liberty-style architecture, leafy streets, and excellent dining. LGBTQ+ friendly and walkable.

Hotel Sanpi Milano. Via Lazzaro Palazzi 18

Charming four-star hotel with a lovely internal garden. Near the park and Corso Buenos Aires shopping district.

Château Monfort. Corso Concordia 1

A fairytale-themed five-star hotel housed in an Art Nouveau building. Dreamlike rooms, refined cuisine, and a romantic atmosphere.

Booking Accommodations for Milan's Festivals

Book early during major events like Fashion Week (February and September), Design Week (April), and the Christmas holidays. Milan is a business city, so rooms fill quickly during conferences and trade fairs.

Best areas during festivals
Centro Storico, Brera, and Porta Venezia provide easy access to event venues, galleries, and public transport.

Accommodation Recommendations beyond Milan

When your travels take you outside Milan, staying overnight can transform a day trip into a richer, more immersive experience. Lombardy's towns and cities are full of charming boutique hotels, elegant historic residences, and welcoming B&Bs where you can slow down and connect with the local rhythm. Whether you're attending a festival, exploring medieval streets, or sampling regional cuisine, choosing the right place to stay allows you to enjoy the evenings when the day-trippers have gone and the atmosphere becomes more intimate and relaxed.

Bergamo Accommodation

For the Bergamo Film Meeting, the Bergamo Jazz Festival, or a general visit, I recommend staying at least two to three nights to enjoy the festivals and explore both the Città Alta and Città Bassa at a relaxed pace.

Relais San Lorenzo. Address: Piazza Mascheroni, 9/A (Città Alta)

A luxury boutique hotel blending contemporary design with medieval architecture. Rooms feature modern comforts and sleek lines, some with views of the Venetian Walls. The on-site restaurant offers gourmet cuisine in an elegant historic setting.

Hotel Piazza Vecchia. Address: Via Colleoni, 3 (Città Alta)

Charming and intimate, this hotel sits just steps from the heart of the Città Alta. Its rooms combine traditional décor with modern amenities, and the warm hospitality makes it a favorite for festivalgoers wanting to stay within the historic walls.

GombitHotel. Address: Via Mario Lupo, 6 (Città Alta)

A stylish, design-forward property next to the medieval Gombito Tower. The interiors pair contemporary art with historic architecture, offering a unique stay in one of Bergamo's most photographed areas.

Hotel Excelsior San Marco. Address: Piazza della Repubblica, 6 (Città Bassa)

Well-positioned near the funicular to the Città Alta, this hotel offers comfortable rooms, a rooftop restaurant with panoramic city views, and easy access to both festival venues and shopping streets.

NH Bergamo. Address: Via Paleocapa, 1/G (Città Bassa)

A modern, centrally located hotel close to the train station and Teatro Donizetti. Ideal for those attending multiple events, it offers comfortable rooms, professional service, and quick transport links.

Bormio Accommodation

For Easter in Bormio, I recommend staying at least four nights, arriving on Thursday or Friday. This allows you to experience the Good Friday and Easter Sunday processions, enjoy traditional holiday meals, and still have time to relax in the town's famous thermal baths or take a spring walk in the surrounding mountains.

Hotel Bagni Vecchi. Via Bagni Vecchi

This historic hotel, set above town, is famous for its thermal baths that have been used since Roman times. Guests stay in rustic Alpine rooms and enjoy access to outdoor hot spring pools with panoramic views of the valley. It is a very atmospheric choice for combining the festival with Bormio's spa heritage.

Hotel Bagni Nuovi. Via Bagni Nuovi

A grand nineteenth-century villa converted into a luxury spa hotel. Rooms are elegant, with high ceilings and period furnishings, and guests have direct access to one of the largest spa complexes in the Alps. Ideal for those seeking relaxation after the bustle of the festival.

Hotel San Lorenzo. Via San Lorenzo 2

A centrally located hotel that blends traditional Alpine style with modern comforts. Just steps from Piazza Cavour and Via Roma, it is perfect for those who want to be close to the heart of the Easter celebrations.

Albergo San Vitale. Via San Vitale 19

A small, family-run hotel located near the church of San Vitale, where the pasquali blessing takes place. Its intimate setting and warm hospitality make it an excellent choice for travelers who want to immerse themselves in the local tradition.

Brescia Accommodation

For the festival or a general visit, I recommend staying for two to three nights in Brescia to fully enjoy the city and nearby attractions.

Hotel Vittoria. Via X Giornate, 20

A five-star art déco hotel in the heart of the historic center. The property offers elegant rooms, a rooftop terrace with panoramic views, and a refined restaurant. Steps from Piazza della Loggia and the principal shopping streets, it is ideal for travelers seeking luxury and convenience.

Centro Paolo VI. Via Gezio Calini, 30

Housed in a 17th-century palace with a beautiful cloister, Centro Paolo VI combines historical charm with modern amenities. Rooms are spacious, and the on-site restaurant serves both Italian and international dishes. The tranquil gardens offer a welcome retreat after a day of sightseeing.

Hotel Ambasciatori. Via Crocefissa di Rosa, 92

Located just outside the historic center, this four-star hotel features modern rooms, a fitness area, and excellent breakfast service. It is within walking distance of key sites and offers on-site parking for those arriving by car.

Il Leoncino. Viale Italia, 19

A charming bed-and-breakfast with bright, contemporary rooms and friendly service. The location is convenient for both the train station and the historic center, making it an excellent base for exploring Brescia and the surrounding area.

Como Accommodation

For the festivals or a general visit, I recommend staying at least two nights in Como to enjoy both the events and the surrounding lake towns.

Palace Hotel. Lungo Lario Trieste, 16

An elegant waterfront hotel with spacious rooms, some offering lake views. Its location next to Piazza Cavour makes it perfect for exploring on foot.

Albergo Terminus Hotel. Lungo Lario Trieste, 14

A historic property with classic interiors and modern comforts. The lakefront setting and proximity to the ferry dock are ideal for day trips.

Hotel Metropole Suisse. Piazza Cavour, 19

Overlooking the lake and ferry terminal, this long-standing hotel offers a mix of traditional and contemporary décor with an in-house restaurant serving Italian classics.

Cremona Accommodation

For the festival or a general visit, I recommend staying two to three nights in Cremona to enjoy both the event and the city's many attractions at a relaxed pace.

Hotel Impero. Piazza della Pace, 21

Located steps from Piazza del Comune, this elegant four-star hotel offers spacious rooms with classic décor and modern comforts. The on-site restaurant serves regional dishes, and many rooms have views of the cathedral or Torrazzo.

Delle Arti Design Hotel. Via Bonomelli, 8

A boutique hotel blending contemporary design with a central location. Stylish rooms feature unique art pieces and modern amenities, while the wellness area offers a sauna and hot tub, ideal after a day of exploring.

Hotel Astoria. Vicolo Bordigallo, 19

Set in the heart of the historic center, this charming hotel occupies a historic building with cozy rooms and friendly service. Perfect for those who want to be within walking distance of Cremona's major landmarks and restaurants.

Locanda Torriani. Via Janello Torriani, 7

Besides its excellent restaurant, this locanda offers a few intimate rooms. Guests enjoy stylish furnishings, a central location near the Museo del Violino, and the convenience of dining on site.

Lago Iseo Accommodation

For the summer festival on Lake Iseo, I recommend staying two to three nights.

Locanda al Lago. Via Peschiera Maraglio 174, Monte Isola

A small family-run inn right on the lakefront, offering simple but comfortable rooms above a restaurant. Guests can enjoy lake views from their windows and step directly into the heart of Peschiera Maraglio's festival atmosphere.

Hotel Sensole. Via Sensole 19, Monte Isola

Overlooking the water in the hamlet of Sensole, this hotel offers cozy rooms and a peaceful setting just a short walk from Peschiera Maraglio. The lakeside terrace is especially inviting at sunset.

Locanda Conti. Via Carzano 40, Monte Isola

Combining a restaurant and guesthouse, this locanda offers a handful of welcoming rooms with traditional décor. Staying in Carzano also places you close to ferry links back to Sale Marasino on the mainland.

Lecco Accommodation

For the Festa di San Nicolò in Lecco, I recommend staying two to three nights but since you are on Lago di Como I would stay seven. Arriving the day before the main celebrations ensures you can enjoy the build-up, including evening concerts and smaller events along the lakeside.

NH Lecco Pontevecchio. Via Azzone Visconti, 84

Near the medieval Ponte Azzone Visconti, this four-star hotel offers elegant rooms with lake and mountain views. Guests appreciate the modern amenities, restaurant, and proximity to both the old town and the lakefront.

Hotel Alberi. Via Lungo Lario Isonzo, 4

A family-run hotel directly overlooking Lake Como, just steps from the promenade. Comfortable rooms, attentive service, and an excellent breakfast make it a favorite for travelers who want central access to festival events.

Legnano Accommodation

For the Knights and Battle of Legnano celebrations, I recommend staying three to four nights. Arriving a day or two before the historic reenactments gives you time to see the preparations, explore the medieval-style parades, and enjoy the atmosphere as the city transforms into a stage for its proud past.

Welcome Hotel. Via Grigna 14

A modern 4-star hotel offering spacious rooms, wellness facilities, and an on-site restaurant. Conveniently located for both business and leisure travelers, with easy access to the town center and train station.

Albergo Al Corso. Corso Magenta 137

Small, family-run hotel near the pedestrian shopping street. Comfortable rooms and warm hospitality make it a practical choice for festival visitors and those wanting to stay in the heart of town.

Palace Hotel Legnano. Via per Castellanza 41

Stylish 4-star hotel featuring a wellness spa, indoor pool, and elegant restaurant. Popular with those looking for a relaxing stay and modern comforts.

BHL Boutique Rooms. Via Venegoni 72

Chic boutique hotel with contemporary rooms designed in a sleek, minimalist style. Offers personalized service and easy access to both central Legnano and transport links to Milan.

Luino Accommodation

Luino, on the eastern shore of Lago Maggiore, is a lively lakeside town known for its historic center, weekly open-air market, and as a gateway to both Italian and Swiss destinations.

Hotel Internazionale Luino. Viale Dante Alighieri 35

A comfortable three-star hotel close to the lakefront and town center, offering classic rooms, a restaurant, and easy access to the train station and ferry dock.

Camin Hotel Luino. Viale Dante Alighieri 29

This charming three-star hotel is set in a historic villa with elegant interiors and a lakeside garden. Guests enjoy a refined restaurant, beautiful common spaces, and proximity to both the lake promenade and Luino's main piazza.

Mantua (Mantova) Accommodation

For Mantua's Patron Saints Festival, I recommend staying four to five nights. This gives you time to enjoy the full rhythm of the celebrations, from solemn Masses and processions honoring Saints Peter and Paul to concerts, markets, and evening events in the city's Renaissance piazzas.

Casa Poli Hotel. Corso Garibaldi, 32

A stylish 4-star boutique hotel blending modern design with comfort. Located just outside the historic walls, it offers spacious rooms, a garden courtyard, and attentive service. Its convenient location makes it an excellent base for exploring Mantua on foot.

Hotel dei Gonzaga. Piazza Sordello, 52

Set directly on Piazza Sordello, this hotel immerses guests in the historic heart of Mantua. Rooms are decorated in a classic style, many with views of the square and the Duomo. Staying here places you steps away from the Palazzo Ducale and other major sites.

Residenza Accademia. Via Accademia, 20

A charming guesthouse in a restored palazzo near Piazza delle Erbe. Rooms are tastefully furnished with period touches, offering a cozy atmosphere that feels authentically Mantuan. Its central location makes it ideal for travelers seeking both comfort and character.

Hotel Broletto. Via Accademia, 1

Nestled in a quiet corner of the centro storico, this small family-run hotel offers warm hospitality and comfortable accommodations. The décor is simple yet elegant, and the welcoming hosts provide helpful advice for exploring Mantua and its surroundings.

Monza Accommodation

For the Monza Grand Prix, Formula One Race, securing a hotel in or near Monza is extremely difficult even when booking a year in advance. I recommend basing yourself near Milano Centrale, where you'll have a wide range of hotel options and quick train connections directly to Monza. If you are fortunate enough to attend the race weekend, plan to stay from Friday through Monday.

Hotel Carol. Via Enrico Arosio 1

A budget-friendly 3-star option close to the train station, offering simple but comfortable rooms. Convenient for travelers seeking easy connections to Milan and the Monza city center.

Hotel Royal Falcone. Corso Milano 5

Centrally located 4-star hotel with modern, spacious rooms and attentive service. A popular choice for both business and leisure stays, within walking distance of shops, restaurants, and the cathedral.

Hotel de la Ville. Viale Regina Margherita di Savoia 15

Elegant 4-star luxury hotel overlooking the Royal Villa of Monza and its park. Known for refined décor, impeccable service, and the award-winning Derby Grill restaurant, it is ideal for a memorable stay.

Locanda San Paolo. Piazza San Paolo, 3

A boutique guesthouse in the historic center with stylish, intimate rooms. Perfect for travelers who want to stay close to Monza's piazzas, cafés, and evening festival life.

Helios Hotel Monza. Viale Elvezia, 4

Near the park, this modern four-star hotel offers spacious rooms, an excellent breakfast, and easy access to the Autodromo. A practical option for visitors focused on attending the race.

Staying in Milan

Because Monza is only 15–20 minutes away by train, many visitors choose to stay in Milan for the broader range of hotels, from luxury palazzi near the Duomo to boutique stays in Brera or Navigli. This option is especially convenient for those combining the Grand Prix with sightseeing in Lombardy's capital. Trains run frequently, even during race weekend, making the commute fast and efficient.

Pavia Accommodation

For the Festa di Sant'Agostino in Pavia, I recommend staying three nights.

Hotel Excelsior. Piazza della Stazione 25

Conveniently located opposite the train station, this hotel offers comfortable rooms with classic furnishings. A practical choice for travelers arriving by rail and exploring the city on foot.

Hotel Aurora. Viale Vittorio Emanuele II 25

Just steps from the historic center, this welcoming hotel combines modern amenities with friendly service. Guests appreciate the easy access to Pavia's main attractions and cafés.

Le Stanze del Cardinale. Piazza Duomo 7

Elegant boutique-style accommodation set in a historic building right on the main square. Offers stylish rooms with frescoed ceilings and a refined atmosphere, perfect for those seeking charm and character.

Polpenazze del Garda Accommodation

For the Festa del Vino or a relaxing visit to the Valtenesi hills, I recommend staying one to three nights in or near Polpenazze. The village itself offers charming agriturismi and small hotels, while nearby Lake Garda towns provide more options within a short drive.

Hotel Riva del Sole. Via Gardesana, 2, Moniga del Garda

Just a 5-minute drive from Polpenazze, this lakeside hotel combines comfort with convenience. Rooms are bright and modern, many with balconies overlooking

Lake Garda. The on-site restaurant serves both Italian classics and local specialties, and the outdoor pool is perfect for unwinding after festival days.

Agriturismo Macesina. Via Macesina, 2, Bedizzole

Set in the countryside a short distance from Polpenazze, this restored farmhouse offers peaceful rooms with rustic-chic décor. Guests can enjoy a hearty breakfast made from local ingredients and relax in the spacious garden. Wine tastings and olive oil sampling are often available on site.

B&B Antiche Mura. Via Roma, 44, Polpenazze del Garda

In the historic center, this charming bed-and-breakfast occupies a building with original stone walls and wooden beams. Rooms are comfortable and individually decorated, and breakfast is served with fresh pastries, fruit, and local cheeses.

Relais Rosa dei Venti. Via del Porto, 10, Moniga del Garda

An apartment-style accommodation ideal for longer stays or those traveling with family. Set in landscaped gardens with two swimming pools, it offers self-catering units just a short drive from Polpenazze and the lakefront.

Agriturismo La Guarda. Via della Selva, 14, Polpenazze del Garda

Also featured in the restaurant section, La Guarda offers cozy rooms in a vineyard setting. Staying here provides a full immersion into the Valtenesi wine country, with the added perk of dining on site and enjoying the wines made from the surrounding vines.

Preghera / Val Taleggio Accommodation

For the Sagra del Taleggio or a general visit, it is best to plan for one or two nights in the area to fully enjoy the festival and the scenic surroundings. While Peghera itself has limited lodging, there are charming options in nearby villages and towns within Val Taleggio.

Agriturismo La Piana. Località La Piana, Val Taleggio

A family-run agriturismo offering comfortable rooms with views of the surrounding pastures. Guests enjoy a warm, home-style breakfast featuring fresh dairy products from the farm, including Taleggio cheese. The peaceful rural location makes it ideal for a relaxing retreat.

Rifugio Sasso di Bosco. Località Sasso di Bosco, Val Taleggio

This rustic mountain lodge offers simple yet cozy rooms above its restaurant. It is popular with hikers and nature lovers who appreciate the proximity to walking trails, fresh alpine air, and hearty meals after a day outdoors.

Hotel Moderno. Piazza Zignoni, San Giovanni Bianco

About 15 minutes from Peghera, this comfortable hotel offers modern amenities in the heart of San Giovanni Bianco. Rooms are bright and well-kept, and the in-house restaurant serves excellent local dishes. Its central location makes it a convenient base for exploring Val Taleggio and nearby valleys.

B&B Casa Arcangeli. Via Roma, Olda, Val Taleggio

A charming bed-and-breakfast set in a historic stone house in the nearby hamlet of Olda. The property offers well-appointed rooms, homemade breakfasts, and friendly hosts who provide tips for exploring the valley.

Sirmione Accommodation

For Sirmione's Christmas markets, I recommend staying two to three nights. This allows you to enjoy the festive atmosphere in the historic center, stroll the lakefront under twinkling lights, and perhaps take a day trip by ferry to another Lake Garda town.

Hotel Eden. Piazza Carducci, 19

A lakeside four-star hotel located directly on the main square, steps from the Christmas markets. Modern rooms with balconies overlook Lake Garda, and guests enjoy a festive atmosphere right in the center of events.

Hotel Sirmione e Promessi Sposi. Piazza Castello, 19

Set beside the castle and overlooking the marina, this historic hotel offers elegant rooms and a spa with thermal pools. The location is unmatched for festival visitors, who can step out directly into the illuminated piazzas and waterfront.

Sondrio Accommodation

For the Festa di San Gervasio in Sondrio, I recommend staying two to three nights.

Grand Hotel della Posta. Piazza Giuseppe Garibaldi, 19

A historic four-star hotel set in an elegant nineteenth century building overlooking the main square. Rooms are refined with classic décor, and the property offers a wellness center, indoor pool, and gourmet restaurant. Its central location makes it ideal for festival visitors who want to be in the heart of Sondrio's celebrations.

Hotel Europa. Via Lungo Mallero Cadorna, 27

Along the Mallero River just steps from Piazza Campello, Hotel Europa offers comfortable modern rooms with views of the old town and surrounding mountains. Guests appreciate the friendly staff, generous breakfast, and easy walking access to the cathedral and main festival routes.

Hotel Vittoria. Via Bernina, 1

A welcoming family-run hotel slightly south of the historic center. Rooms are simple but well kept, with an emphasis on warm service and local hospitality. The on-site restaurant serves traditional Valtellina dishes, making it a convenient choice for travelers who want authentic food without leaving the property.

Varese Accommodation

For the Festa di San Vittore in Varese, I recommend staying five nights, or even seven if you can.

Vecchia Riva Hotel & Restaurant. Via Giovanni Macchi 146

Set beside Lake Varese, this hotel offers comfortable rooms with lake views and a terrace restaurant serving traditional Lombard dishes. Guests appreciate the peaceful setting, walking and cycling paths nearby, and friendly service.

Palace Grand Hotel. Via Luciano Manara 11

An elegant Liberty-style villa set in a hillside park overlooking Lake Varese and the Alps. Features refined rooms, a swimming pool, and a gourmet restaurant, ideal for a more luxurious stay.

Albergo Ristorante Bologna. Via Broggi 7

Family-run hotel in the heart of town with an on-site restaurant known for homemade pasta and Lombard specialties. A favorite with locals and visitors looking for authentic regional flavors.

Vigevano Accommodation

For the Renaissance Fair in Vigevano, I recommend staying two to three nights. This gives you time to enjoy the historic reenactments, parades in period costume, and lively markets that fill Piazza Ducale, one of Italy's most beautiful Renaissance squares.

Nuovo Hotel Vigevano. Corso Milano 150

This 3-star hotel sits near the Ticino Valley Nature Reserve and offers a peaceful stay with free parking and air-conditioned rooms. It's a short drive from the city center and Piazza Ducale, making it a good choice for those arriving by car. The hotel features a bar, breakfast service, and friendly reception staff.

Hotel Locanda Da Carla. Via Mortara 2

A charming 4-star property located in a quiet area just outside the center, offering spacious rooms, a garden, and an on-site restaurant. Known for its homey atmosphere and accommodating staff, the hotel also provides free bikes and private parking.

Villimpenta Accommodation

For the Risotto Festival in Villimpenta, an overnight stay isn't strictly necessary; many visitors come just for the evening to enjoy generous plates of risotto prepared in giant copper pots. However, if you'd like to linger, consider staying three to four nights.

Agriturismo Trebis. Strada Trebis 20, Villimpenta

A family-run agriturismo on the edge of the town, surrounded by rice fields. Rooms are simple yet comfortable, and the on-site restaurant serves traditional Mantuan dishes, including risotto prepared with rice from the farm's own harvest.

B&B 3 Tesori. Via Roma 40, Villimpenta

In the town center, this B&B offers a handful of cozy rooms within walking distance of the Scaligeri Castle and festival piazzas. Known for warm hospitality and convenient location during festival days.

CHAPTER FORTY-SEVEN

Transportation Detail

Planes, Trains, Ferries, Buses, Cars

Airports in Milan and Lombardy

Milan and the Lombardy region are served by three main airports, all of which connect travelers to destinations throughout Italy and Europe.

Milan Malpensa Airport (MXP)
The largest international airport in northern Italy, Malpensa is located 50 kilometers (31 miles) northwest of Milan. It offers direct flights to North America, Asia, and all major European cities. Malpensa is ideal for international travelers and long-haul flights.

Milan Linate Airport (LIN)
Located just 7 kilometers (4.3 miles) from the city center, Linate is Milan's most convenient airport for domestic and short European flights. It is perfect for those staying in the city or traveling between Italian cities.

Orio al Serio Airport (BGY)
Also known as Milan Bergamo Airport, this is a hub for low-cost carriers like Ryanair. Located near the city of Bergamo, about 45 kilometers (28 miles) northeast of Milan, it is a good option for budget-conscious travelers or those heading to Lake Iseo or the eastern part of Lombardy.

Choosing the Right Airport

Itinerary: If your trip centers on Milan, Linate is the most convenient. For exploring Lake Como or the northern Alpine areas, Malpensa is ideal. For Bergamo, Brescia, or Lake Iseo, consider flying into Orio al Serio.

Transportation options: Malpensa and Orio al Serio both offer regular shuttle buses and train connections. Linate has quick bus and taxi access to Milan's center.

Budget: Linate is closest but may cost more. Orio al Serio is often the most affordable for flights, but be prepared for longer ground transfers.

Getting Around Milan

Metro and Suburban Trains
Milan's metro system is extensive, efficient, and easy to use. With five metro lines (M1 to M5), it connects all major areas including the Duomo, Brera, Navigli, and Porta Garibaldi. Tickets are valid on the metro, buses, and trams, making it simple to switch between different modes of transport.

You can purchase tickets at metro station vending machines, newsstands, and tobacco shops marked with a "T" sign. Tickets can also be bought through official ATM Milano mobile apps or by tapping a contactless credit card at metro turnstiles. It is important to validate your ticket before boarding by stamping it in the machines located at the station or on the vehicle for buses and trams.

Suburban trains (Passante Ferroviario) run through underground city stations and connect to outlying suburbs and regional hubs.

Trams and Buses
ATM (Azienda Trasporti Milanesi) operates Milan's elegant old trams and modern buses. Trams are a scenic way to travel between neighborhoods. Tickets can be purchased at metro stations, newsstands, or via the ATM Milano app.

Taxis
Taxis in Milan must be picked up at a taxi stand or reserved. They do not stop if hailed from the street.

RideShare Apps

While Milan has excellent public transportation, sometimes you may want the convenience of a car. One of the easiest ways to arrange this is with **Free Now or IT Taxi**, popular ride-hailing apps that connect you directly with licensed taxis. The service is widely used by locals and visitors alike, and it offers the reassurance of regulated fares with the flexibility of modern app-based booking.

Download the app, set your pickup location, and request a ride. You will see your driver's details, the estimated fare, and the expected arrival time before you confirm. Payment can be handled directly through the app, so there is no need to carry cash unless you prefer to. Free Now works seamlessly across many Italian cities, so you can continue using it if your travels take you beyond Milan.

Compared to Uber, which in Milan is typically limited to higher-cost chauffeur services such as Uber Black or Uber Lux, Free Now provides greater availability and more competitive pricing. It is especially useful late at night, during rainy weather, or when carrying luggage, offering a comfortable and reliable alternative to public transport.

Bikes and E-Scooters

BikeMi is Milan's public bike-sharing system. E-scooters and electric bikes can also be rented through apps like Lime, Dott, and Bird. They are convenient for quick trips within neighborhoods like Isola, Brera, and Porta Venezia.

Navigating Lombardy by Train

Trains are the best way to travel between Milan and other cities and lakes in Lombardy. Trenitalia and Trenord operate most regional routes.

High-speed Frecciarossa and Italo trains connect Milan with other major Italian cities, while slower regional trains reach smaller towns and lakefront stations.

Trains in Detail: Cities and Towns in Lombardy with Trenitalia and Trenord Stations

Lombardy has one of the most extensive and efficient regional train networks in Italy, served primarily by **Trenitalia** and **Trenord**. High-speed services link

Milan to cities across the country, while regional and suburban lines reach towns throughout the lakes, valleys, and foothills.

You can check timetables and purchase tickets at:
www.trenitalia.com
www.trenord.it

Main Cities in Lombardy with Major Train Stations

- **Milan**:

  - *Milano Centrale*: High-speed hub and regional gateway

  - *Milano Porta Garibaldi*: Suburban and regional services

  - *Milano Cadorna*: Trenord lines to Como, Varese, and Malpensa Airport

  - *Milano Rogoredo and Lambrate*: Regional and high-speed connections

- **Bergamo**

- **Brescia**

- **Como**:

  - *Como San Giovanni*: Main station with regional and cross-border trains

  - *Como Lago*: Convenient for travelers from Milan Cadorna via Trenord

- **Lecco**

- **Pavia**

- **Varese**

- **Mantua (Mantova)**

- **Cremona**

Smaller Towns in Lombardy with Train Access

- **Desenzano del Garda**

- **Peschiera del Garda**

- **Bellano and Varenna (Lake Como)**

- **Tirano**

- **Chiavenna**

- **Edolo**

- **Sondrio**

Insider Tips for Train Travel in Lombardy

- Validate your regional ticket before boarding using the green or yellow machines in the station.

- For high-speed trains (Frecciarossa or Italo), no validation is needed, your assigned seat and time are printed on the ticket.

- Keep your ticket during the entire ride, as onboard inspectors will often check it.

- Seats on regional trains are usually first come, first served.

- Trains to Lake Como (Como or Varenna) are frequent, making them perfect for day trips.

Whether you are gliding through Alpine valleys or zipping between cities on high-speed tracks, Lombardy's rail network offers one of the easiest and most scenic ways to explore the region.

Train Tip: Most stations are near historic centers, making train travel ideal for day trips and short stays. Always validate regional train tickets before boarding using the yellow or green machines at the station.

Car Rentals in Lombardy

While a car is unnecessary in Milan itself, it can be useful for exploring the countryside, lakes, and wine regions.

Best for: Lake Como scenic drives, visiting the Franciacorta wine region, exploring Lake Iseo and the Camonica Valley, or reaching small towns in the Oltrepò Pavese.

Rental locations: Cars can be rented at all three airports or in the city near Milan Central Station.

Driving Notes

- Watch for ZTL zones (limited traffic zones) in historic centers like Bergamo Alta, Como, and Pavia.

- Highways are toll roads. Use the "Telepass" lane only if your car is equipped.

- Automatic cars are available but limited. Reserve early if preferred.

- Parking in cities can be difficult. Use paid garages or park on the outskirts and use public transport.

It seems that whenever we rent a car for a few weeks in Italy, a ticket eventually arrives in the mail for a ZTL entry or parking violation. These fines must be paid by bank transfer and can be a bit confusing to handle from abroad. We always pay them promptly and simply accept that it's part of the experience of renting a car in Italy.

Getting to the Lakes and Mountains

Lake Como
By train from Milan Cadorna to Como Lago or Milan Centrale to Como San Giovanni. From Como, ferries and buses serve lake towns.

Lake Garda
Take a train to Desenzano or Peschiera del Garda. Ferries connect lake towns, and buses reach Sirmione and Limone.

Lake Maggiore
From Milan Centrale, trains go to Stresa, Arona, and Verbania. Boat services run to the Borromean Islands.

Alpine towns
Varenna, Tirano, and Chiavenna are reachable by train. From Tirano, connect to the Bernina Express for one of the most scenic rail journeys in Europe.

Ferries and Boats on the Lakes

Lombardy's lakes are well connected by ferry. This is a scenic and enjoyable way to travel between towns.

Navigazione Laghi operates ferry services on:

- **Lake Como**: Como to Bellagio, Varenna, Menaggio, and more

- **Lake Garda**: Desenzano, Sirmione, Bardolino, Limone, and Riva

- **Lake Maggiore**: Stresa, Isola Bella, Isola dei Pescatori, and Verbania

Fast hydrofoils and car ferries are available. Schedules vary by season, with more frequent services in spring and summer.

Websites:
www.navigazionelaghi.it
www.trenitalia.com
www.trenord.it

Whether arriving by plane, exploring cities by train, cruising the lakes by boat, or driving through vineyard-covered hills, Lombardy offers multiple ways to move at your own pace. Each mode of transport reveals a different side of this elegant and diverse region.

Buon viaggio!

CHAPTER FORTY-EIGHT

Healthy, Safe, and Responsible Travel

What You Need to Know

Traveling through Milan and Lombardy is an unforgettable experience, but it's always wise to prepare for a safe and healthy trip. A few practical steps will ensure your journey is both smooth and enjoyable.

Drinkable Water and Responsible Travel

Across Lombardy, tap water is safe to drink. In fact, many cities provide public fountains where you can refill your bottle with fresh water. Bringing a refillable water bottle is a way to travel responsibly. Consider the scale: Venice alone has reported collecting over a million discarded plastic bottles each month. Choosing to refill instead of buying bottled water helps reduce waste and protects Italy's treasured landscapes.

Pharmacies in Italy

Pharmacies, marked by a green cross, are easy to find in every city and town. Italian pharmacists are highly trained and often act as a first stop for medical concerns. They can suggest treatments, prescribe medications for minor illnesses, and help you avoid a costly and unnecessary doctor's visit.

I learned this firsthand when my son, Augustus, developed an eye infection while we were in Italy. We stopped at a pharmacy, showed the pharmacist his symptoms, and for just three euros received the exact same medication we had once paid seventy dollars for back home in the United States. It was a reminder of how accessible and practical Italian healthcare can be for travelers.

Avoiding Theft and Scams

Like in any major European city, pick-pocketing can be an issue in Milan, especially in crowded places like train stations, markets, and popular piazzas. Keep valuables secured in a crossbody bag or money belt and always be aware of your surroundings.

Be alert for scams that prey on tourists. A common one involves someone trying to slip a bracelet onto your wrist or pressing a trinket into your hand. Once you take it, they will demand payment. The best response is a firm "No, grazie" and to keep walking. As a rule, never accept items from strangers on the street, no matter how insistent they may be.

Nighttime Safety

Milan is generally safe, but it is best to avoid being out late at night in unfamiliar areas. Exercise particular caution around Milano Centrale train station after dark, and try not to arrive there after midnight. If your train or flight schedule means a late arrival, consider arranging a taxi or private transfer in advance to ensure a secure and smooth journey.

Emergency Numbers in Italy

If you need urgent help, dial 112 from any phone. This is the EU-wide emergency number and connects you to police, ambulance, or fire services. Operators can provide assistance in multiple languages.

Other helpful numbers:

113– Police (Polizia di Stato)

118 – Ambulance / Medical Emergency

115 – Fire Brigade (Vigili del Fuoco)

For travelers, remembering 112 is usually enough, since it covers all services. Mobile users in Italy can dial these numbers even without local SIM credit.

Accessible Travel

Milan has made significant efforts to become one of Italy's most accessible cities. Metro stations and buses increasingly include elevators, ramps, and priority seating, while most major museums and attractions provide barrier-free access. The Duomo, for example, has an elevator to the rooftop terraces for visitors with limited mobility. Sidewalks in the historic center are often uneven, but many have been adapted with ramps at crosswalks.

If you or someone in your group requires assistance, look for signs marked "accessibile" or ask staff for help. Italians are generally kind and quick to accommodate. Planning ahead is still recommended, particularly for smaller towns in Lombardy where infrastructure may not yet be as modernized as Milan.

Lost Property in Milan

If you lose belongings while in Milan, there is an official Ufficio Oggetti Smarriti (Lost Property Office). At Milano Centrale railway station, Trenitalia operates a lost and found service where you can report or reclaim items left on trains or within the station.

Location: Ground floor of Milano Centrale (look for signs to "Oggetti Smarriti")

Hours: Typically weekdays during business hours (check ahead, as times may change)

What you'll need: Identification and a clear description of the lost item

For items lost elsewhere in the city, you can contact the Comune di Milano Ufficio Oggetti Smarriti at Via Friuli 30. They maintain a database of lost items turned in across the city.

Quick Reference Guide

Calendar, Alphabetical City Index, Rulers & Dynasties, Glossary

CHAPTER FORTY-NINE

Rulers and Dynasties of Lombardy

A Traveler's Timeline

E arly Communes and Imperial Rule

Before 1277, Milan and other Lombard cities were part of the Lombard League, a confederation of northern Italian city-states that resisted control by the Holy Roman Emperors. Milan emerged as a powerful commune, governed by its own consuls and later by a podestà (chief magistrate). This era laid the groundwork for the rise of the Visconti, who consolidated power and transformed Milan from a free commune into a duchy.

Visconti Family

The Visconti were a dominant noble family who ruled Milan from 1277 until 1447. They transformed Milan into a major power in northern Italy, consolidating surrounding territories into a duchy. Under their rule, Milan saw the construction of important landmarks, including the original fortifications of the Castello Sforzesco and the beginning of the Duomo di Milano. The Visconti promoted Gothic architecture and established Milan as a center of political and military influence in the late Middle Ages.

Sforza Family

The Sforza dynasty succeeded the Visconti in 1450 and ruled Milan until 1535. They ushered in a golden age of Renaissance art and culture. Ludovico il Moro's court attracted figures such as Leonardo da Vinci and Donato Bramante, leading to masterpieces like The Last Supper and the design of Santa Maria delle Grazie. The Sforza family strengthened Milan's fortifications and transformed it into a flourishing Renaissance city, leaving a legacy of patronage and monumental architecture.

Spanish Habsburgs

After the death of the last Sforza duke in 1535, Milan came under Spanish Habsburg control until 1706. This period was marked by the Counter-Reformation, during which the city became a center of Catholic renewal. The Spanish rulers strengthened religious institutions, built new churches, and reinforced the city's defenses. Spanish governance also brought Baroque influences that shaped the city's architecture and art.

Austrian Habsburgs

From 1706 to 1796, Lombardy passed under Austrian Habsburg rule. This era saw significant Enlightenment-era reforms under Empress Maria Theresa and her son Joseph II, including improvements in education, infrastructure, and administration. Austrian rule modernized Milan and its surrounding territories, laying the groundwork for the region's economic and cultural growth leading up to the Napoleonic era.

Gonzaga Family

The Gonzaga family ruled Mantua from 1328 to 1708, turning the city into one of Italy's great Renaissance courts. They commissioned magnificent palaces, including the Palazzo Ducale and Palazzo Te, and attracted leading artists such as Andrea Mantegna. The Gonzaga were patrons of music, literature, and theater, making Mantua a cultural beacon that continues to draw visitors today.

Scaligeri Family (della Scala)

A powerful noble dynasty that ruled Verona and much of the surrounding territory from the mid-thirteenth to the late fourteenth century. Known as the

Lords of Verona, the Scaligeri expanded their influence around Lake Garda and built an extensive network of castles and fortifications, including those in Sirmione, Malcesine, and Lazise. Their emblem was the ladder (scala in Italian), a symbol still visible in the architecture and heraldry of the region. The Scaligeri left a lasting legacy of medieval military architecture and cultural patronage in northern Italy.

Napoleonic Rule

From 1796 to 1814, Lombardy was occupied by Napoleon's forces and reorganized into the Cisalpine Republic and later the Kingdom of Italy under Napoleon's rule. French reforms modernized administration, abolished feudal privileges, and introduced the Napoleonic Code, creating a foundation for a more centralized and secular state. Milan became the capital of Napoleon's Italian Kingdom, and the city gained new monuments such as the Arch of Peace (Arco della Pace) and improvements to its infrastructure, many of which still shape its layout today.

Austrian Restoration and Risorgimento

After Napoleon's defeat, Lombardy returned to Austrian rule as part of the Kingdom of Lombardy-Venetia (1815–1859). The period saw industrial growth but also rising nationalist sentiment. Milan became a center of resistance during the 1848 Five Days of Milan uprising, a key moment in the Risorgimento (Italian unification movement).

House of Savoy

The House of Savoy ruled the Kingdom of Sardinia, which became the driving force behind the unification of Italy. After Lombardy was ceded from Austria to Sardinia in 1859 following the Second Italian War of Independence, King Victor Emmanuel II of Savoy became the central figure in uniting the Italian states. Under his reign, Lombardy was integrated into the growing Kingdom of Sardinia, which soon became the Kingdom of Italy in 1861.

Remarkably, the House of Savoy still exists today as a royal dynasty in exile, its members occasionally appearing in Italian public life and reminding visitors that the story of Italy's kings is not as distant as it may seem.

CHAPTER FIFTY

Glossary of Terms and Useful Italian Words

Agriturismo: An agriturismo, or farm stay, is a type of accommodation in Italy that allows you to enjoy the peace and quiet of the countryside. Often functioning farms, these accommodations often include breakfast, a pool and spa, and luxurious rooms (4 and 5 star) or they an offer affordable accommodation with the family who enjoys having you. This type of stay helps to support farmers. The farm can be olive groves, orange groves, wineries, or farms with animals.

Apericena: A Milanese variation of the traditional aperitivo, where the drinks are accompanied by an abundant buffet of food, often enough to serve as dinner.

Aperitivo/Aperitif: Aperitivo is an Italian tradition of enjoying a light drink and small snacks in the early evening to stimulate the appetite before dinner. It is both a social ritual and a relaxing pause in the day, often shared with friends in cafés, bars, or piazzas.

Ascension (Feast of the Ascension): Jesus Christ was taken up to Heaven in body and spirit. Acts of the Apostles (Acts 1:9–11). In Christian belief, the Ascension refers to the event in which, forty days after His Resurrection. It is described in the, where Jesus blesses His disciples on the Mount of Olives before rising into the sky, received by a cloud and no longer visible to them.

Bàcari (singular: bàcaro): Bàcari are traditional Venetian wine bars known for their casual, friendly atmosphere and small bites called cicchetti. These humble establishments are scattered throughout Venice and are a beloved part of the city's culinary culture.

Basilica: A term derived from the official building of a Greek magistrate, Basileus. In antiquity, it was a roofed building with a double colonnade used for law courts, assemblies, or markets. In the Christian era, it meant a characteristic type of church building with a high nave and two or four aisles. Usually oriented to the west. basilicas usually have windows on the elevated part of the walls (clerestory) where the roof meets the wall. A basilica is the shape of Catholic churches since the 4th century. The Pope has given the basilica special privileges as a major church.

Benedictines: St. Benedict of Nursia (c. 480-547) founded the oldest order of Western monks. 529AD. The Benedictine rule formed the basis of Western monasticism. The primary task was to cultivate liturgy and prayer. Physical labor, scholarly and artistic work supplemented this.

Blue Flag Beaches: The Blue Flag is an international certification awarded to beaches, marinas, and sustainable boating tourism operators that meet high environmental and safety standards. It is granted by the Foundation for Environmental Education (FEE), a non-profit organization, and is recognized worldwide as a symbol of clean and well-managed beaches.

Brotherhoods: The brotherhoods, or "confraternite" in Italian, are religious lay organizations that play a crucial role in preserving and celebrating local traditions of the region. These brotherhoods have deep historical roots, often dating back centuries, and are named after various saints or religious concepts.

Buongiorno: Pronunciation: [bwon-'jor-no]. Literally "good day." In Italian, it is the standard greeting used from early morning until late afternoon, similar to saying "good morning" or "good day" in English. In the late afternoon or evening, Italians typically switch to buonasera ("good evening").

Byzantine architecture: This style relates to the architecture developed in the Byzantine or Eastern Roman Empire. Characterized by enormous domes, mosaics, rounded arches, and spires.

Campanile: A bell tower of an Italian church. Sometimes a watchtower for the town, the bell tower grew in importance during the Renaissance.

Centro Storico: The historic center of town.

Chiesa di: Church of followed usually by a saint's name.

Chiesa Madre: Mother church or the most important church in town. This is not a duomo or cathedral.

Cinquecento: A term shortened in Italian from mille-cinquecento. It means the 1500s or the 16th century.

Cistercians: The Cistercians are a monastic Catholic order that has its origins in the reformed Benedictine monastery of Citaeux founded in 1098. The new order set out to achieve fully the ideal from the Rule of St. Benedict.

Confraternite: Religious brotherhoods composed of laypeople dedicated to prayer, charity, and community service, especially within Catholic traditions. Confraternities in Italy, including those in Sicily, are often responsible for organizing and participating in religious processions during major festivals. During events such as the Festa di Santa Rosalia in Palermo, the confraternities don traditional garments—typically long tunics and capes, carrying banners and religious symbols. They play a key role in maintaining the solemnity and spiritual focus of the event, embodying centuries-old traditions of faith and devotion.

Consul: A Roman consul was one of the highest-ranking elected officials in the Roman Republic. After the overthrow of the Roman monarchy, the Romans introduced the office of consul around 509 BC. The Roman Republic elected two consuls each year to serve jointly for a one-year term. They held significant power and responsibility.

Corpus Domini: Corpus Domini is the Latin term for the Solemnity of the Most Holy Body and Blood of Christ, a major feast in the Catholic Church. Commonly referred to as Corpus Christi in English, this celebration honors the real presence of Jesus Christ in the Eucharist. It is traditionally celebrated on the

Thursday after Trinity Sunday or, in many places, moved to the following Sunday to encourage broader participation.

Corso & Via: Street.

DOC: DOC stands for Denominazione di Origine Controllata (Designation of Controlled Origin) in Italian. It is a quality assurance label for Italian wines, cheeses, and other agricultural products. This classification guarantees that the product meets strict production standards and comes from a specific geographic area.

DOCG (Denominazione di Origine Controllata e Garantita): Italy's highest classification for wines, indicating strict government guarantees of quality and origin. The label means "Controlled and Guaranteed Designation of Origin." DOCG wines must meet rigorous standards in terms of grape variety, production methods, aging, and geographic origin. They are subject to official taste testing and analysis before bottling, and each bottle is sealed with a numbered governmental label. Famous examples include Prosecco Superiore DOCG from Conegliano and Valdobbiadene, Brunello di Montalcino, and Barolo. When travelers see a DOCG label, they can expect a wine tied closely to its region, crafted with tradition, and held to the highest standards of Italian winemaking.

Duomo or Cattedrale: These are all referred to as the town's cathedral, but they have different significance. Cathedral means the main church of the diocese where the bishop's seat is located. Duomo is the Italian word for cathedral, but both Duomo and Cattedrale are used when seeking the bishop's seat in Italy.

Gianduja: Gianduja (also spelled gianduia) is a sweet Italian chocolate-hazelnut mixture from Piedmont, particularly associated with Turin.

Grazie: Thank you.

Hydrofoil: A fast passenger boat fitted with winglike foils beneath the hull that lift it out of the water as speed increases, reducing drag and allowing greater velocity. Hydrofoils operate on several Italian lakes, including Garda, Como, and Maggiore, and are a popular way for travelers to move quickly between towns while enjoying panoramic views from the water.

Loggia: A loggia is an open-sided gallery or corridor, often on the ground floor or upper level of a building, with a series of columns or arches supporting the roof. It is typically open to the air on at least one side and used for shade, shelter, or enjoying views. Loggias are common in Italian Renaissance architecture and can be found in palaces, villas, and public buildings, often facing a courtyard or piazza.

Municipio: Town hall or city hall.

Navigli: The historic canal district in Milan, originally designed in part by Leonardo da Vinci, known for its scenic waterways, lively nightlife, art galleries, and dining along the canals.

Piazza: Square, as an element of urban layout.

Reformation: A major religious movement from within the Catholic Church that began in Germany in 1517 at the instigation of Martin Luther. His challenge of the practices and doctrines of the Roman Catholic Church ultimately led to the establishment of the Protestant churches.

Rifugio: A rifugio is a mountain refuge or hut, typically found in the Italian Alps and Apennines, that provides shelter, simple lodging, and hearty meals for hikers, climbers, and outdoor enthusiasts. Positioned at strategic high-altitude locations, often near trails, passes, or summits, rifugi are staffed during the trekking season and may offer dormitory-style rooms or bunks, a communal dining area serving regional specialties (polenta, soups, cured meats, cheeses), potable water, and basic facilities (toilets, hot water).

Risorgimento: A 19th-century political and cultural movement that sought the unification and liberation of the Italian states from foreign rule. Beginning in the early 1800s and culminating in 1871 with the establishment of the Kingdom of Italy, it fostered a renewed sense of national identity and independence.

Romanesque: A term used to describe forms of Roman architecture such as rounded arches, columns, capitals, and vaults that were used in buildings in the early Middle Ages. The term Romanesque covers the period from about 1000 to the point when Gothic began.

Traghetto: Ferry

CHAPTER FIFTY-ONE

Festival Calendar

Dates, Cities, and Celebrations Across Milan and Lombardy

These are the festivals included in this guide, but each chapter offers more information about these events.

Date / City Name / Festival Name

January Events

January 6. Milan. Festa dell'Epifania. Costumed figures in rich medieval robes gather, their crowns catching the winter light as they prepare to recreate one of history's most sacred journeys.

February Events

February 15. Brescia. Festa di San Faustino e Giovita. Brescia's most beloved civic and religious celebration is the Festa di San Faustino, a vibrant day honoring the city's patron saint.

Cities with Carnival Events which can be February or March depending on Easter date. Varese, Legnano, Sondrio, Sabbioneta, Luino, Pavia, Lecco,

Mantua, Milan, Bagolino, Crema, Schignano, Soncino, Cantu, and Castiglione delle Stiviere.

February / March / September. Milan Fashion Week. During Fashion Week, Milan fills with more than one hundred and fifty official events.

March Events

March 18. Mantua. Festa di Sant'Anselmo. Mantua's most heartfelt civic and religious celebration is this event, honoring the city's patron saint.

2nd week, 3rd week. Bergamo. FestaFusion.

#1. Bergamo Film Meeting.

#2. Bergamo Jazz Festival.

April Events

Easter. Bormio. Easter I Pasquali. The tradition of I Pasquali is one of the most distinctive Easter celebrations I have ever seen. It blends religious devotion with Alpine craftsmanship with community pride.

April 25. All of Italy. Festa della Libreazione. Liberation Day festival is a national holiday that celebrates the liberation of Italy at the end of World War II.

April. Milan. Salone del Mobile & Fuorisalone (Design Week). Major international furniture and design fair.

May Events

May 8. Varese. Festa di San Vittorio. The Festa di San Vittore in Varese honors the city's patron saint with solemn religious processions.

May 10. Vigevano. Festa di San Maiolo. This festival honors Saint Maiolus of Cluny, one of Vigevano's patron saints, who is celebrated with a religious procession through Piazza Ducale and Mass in the Cathedral of Sant'Ambrogio.

Last weekend of May. Villimpenta. Festa del Risotto. While risotto remains the star, the festival has expanded into a broader showcase of rural culture.

Last Sunday of May. Legnano. Palio di Legnano. The Palio di Legnano emerged from that peculiarly Italian genius for transforming memory into spectacle, inspired by the wave of historical celebrations sweeping the peninsula and fueled by a community's unshakeable pride in their defining moment.

May with Dates that Vary

Late May to early June. Polpenazze del Garda. Festa del Vino (Wine Festival). The Festa del Vino is the village's signature celebration, attracting thousands of visitors eager to sample the rich winemaking heritage of the Valtenesi hills.

June Events

June / August / September. Milan. Estate Sforzesca at Castello Sforzesco. Every summer, the Castello Sforzesco is reborn as Milan's largest open-air cultural stage during Estate Sforzesca.

June / July / August / September. Legnano. Estate Legnanese. A summer cultural program that fills Legnano with concerts, outdoor cinema, theater, and exhibitions.

First Sunday. Milan. Festa del Naviglio. A lively celebration along the Navigli canals, with music, dancing, and food stalls.

June 6. Monza. Festa di San Gerardo dei Tintori. Honoring Monza's co-patron saint, this local celebration includes religious ceremonies, a solemn procession, and community gatherings.

June 19. Sondrio and Bormio. Festa di San Gervasio. For centuries, this Alpine town has placed its fate in the hands of the twin martyrs Gervasius and Protasius, those early Christian brothers whose devotion proved stronger than Roman steel.

June 24. Legnano, Monza, Lecco, and Peghera. Festa di San Giovanni. One of the city's traditional summer feasts, held with open-air concerts, food stalls, and a festive market.

June 27-29. Luino. FestaFusion.

#1. Festa Patronale di Santi Pietro e Paolo. Luino's grand patronal feast blends solemn liturgy, processions, music, and fireworks on June 29.

#2. Festa del Miracolo. A local religious celebration on June 27, recalling a miracle attributed to the Virgin Mary, with Mass and community prayers.

#3. Palio Remiero. A spirited rowing competition among Luino's nine districts on Lake Maggiore is a highlight of the patronal festivities.

June with Dates that Vary

Last Weekend of June or Early July. Varese. Sacro Monte Festival. The week features evening torchlight processions along the cobbled Via Sacra that leads past fourteen Renaissance chapels to the sanctuary at the summit, creating an evocative atmosphere that recalls the journeys of medieval pilgrims.

Early June. Lecco. ResegUp Mountain Race. For sports lovers and hiking enthusiasts alike, ResegUp is an exhilarating mountain race that starts in the center of Lecco, climbs through woods and mountain trails to the summit of Monte Resegone, then returns.

June. Pavia. Palio del Ticino (Rowing Race). A historic regatta and medieval-themed festival with costumed processions, rowing competitions on the Ticino River, and reenactments.

June. Mid-June. Mille Miglia: Brescia's Legendary Vintage Car Rally. The Mille Miglia began in 1927, conceived by two young Brescian counts, Aymo Maggi and Franco Mazzotti, who wanted to elevate their hometown's prestige with an epic road race.

June. Mantua. Mantova Chamber Music Festival. Mantua's historic palaces and piazzas host intimate chamber music concerts, combining classical repertoire with the city's Renaissance atmosphere.

June. Verona. Verona Opera Festival. Each summer, Verona's ancient Roman Arena becomes the stage for one of the world's most iconic opera festivals.

June. Moniga del Garda Chiaretto Festival (Italia in Rosa Wine Festival). Held in neighboring Moniga del Garda, this festival is dedicated entirely to rosé wines, with a special emphasis on the local Chiaretto.

June. Milano Monza Open-Air Motor Show (MIMO). An innovative auto show where the latest cars and prototypes are displayed outdoors in Milan and Monza.

Late June or Early July. Brescia and nearby towns. Notte Bianca di Brescia. Brescia stays awake until dawn during this lively summer night festival. Shops remain open late, street performers fill the squares, and music stages offer entertainment from rock bands to folk ensembles. Food stalls and pop-up bars ensure that the city's energy never dips.

Late June to Early July. Peghera. FestaFusion: Sagra del Taleggio and Festunt.

#1. Sagra del Taleggio. A celebration of the famed Lombard cheese held in the Taleggio Valley.

#2. Festunt. Treviglio's summer festival of beer, food, and live music.

Late June. Milano Pride. A vibrant week of cultural events, debates, and performances culminating in a massive parade through central Milan.

Late June to Early July. Luino. Settimana del Santuario. In the days surrounding the Feast of Saints Peter and Paul, Luino also honors its Sanctuary with special liturgies and gatherings.

June / July. Lake Iseo. Onde Musicali sul Lago d'Iseo (Waves of Music Festival). This music festival features classical and contemporary performances staged in churches, villas, and piazzas around the lake.

July Events

July 25. Milan Naviglio District. Sagra di San Cristoforo. Celebrated in the picturesque Naviglio district, this traditional festival honors Saint Christopher, patron saint of travelers.

July / August. Desenzano del Garda Summer Festival. A series of concerts, markets, and cultural events spread throughout the summer months in Desenzano.

July / August. Brescia Summer Music. A series of open-air concerts and cultural events held in piazzas, courtyards, and historic venues across the city.

July / August. Bormio. Stelvio Festival. A summer cultural festival that brings classical music, chamber concerts, and art events to Bormio and neighboring villages in the Stelvio National Park.

July / August / September. Milan. Estate all'Umanitaria. Hosted at the Società Umanitaria, this long-running series features open-air concerts, theater, and film screenings in a beautiful cloister setting.

July with Dates that Vary

July / August / September. Milan. AriAnteo. A beloved summer cinema festival with outdoor screenings in historic courtyards and piazzas.

July / August. Milan. Festival Latinoamericano. One of Europe's largest Latin American festivals, held at the Assago Forum. Concerts, dance, food, and cultural performances bring Latin rhythms and flavors to Milan's summer nights.

July. Lake Iseo. Sagra delle Sardine, Peschiera Maraglio (Monte Isola). This beloved food festival celebrates the island's age-old tradition of drying and grilling sardines over open fires.

July. Lake Iseo. Iseo Jazz Festival. A long-standing cultural event, the Iseo Jazz Festival brings international musicians to the town of Iseo and surrounding villages.

August Events

August 5. Bormio. Festa della Madonna della Neve, Santa Caterina Valfurva. In the mountain village of Santa Caterina Valfurva, locals honor the Madonna of the Snow with an outdoor Mass, processions, and traditional food stalls.

August 9, closest weekend. Monte Isola in Lago Iseo. Festa di San Fermo. Patron saint celebration on lake Iseo.

August 15. Ferragosto. Varese. Feast of the Assumption of Mary and Ferragosto, a national holiday.

August 20. Vigevano. Festa di San Bernardo. Dedicated to Saint Bernard of Clairvaux, another of Vigevano's patron saints, this festival includes religious services, processions, and civic events.

August 26. Bergamo. Festa di Sant'Alessandro. Bergamo's patron saint is honored with a full day of celebrations that blend devotion and festivity.

August 28. Pavia. Festa di Sant'Agostino. Each year on the twenty-eighth day of the month, pilgrims pour through medieval gates like tributaries flowing toward a sacred sea, drawn by the same magnetic pull that has summoned the faithful for thirteen centuries.

Late August around August 28. Como. Sant'Agostino Fair. In late summer, the Sant'Agostino district comes alive with this traditional fair, which has roots stretching back centuries.

August 31. Como. Festa Fusion Como.

#1. Fiera di Sant'Abbondio. Como's celebration of its patron saint, combining solemn religious rites, traditional markets, music, and food.

#2. Palio del Baradello. A grand historical reenactment and medieval games event commemorating Emperor Frederick Barbarossa's visit to Como in 1159.

September Events

September / October. Varese. Autunno Gastronomico Varesino. Dozens of restaurants, trattorie, and agriturismi join in by offering seasonal menus designed to showcase the region's best products.

2nd weekend in September. Lake Iseo. Just south of the lake, the celebrated Franciacorta wine region hosts its signature event.

September with Dates that Vary

Early September. Monza, Gran Premio di Monza, Formula One Race. First held in 1921 near Brescia and permanently moved to Monza in 1922, the race is one of the oldest on the Formula 1 calendar and the only event, besides the British Grand Prix, to be held every year since the championship's founding in 1950.

Early September. Mantua. Festivalletteratura (Literary Festival). Mantua's most celebrated cultural event, this international literary festival transforms the city into an open-air stage for authors, poets, and thinkers from around the globe.

Early September. Puegano. Festa dell'Uva di Puegnago del Garda (Grape Harvest Festival). Events include grape pressing demonstrations, wine tastings, food stands, and music, all set against panoramic views of the Valtenesi hills and Lake Garda.

Early September. Brescia. Festa dell'Uva di Puegnago (Wine Festival). The event features wine tastings, local food stands, music, and contests. It is a great opportunity to explore the surrounding countryside while enjoying regional flavors.

Early September. Pavia. Mercato Europeo di Pavia. A traveling European market with international food, crafts, and cultural performances, adding a global flair to the city's festivities.

Early September. Pavia. Festa del Ticino (River Fest). Events include river regattas, concerts, open-air markets, and food stalls along the riverbank.

Mid-September. Lake Iseo. Festa dell'Uva di Capriolo (Grape Harvest, Wine Festival, part of the Franciacorta harvest events). In the town of

Capriolo, near the western shore of Lake Iseo, this lively grape festival celebrates the harvest with wine tastings, parades, artisan markets, and music.

September. Sondrio. La Valtellina in Festa. A celebration of the valley's harvest traditions, held throughout Sondrio and neighboring villages. Markets feature wines made from Nebbiolo grapes, cheeses from the Alpine pastures, and local specialties like pizzoccheri and bresaola.

Late September. Lugana di Sirmione. Festival della Lugana (part of Festa del Lago, Lake Festival). Tastings, food pairings, concerts, and markets highlight the wine culture of the southern shores of Lake Garda.

Late September. Cremona. Cremona Musica International Exhibition. Cremona's most prestigious cultural event, the Cremona Musica International Exhibition, is a celebration of sound, craftsmanship, and the enduring legacy of the city's world-famous luthiers.

September. Quistello. Festa dell'Uva di Quistello (Wine Festival). Visitors enjoy tastings of local wines, grape-themed sweets, and festive parades. The event highlights the agricultural richness of the Mantovano countryside.

September. Bormio. Sagra dei Pizzoccheri, Teglio. Teglio, considered the birthplace of the iconic Valtellina dish pizzoccheri, celebrates its culinary heritage with a popular food festival each autumn.

September. Bergamo. Palio di Citta Alta. A lively neighborhood competition in the upper town, featuring costumed participants, traditional games, and parades through the medieval streets.

October Events

2nd weekend of October. Peghera. Sagra dello Strachitunt in Vedeseta. Just a short drive from Peghera, the nearby village of Vedeseta hosts a festival dedicated to Strachitunt, a rare blue-veined cheese produced in Visitors can enjoy tastings, see cheese-making demonstrations, and learn about the centuries-old techniques behind this Slow Food protected specialty.

2nd weekend in October. Vigevano. Rievocazione Storica Rinascimentale di Vigevano (Renaissance Fair). What began in the early 1980s as a modest tribute by local cultural groups has grown into the Rievocazione Storica Rinascimentale di Vigevano, one of Lombardy's most spectacular celebrations, drawing thousands who come to witness history breathing again in the very stones where it was first written.

November Events

November 1. Bormio. Fiera di Ognissanti, Bormio (All Saints Day). Held on All Saints' Day, this historic fair fills Bormio's streets with stalls selling produce, livestock, crafts, and seasonal foods.

November 4. Milan. Festa di San Carlo Borromeo. Celebrated annually on November 4, it honors the city's beloved 16th-century archbishop, canonized in 1610, whose leadership during the Counter-Reformation and selfless care for plague victims left an indelible mark on both Church and city.

November 5. Legnano. Festa di San Magno. Dedicated to Legnano's patron saint, San Magno, this feast day is celebrated with solemn Masses in the basilica and civic ceremonies in the piazza.

November 11. Peghera. Fiera di San Martino. Visitors can enjoy roasted chestnuts, mulled wine, and folk performances while processions through the streets honor the saint.

November 13. Cremona, Festa di Sant'Omobono. Dedicated to Sant'Omobono, the patron saint of Cremona, this feast day includes religious processions, special Masses, and a traditional fair.

November with Dates that Vary

November. Sondrio. Sondrio Festival. An international documentary film festival dedicated to nature and the environment.

November. Vigevano. Fiera dell'Oca. A traditional fair dedicated to the goose, an animal long associated with the agricultural heritage of Lomellina.

November. Bergamo. Donizetti Opera Festival. Celebrating Bergamo's most famous composer, Gaetano Donizetti, this festival stages opera productions, concerts, and recitals in theaters across the city.

Mid to late November. Cremona. Festa del Torrone. Cremona's sweetest festival celebrates the city's claim to fame: torrone, the traditional nougat made with honey, sugar, egg whites, and almonds.

December Events

December 6. Lecco. Festa di San Nicolo. Patron saint festival in Lecco. The festival now weaves together solemn liturgies with joyous processions, sacred concerts with community feasts.

December 7. Milan. Festa di Sant'Ambrogio. For over fifteen centuries, longer than most nations have existed, the city has gathered to honor Saint Ambrose, their beloved patron saint, in what may be Italy's most enduring celebration.

December 8 to January 6. Christmas Markets. Varese, Legnano, Polpenazze del Garda, Brescia, Sondrio, Luino, Peghera, Como, Lecco, Sirmione, Milan, Bergamo.

December 9. Pavia. Festa di San Siro. Honors Pavia's patron saint with religious services, food stalls, and a small winter fair in the historic center.

CHAPTER FIFTY-TWO

Alphabetical Listing of Cities in this Guide

Cities and their Chapters

 lphabetical Listing of Cities / Chapter Number

Festival Chapters

Day Trip Cities

City / Chapter Number

CHAPTER FIFTY-THREE

Preserving the Spirit of Italy

The Story Behind this Guide

I 've always believed travel is more than sightseeing. It's about connection to people, history, and the spirit that lingers after you arrive home.

Like most visitors to Italy, I stood in awe before the Colosseum, wandered beneath Venice's golden mosaics, and gazed from Florence's towers. But I found myself wanting more. Why did Italians dance in the streets? Why carry saints through piazzas? What drove these festivals of music and light?

That curiosity became my calling: to be the documentarian of these living traditions. Yet I never wanted just a history book. I wanted readers to feel the warmth of a village at dusk, smell roasted chestnuts, hear laughter drifting from festival squares.

This book is for travelers who are ready to wander further, those seeking not only beauty but belonging. Because somewhere between the processions and shared meals, you discover a deeper kind of travel that stays with you long after you return home.

CHAPTER FIFTY-FOUR

Editing and Photo Credits

Acknowledgment to my beloved Editor

My heartfelt thanks go to **Pamela Zale** for her thoughtful reviews, insights, comments, questions, challenges, and suggestions. Her careful eye and generous spirit have strengthened this work at every stage, and I am deeply grateful for her guidance and encouragement throughout the process.

Photo Credits

Cremona Cathedral and Main Piazza. Marcelaisabel98, CC0, via Wikimedia Commons.

Peschiera del Garda. Ponte Voltoni. W2k2, CC BY 4.0

https://creativecommons.org/licenses/by/4.0>, via Wikimedia Commons.

Bastions at Peschiera del Garda. W2k2, CC BY 4.0

https://creativecommons.org/licenses/by/4.0>, via Wikimedia Commons.

Lecco from above.

CHAPTER FIFTY-FIVE

Select Bibliography

Great Reads for those Traveling to Italy

Ady, Cecilia Mary. A History of Milan Under the Sforza.

Bowen, Marjorie. The Viper of Milan: A Romance of Lombardy.

Cartwright, Julia Mary. Beatrice D'Este, Duchess of Milan, 1475–1497: A Study of the Renaissance.

Daverio, Philippe. Lombardy: 127 Destinations for Discovering Art, History, and Beauty.

Lombard Towns of Italy: Or The Cities of Ancient Lombardy.

Manzoni, Alessandro. The Betrothed (I promessi sposi).

Mauro. Secret Stories of the History of Milan: Anecdotes, Curiosities, Mysteries, and Legends of the Ambrosian City.

Various Authors. Blue Guide Lombardy, Milan & the Italian Lakes.

CHAPTER FIFTY-SIX

Thank You & Please Leave a Review

Reviews Enhance Discoverability

Thank you for reading this *Ultimate Festival & Travel Guide*. It is the sixth volume in the Travel Italy Series.

If this guide has helped you plan your travels, I would be truly grateful if you left a review on Amazon. Your feedback not only assists fellow travelers in discovering authentic experiences but also supports the continued success of this series.

I hope you have enjoyed exploring Milan and Lombardy through their vibrant festivals, hidden gems, and timeless traditions. I would love to hear about your own journeys; whether you've wandered the streets of Milan, sipped wine in Franciacorta, or explored the lakes and mountain towns that make this region so special.

Thank you for being part of this journey. I look forward to hearing about your adventures, and I wish you safe and joyful travels wherever the road leads!

Wishing you the safest and happiest travels!

Katerina Ferrara

CHAPTER FIFTY-SEVEN

Connect with Me for Exclusive Insights

Free Travel Resources and More

Newsletter / Travel News

Sign up for my FREE newsletter and stay updated with insider secrets about Milan and Lombardy, historic neighborhoods, authentic trattorie, elegant cafés, and charming small towns beyond the city. Discover seasonal festivals, lakeside traditions, and cultural treasures you won't find in standard travel guides. Stay informed about local events, curated itineraries, podcast episodes, and unique insights that go beyond the book!

KaterinaFerrara.
com

Immersion Travel by Katerina Ferrara Blog

Looking for even more hidden treasures in Milan and Lombardy?

My blog is filled with insider tips. From elegant courtyards tucked behind unassuming facades in Milan to self-guided walking tours through charming towns like Bergamo, Mantua, and Pavia. Explore family-run osterias serving classic Lombard dishes, artisan ateliers keeping centuries-old traditions alive, and serene spots along Lakes Como, Garda, and Iseo perfect for a peaceful retreat.

Whether you're planning a stylish city getaway or a lakeside escape, you'll find everything you need to craft unforgettable memories in this culturally rich region. Subscribe at KaterinaFerrara.com for exclusive travel insights and start uncovering Milan and Lombardy's best-kept secrets!

Immersion Travel Podcast and YouTube

Looking for the real Italy? Step beyond the tourist trail with the Immersion Travel Podcast and YouTube series, where I take you deep into Italy's most captivating regions. From hidden festivals and authentic food spots to spiritual walks and backstreet wonders, each episode brings you insider stories, expert tips, and cultural treasures you won't find in typical travel guides.

Corrections / Updates / Suggestions Oops!

Even with the most careful research, details about Italy's ever-changing events and venues can shift like the tides in the lagoon. I would appreciate your help in keeping my content current and accurate. Please visit the book page here: https://katerinaferrara.com.

CHAPTER FIFTY-EIGHT

About the Author

Travel Blogger and Festival Follower

Katerina Ferrara first arrived in Milan more than two decades ago, drawn by the magnetic blend of fashion, art, history, and elegance that pulses through Italy's most cosmopolitan city. What began as a short cultural escape quickly blossomed into a lifelong love affair with Milan and the wider Lombardy region.

Over the years, she has returned again and again, exploring Milan in every season, attending art fairs and local festivals, lingering over espresso beneath Gothic spires, and uncovering hidden gems far from the well-trodden tourist path. From sunrise strolls along the Navigli to evenings spent listening to opera in historic theaters, her bond with Milan is one of discovery, creativity, and deep affection.

As the founder of **Immersion Travel Italy** and author of multiple travel guides, Katerina has spent countless hours exploring Lombardy's diverse landscapes, from the majestic lakes of Como, Garda, and Iseo to medieval hill towns and Alpine villages near the Swiss border. She has wandered through frescoed villas, sampled award-winning cheeses on mountain farms, followed in the footsteps of Leonardo da Vinci, and learned traditional recipes from nonnas in small-town trattorias. Whether hiking above Lake Como or exploring the hidden courtyards of Milan, she embraces each experience with curiosity and reverence.

Fluent in Italian, Katerina navigates Lombardy with ease, striking up conversations with artisans, historians, chefs, and locals who have generously shared their stories, traditions, and the best spots for risotto alla milanese. Her ultimate mission is to inspire fellow travelers to become "Festival Followers", those who align their journeys with Italy's vibrant celebrations, from city-wide events in Milan to lesser-known sagre in the countryside, uncovering the soul of each place through its seasonal rhythms.

Website: https://katerinaferrara.com

Follow the Immersion Travel Podcast on Spotify and Apple iTunes.

Podcast links available at: https://katerinaferrara.com/video-podcast

Katerina's YouTube Channel:

https://www.youtube.com/@ImmersionTravelItaly

Katerina on Instagram

@KaterinaFerraraAuthor

www.ingramcontent.com/pod-product-compliance
Lightning Source LLC
Chambersburg PA
CBHW051256120626
46547CB00015B/1968